DATE DUE

APR 21 '90			
JL 5 '90	NOV 0 5 1998		
FEB 25 '9	MAR 2 2 2000		
APR 10 '9	DEC 0 5 2000		
NOV 1 '93	FEB 2 7 2001		
NOV 1 '93	JUL 0 2 2003		
MAY 04 '94	OCT 2 3 2003		
JUN 14 '94	FEB 1 0 2004		
MAY 3 '95	3|7|11		
DEC 18 '95			
NOV 04 '96	3|30|11		
APR 03 '97			
OCT 31 '97			
OCT 31 '97			
AUG 3 1998			

A Short History of Women's Rights

From the Days of Augustus to the Present Time. With Special Reference to England and the United States

By

Eugene A. Hecker

SECOND EDITION REVISED, WITH ADDITIONS

GREENWOOD PRESS, PUBLISHERS
WESTPORT, CONNECTICUT

HQ
1121
.H4
1971

The Library of Congress cataloged this book as follows:

Hecker, Eugene Arthur, 1884-
   A short history of women's rights from the days of Augustus
to the present time. With special reference to England and the
United States, by Eugene A. Hecker.   2d ed. rev., with additions.   Westport, Conn., Greenwood Press [1971]

   xii, 313 p.   23 cm.

   Reprint of the 1914 ed.
   Includes bibliographical references.

   1. Woman—Rights of women.   I. Title.

HQ1121.H4   1971   301.41'2   72-98839
ISBN 0-8371-3106-5   MARC

Library of Congress   71

Originally published in 1914 by G. P. Putnam's Sons, N.Y.

Reprinted in 1971 by Greenwood Press, Inc., 51 Riverside
Avenue, Westport, Conn. 06880

Library of Congress catalog card number 72-98839
ISBN 0-8371-3106-5

Printed in the United States of America

10 9 8 7 6 5 4 3

To

MY MOTHER

PREFACE TO THE SECOND EDITION

IN this edition a chapter has been added, bringing down to date the record of the contest for equal suffrage. The summary on pages 175–235 is now largely obsolete; but it has been retained as instructive evidence of the rapid progress made during the last four years.

E. A. H.

CAMBRIDGE, MASS.
August, 1914.

PREFACE

WHILE making some researches in the evolution of women's rights, I was impressed by the fact that no one had ever, as far as I could discover, attempted to give a succinct account of the matter for English-speaking nations. Indeed, I do not believe that any writer in any country has essayed such a task except Laboulaye; and his *Recherches sur la Condition Civile et Politique des Femmes*, published in 1843, leaves much to be desired to one who is interested in the subject to-day.

I have, therefore, made an effort to fill a lack. This purpose has been strengthened as I have reflected on the great amount of confused information which is absorbed by those who have no time to make investigations for themselves. Accordingly, in order to present an accurate historical review, I have cited my authorities for all statements regarding which any question could be raised. This is particularly so in the chapters which deal with the condition of women under Roman Law, under the early Christian Church, and under Canon Law. In all these instances I have gone directly to primary sources, have investigated them myself, and have admitted no second-hand evidence. In connection with women's rights in England and in the United States I have either consulted the statutes or studied the commentaries of jurists, like Messrs. Pollock and Maitland, whose authority cannot be doubted. To such I have given the exact references whenever they have been used. In preparing the chapter on the progress of women's rights in the United States I derived great assistance from the very exhaustive *History of Woman Suffrage*, edited by Miss Susan B. Anthony, Mrs. Ida H. Harper, and others to whose unselfish labours we are for ever indebted. From their volumes I have drawn freely; but I have not given each specific reference.

The tabulation of the laws of the several States which I have given naturally cannot be entirely adequate, because the laws are being changed constantly. It is often difficult to procure the latest revised statutes. However, these laws are recent enough to illustrate the evolution of women's rights.

Finally, this volume was written in no hope that all readers would agree with the author, who is zealous in his cause. His purpose will be gained if he induces the reader to reflect for himself on the problem in the light of its historical development.

E. A. H.

CAMBRIDGE, MASS., 1910.

CONTENTS

CHAPTER I

CHAPTER II

WOMEN AND THE EARLY CHRISTIAN CHURCH

CHAPTER VII

WOMEN'S RIGHTS IN ENGLAND

CHAPTER VIII

WOMEN'S RIGHTS IN THE UNITED STATES

CHAPTER IX

GENERAL CONSIDERATIONS

Contents

A Short History of Women's Rights

A Short History of
Women's Rights

CHAPTER I

WOMEN'S RIGHTS UNDER ROMAN LAW, FROM AUGUSTUS TO JUSTINIAN—27 B.C. TO 527 A.D.

THE age of legal capability for the Roman woman was after the twelfth year, at which period she was permitted to make a will. [1] However, she was by no means allowed to do so entirely on her own account, but only under supervision. [2] This superintendence was vested in the father or, if he was dead, in a guardian [3]; if the woman was married, the power belonged to the husband. The consent of such supervision, whether of father, husband, or

Guardian-
ship.

[1] Paulus, iii, 4a, 1.
[2] Ulpian, Tit., xx, 16. Gaius, ii, 112.
[3] Male relatives on the father's side—agnati—were guardians in such cases; these failing, the judge of the supreme court (praetor) assigned one. See Ulpian, Tit., xi, 3, 4, and 24. Gaius, i, 185, and iii, 10. Libertae (freedwomen) took as guardians their former masters.

I

guardian, was essential, as Ulpian informs us,[1] under these circumstances: if the woman entered into any legal action, obligation, or civil contract; if she wished her freedwoman to cohabit with another's slave; if she desired to free a slave; if she sold any things *mancipi*, that is, such as estates on Italian soil, houses, rights of road or aqueduct, slaves, and beasts of burden. Throughout her life a woman was supposed to remain absolutely under the power[2] of father, husband, or guardian, and to do nothing without their consent. In ancient times, indeed, this authority was so great that the father and husband could, after calling a family council, put the woman to death without public trial.[3] The reason that women were so subjected to guardianship was "on account of their unsteadiness of character,"[4] "the weakness of the sex," and their "ignorance of legal matters."[5] Under certain circumstances, however, women became *sui iuris* or entirely independent: I. By the birth of three children (a freedwoman by four)[6]; II. By becoming a Vestal Virgin, of whom there were but six[7]; III. By a formal emancipation, which took place

---

[1] Ulpian, Tit., xi, 27.

[2] The power of the father was called *potestas;* that of the husband, *manus.*

[3] Aulus Gellius, x, 23. Cf. Suetonius, *Tiberius*, 35.

[4] Gaius, i, 144.

[5] Ulpian, Tit., xi, 1.

[6] Ulpian, Tit., xi, 28a. Gaius, i, 194. Paulus, iv, 9, 1–9.

[7] Gaius, i, 145. Ulpian, Tit., x, 5.

rarely, and then often only with a view of trans-
ferring the power from one guardian to another.[1]
Even when *sui iuris* a woman could not acquire
power over any one, not even over her own children[2]; for these an agnate—a male relative on the
father's side—was appointed guardian, and the
mother was obliged to render him and her children an account of any property which she had
managed for them.[3] On the other hand, her
children were bound to support her.[4]

So much for the laws on the subject. They
seem rigorous enough, and in early times were
doubtless executed with strictness. A Digression on
the growth of
respect for
women
marked feature, however, of the Roman
character, a peculiarity which at once
strikes the student of their history as compared
with that of the Greeks, was their great respect
for the home and the *materfamilias*. The stories
of Lucretia, Cloelia, Virginia, Cornelia, Arria,
and the like, familiar to every Roman schoolboy,
must have raised greatly the esteem in which
women were held. As Rome became a world
power, the Romans likewise grew in breadth of
view, in equity, and in tolerance. The political

[1] Gaius, i, 137. For an example see Pliny, *Letters*, viii, 18. Cf.
Spartianus. *Didius Iulianus*, 8: filiam suam, potitus imperio,
dato patrimonio, emancipaverat. See also Dio, 73, 7 (Xiphilin).

If emancipated children insulted or injured their parents,
they lost their independence—Codex, 8, 49 (50), 1.

[2] Ulpian, Tit., viii, 7a.

[3] Paulus, i, 4, 4: Mater, quae filiorum suorum rebus inter-
venit, actione negotiorum gestorum et ipsis et eorum tutoribus
tenebitur.   [4] Ulpian in Dig., 25, 3, 5.

influence wielded by women [1] was as great during
the first three centuries after Christ as it has ever
been at any period of the world's history; and the
powers of a Livia, an Agrippina, a Plotina, did not
fail to show pointedly what a woman could do.
In the early days of the Republic women who
touched wine were severely punished and male
relatives were accustomed solemnly to kiss them,
if haply they might discover the odour of drink on
their breath. [2] Valerius Maximus tells us that

[1] For Livia's great influence over Augustus see Seneca, *de
Clementia*, i, 9, 6.   Tacitus, *Annals*, i, 3, 4, and 5, and ii, 34.
Dio, 55, 14–21, and 56, 47.

Agrippina dominated Claudius—Tacitus, *Annals*, xii, 37.
Dio, 60, 33.   Caenis, the concubine of Vespasian, amassed great
wealth and sold public offices right and left—Dio, 65, 14.   Plotina, wife of Trajan, engineered Hadrian's succession—Eutro-
pius, viii, 6.   Dio, 69, 1.   A concubine formed the conspiracy
which overthrew Commodus—Herodian, i, 16–17.   The plotting
of Maesa put Heliogabalus on the throne—Capitolinus, *Macri-
nus*, 9–10.   Alexander Severus was ruled by his mother Mam-
maea—Lampridius, *Alex. Severus*, 14; Herodian, vi, 1, 1 and 9.
Gallienus invited women to his cabinet meetings—Trebellius
Pollio, *Gallienus*, 16.   The wives of governors took such a strenu-
ous part in politics and army matters that it caused the Senate
grave concern—see examples in Tacitus, *Annals*, iii, 33 and 34,
and iv, 20; also i, 69, and ii, 55; id. *Hist.*, iii, 69.   Velleius Paterculus, ii, 74 (Fulvia).

Of course, no woman ever had a right to vote; but neither did
anybody else, since the Roman government had become an
absolute despotism.   The first woman on the throne was Pulcheria, who, in 450 A.D., was proclaimed Empress of the East,
succeeding her brother, Theodosius II.   But she soon took a
husband and made him Emperor.   She had been practically sole
ruler since 414.

[2] Plutarch, *Roman Questions*, 6.   Aulus Gellius, x, 23.   Athenaeus, x, 56.

Egnatius Mecenas, a Roman knight, beat his wife to death for drinking wine. [1] Cato the Censor (234–149 B.C.) dilated with joy on the fact that a woman could be condemned to death by her husband for adultery without a public trial, whereas men were allowed any number of infidelities without censure. [2] The senator Metellus (131 B.C.) lamented that Nature had made it necessary to have women. [3]

The boorish cynicism of a Cato and a Metellus —though it never expressed the real feelings of the majority of Romans—gave way, however, under the Empire to a generous expression of the equality of the sexes in the realms of morality and of intellect. "I know what you may say," writes Seneca to Marcia, [4] "'You have forgotten that you are consoling a woman; you cite examples of fortitude on the part of men.' But who said that Nature had acted scurvily with the characters of women and had contracted their virtues into a narrow sphere? Equal force, believe me, is possessed by them; equal capability for what is

---

[1] Valerius Maximus, vi, 3, 9. For this he was not even blamed, but rather received praise for the excellent example.

[2] Aulus Gellius, x, 23. A woman in the *Menaechmi* of Plautus, iv, 6, 1, complains justly of this double standard of morality:

> Nam si vir scortum duxit clam uxorem suam,
> Id si rescivit uxor, impune est viro.
> Uxor viro si clam domo egressa est foras,
> Viro fit causa, exigitur matrimonio.
> Utinam lex esset eadem quae uxori est viro!

[3] Aulus Gellius, i, 6.

[4] De Consolatione ad Marciam, xvi, 1.

honorable, if they so wish." The Emperor Marcus
Aurelius gratefully recalls that from his mother he
learned piety and generosity, and to refrain not
only from doing ill, but even from thinking it,
and simplicity of life, far removed from the
ostentatious display of wealth. [1] The passionate
attachment of men like Quintilian and Pliny to
their wives exhibits an equality based on love that
would do honour to the most Christian households. [2]
All Roman historians speak with great admiration
of the many heroic deeds performed by women
and are fond of citing conspicuous examples of
conjugal affection. [3] The masterly and sym-

---

[1] *Commentaries*, A, γ'.

[2] Quintilian, *Instit. Orat.*, vi, 1, 5.　Pliny, *Letters*, vi, 4 and 7,
and vii, 5.

[3] Great admiration expressed for Paulina, wife of Seneca, who
opened her veins to accompany her husband in death—Tacitus,
Annals, xv, 63, 64.　Story of Arria and Paetus—Pliny, *Letters*,
iii, 16.　Martial, i, 13.　The famous instance of Epponina,
under Vespasian, and her attachment to her condemned husband—Tacitus, *Hist.*, iv, 67.　Tacitus mentions that many
ladies accompanied their husbands to exile and death—*Annals*,
xvi, 10, 11.　Numerous instances are related by Pliny of tender
and happy marriages, terminated only by death—see, e.g., *Letters*, viii, 5.　Pliny the elder tells how M. Lepidus died of regret
for his wife after being divorced from her—*N. H.*, vii, 36.　Valerius Maximus devotes a whole chapter to Conjugal Love—
iv, 6.　But the best examples of deep affection are seen in tomb
inscriptions—e. g., CIL i, 1103, viii, 8123, ii, 3596, v, 1, 3496, v, 2,
7066, x, 8192, vi, 3, 15696, 15317, and 17690.　Man and wife
are often represented with arms thrown about one another's
shoulders to signify that they were united in death as in life.
The poet Statius remarks that "to love a wife when she is living
is pleasure; to love her when dead, a solemn duty" (Silvae,

pathetic delineation of Dido in the *Aeneid* shows
how deeply a Roman could appreciate the character of a noble woman. In the numerous provisions
for the public education at the state's expense
girls were given the same opportunities and
privileges as boys; there were five thousand boys
and girls educated by Trajan alone.[1]

Such are a few examples of the growth of respect
for women; and we should naturally conclude
that, as time progressed, the unjust Decay of the
laws of guardianship would no longer power of the
guardian.
be executed to the letter, even though
the hard statutes were not formally expunged.
This was the case during the first three centuries
after Christ, as is patent from many sources. It
is to be borne in mind that because a law is on the
books, does not mean necessarily that it is enforced. A law is no stronger than public opinion.
Of this anomaly there are plenty of instances even
to-day—the Blue Laws of Massachusetts, for
example. "That women of mature age should be
under guardianship," writes the great jurist
Gaius[2] in the second century, "seems to have no
valid reason as foundation. For what is commonly believed, to the effect that on account of
unsteadiness of character they are generally

in prooemio). Yet some theologians would have us believe that
conjugal love and fidelity is an invention of Christianity.

[1] Pliny, *Panegyricus*, 26. For other instances see Capitolinus, *Anton. Pius*, 8; Lampridius, *Alex. Severus*, 57; Spartianus,
Hadrian, 7, 8, 9; Capitolinus, *M. Anton. Phil.*, 11.

[2] Gaius, i, 190.

hoodwinked, and that, therefore, it is right for them to be governed by the authority of a guardian, seems rather specious than true. As a matter of fact, women of mature age do manage their own affairs, and in certain cases the guardian interposes his authority as a mere formality; frequently, indeed, he is forced by the supreme judge to lend his authority against his will." Ulpian, too, hints at the really slight power of the guardian in his day, that is, the first three decades of the third century. "In the case of male and female wards under age, the guardians both manage their affairs and interpose their authority; but in the case of mature women they merely interpose their authority."[1] The woman had, in practice, become free to manage her property as she wished; the function of the legal guardian was simply to see to it that no one should attempt a fraud against her. Adequately to observe the decay of the vassalage of women, we must investigate the story of their rights in all its forms; and the position of women in marriage will next occupy our attention.

As in all Southern countries where women mature early, the Roman girl usually married

---

[1] Ulpian, Tit. xi, 25.   Cf. Frag. iur Rom. Vatic. (Huschke, 325): Divi Diocletianus et Constantius Aureliae Pontiae: Actor rei forum sequi debet et mulier quoque facere procuratorem *sine tutoris auctoritate* non prohibetur. So Papinian, lib. xv, Responsorum (Huschke, 327).   I shall discuss these matters at greater length when I treat of women and the management of their property.

young; twelve years were required by custom for her to reach the marriageable age.[1] In the earlier period a woman was acquired Women and as wife in three different ways: I. By marriage. *coemptio*—a mock sale to her husband[2]; II. By *confarreatio*—a solemn marriage with peculiar sacred rites to qualify men and women and their children for certain priesthoods[3]; III. By *usus*, or acquisition by prescription. A woman became a man's legal wife by *usus* if he had lived with her one full year and if, during that time, she had not been absent from him for more than three successive nights.[4]

All these forms, however, had either been abolished by law or had fallen into desuetude during the second century of our era, as is evident from Gaius.[5] A man could marry even if not present personally; a woman could not.[6] The woman's parents or guardians were accustomed to arrange a match for her,[7] as they still do in many parts of Europe. Yet the power of the

[1] Dio, 54, 16. Pomponius in Dig., 23, 2, 4.

[2] Gaius, i, 113.

[3] Ulpian, Tit., ix, 1: Farreo convenit uxor in manum certis verbis et testibus X praesentibus et sollemni sacrificio facto, in quo panis quoque farreus adhibetur. Cf. Gaius, i, 112.

[4] Aulus Gellius, iii, 2, 12. Gaius, i, 111.

[5] Gaius, i, 110 and 111.

[6] Paulus, ii, xix, 8.

[7] Pliny, *Letters*, i, 14, will furnish an example; cf. id. vi, 26, to Servianus: Gaudeo et gratulor, quod Fusco Salinatori filiam tuam destinasti. Note the way in which Julius Caesar arranged a match for his daughter—Suetonius, *Divus Julius*, 21.

father to coerce his daughter was limited. Her consent was important. "A marriage cannot exist," remarks Paulus, "unless all parties consent."[1] Julianus writes also that the daughter must give her permission[2]; yet the statement of Ulpian which immediately follows in the Digest shows that she had not complete free will in the matter: "It is understood that she who does not oppose the wishes of her father gives consent. But a daughter is allowed to object only in case her father chooses for her a man of unworthy or disgraceful character."[3] The son had an advantage here, because he could never be forced into a marriage against his will.[4] The consent of the father was always necessary for a valid marriage.[5] He could not by will compel his daughter to marry a certain person.[6] After she was married, he still retained power over her, unless she became independent by the birth of three children; but this was largely to protect her and represent her in court against her husband if necessity should arise.[7] A father was not per-

[1] Paulus in Dig., 23, 2, 2: Nuptiae consistere non possunt, nisi consentiunt omnes, id est, qui coeunt quorumque in potestate sunt.

[2] Julianus in Dig., 23, 1, 11.

[3] Ulpian in Dig., 23, 1, 12.

[4] Paulus in Dig., 23, 1, 13.   Terentius Clemens in Dig., 23, 2, 21.

[5] Paulus, ii, 19, 2.

[6] Ulpian, 24, 17.

[7] Cf. Ulpian, Tit., vi, 6: Divortio facto, si quidem sui iuris sit mulier, ipsa habet rei uxoriae actionem, id est, dotis repetitionem;

mitted to break up a harmonious [1] marriage; he could not get back his daughter's dowry without her consent, [2] nor force her to return to her husband after a divorce [3]; and he was punished with loss of citizenship if he made a match for a widowed daughter before the legal time of mourning for her husband had expired. [4] A daughter passed completely out of the power of her father only if she became *sui iuris* by the birth of three children or if she became a Vestal, or again if she married a special priest of Jupiter (*Flamen Dialis*), in which case, however, she passed completely into the power of her husband. Under all circumstances a daughter must not only show respect for her father, but also furnish him with the necessaries of life if he needed them. [5]

Under the Empire no such thing as a "breach of promise" suit was permitted, although in the

---

quodsi in potestate patris sit, pater adiuncta filiae persona habet actionem.

The technical recognition of the father's power was still strong. Cf. Pliny, *Panegyricus*, 38: Tu quidem, Caesar . . . intuitus, opinor, vim legemque naturae, quae semper in dicione parentum esse liberos iussit. The same writer, on requesting Trajan to give citizenship to the children of a certain freedman, is careful to add the specification that they are to remain in their father's power—see Pliny to Trajan, xi (vi).

[1] Paulus, vi, 15. Codex, v, 4, 11, and 17, 5.
[2] Paulus, in Dig., 23, 3, 28. Codex, v, 13, 1, and 18, 1.
[3] Codex, v, 17, 5.
[4] Salvius Julianus: Frag. Perp. Ed.: Pars Prima, vii—under "De is qui notantur infamia."
[5] Codex, 8, 46 (47), 5.

days of the Republic the party who broke a promise to marry had been liable to a suit for dam-
" Breach of ages.[1]   But this had now disappeared,
Promise." and either party could break off the
betrothal at pleasure without prejudice.[2]   Whatever gifts had been given might be demanded
back.[3]   The engagement had to be formally
broken off before either party could enter into marriage or betrothal with another; otherwise he or she
lost civil status.[4]   While an engagement lasted,
the man could bring an action for damages against
any one who insulted or injured his fiancée.[5]

The Roman marriage was a purely civil contract based on consent.[6]   The definition given by
Husband and the law was a noble one.   "Marriage is
Wife. the union of a man and a woman and
a partnership of all life; a mutual sharing of laws
human and divine."[7]   The power of the husband
over the wife was called *manus;* and the wife
stood in the same position as a daughter.[8]   No
husband was allowed to have a concubine.[9]   He
was bound to support his wife adequately, look

[1] Aulus Gellius, iv, 4.

[2] Juvenal, vi, 200–203. Gaius in Dig., 24, 2, 2. Ulpian, ibid.,
23, 1, 10. Codex, v, 17, 2, and v, 1, 1.

[3] Codex, v, 3, 2.

[4] Dig., 3, 2, 1.

[5] Ulpian in Dig., 47, 10, 24.

[6] Cf. Alexander Severus in Codex, viii, 38, 2: Libera matrimonia
esse antiquitus placuit, etc.   Also Codex, v, 4, 8 and 14.

[7] Modestinus in Dig., xxiii, 2, 1.

[8] Gaius, ii, 159.

[9] Paulus, ii, xx, 1.

out for her interests, [1] and strictly to avenge any insult or injury offered her [2]; any abusive treatment of the wife by the husband was punished by an action for damages. [3] A wife was compelled by law to go into solemn mourning for a space of ten months upon the death of a husband. [4] During the period of mourning she was to abstain from social banquets, jewels, and crimson and white garments. [5] If she did not do so, she lost civil status. The emperor Gordian, in the year 238, remitted these laws so far as solemn clothing and other external signs of mourning above enumerated were concerned. [6] But a husband was not compelled to do any legal mourning for the death of his wife. [7]

The wife was, as I have said, in the power of her husband. Originally, no doubt, this power was absolute; the husband could even put his wife to death without a public trial. But the world was progressing, and that during the first three centuries after Christ the power of the husband was reduced in practice to absolute nullity I shall

[1] Note the rescript of Alexander Severus to a certain Aquila (Codex, ii, 18, 13): Quod in uxorem tuam aegram erogasti, non a socero repetere, sed adfectioni tuae debes expendere.

[2] See, e.g., Dig., 47, 10, and Ulpian, ibid., 48, 14, 27.

[3] Cf. Gaius, i, 141: In summa admonendi sumus, adversus eos, quos in mancipio habemus, nihil nobis contumeliose facere licere; alioquin iniuriarum (actione) tenebimur.

[4] Paulus, i, 21, 13.

[5] Paulus, i, 21, 14.

[6] Codex, ii, 11, 15.

[7] Paulus in Dig., iii, 2, 9.

make clear in the following pages. I shall, accordingly, first investigate the rights of the wife over her dowry, that is, the right of managing her own property.

Even from earliest times it is clear that the wife had complete control of her dowry. The henpecked husband who is afraid of offending his wealthy wife is a not uncommon figure in the comedies of Plautus and Terence; and Cato the Censor growled in his usual amiable manner at the fact that wives even in his day controlled completely their own property.[1]   The attitude of the Roman law on the subject is clearly expressed. "It is for the good of the state that women have their dowries inviolate."[2]   "The dowry is always and everywhere a chief concern; for it is for the public good that dowries be retained for women, since it is highly necessary that they be dowered in order to bring forth offspring and replenish the state with children."[3]   "It is just that the income of the dowry belong to the husband; for inasmuch as it is he who stands the burdens of the married state, it is fair that he also acquire the interest."[4]   "Nevertheless, the dowry belongs

[1] Aulus Gellius, xvii, 6, speech of Cato: Principio vobis mulier magnam dotem adtulit; tum magnam pecuniam recipit, quam in viri potestatem non committit, eam pecuniam viro mutuam dat; postea, ubi irata facta est, servum recepticum sectari atque flagitare virum iubet.

[2] Paulus in Dig., 23, 3, 2.

[3] Pomponius in Dig., 24, 3, 1.

[4] Ulpian in Dig., 23, 3, 7.

to the woman, even though it is in the goods of the husband."[1] "A husband is not permitted to alienate his wife's estate against her will."[2] A wife could use her dowry during marriage to support herself, if necessary, or her kindred, to buy a suitable estate, to help an exiled parent, or to assist a needy husband, brother, or sister. The numerous accounts in various authors of the first three centuries after Christ confirm the statement that the woman's power over her dowry was absolute.[3] Then as now, a man might put his property in his wife's name to escape his creditors,[4]—a useless proceeding, if she had not had complete control of her own property.

When the woman died, her dowry, if it had been given by the father (*dos profecticia*) returned to the latter; but if any one else had given it (*dos adventicia*), the dowry remained with the husband, unless the donor had expressly stipulated that it was to be returned to himself at the woman's death (*dos recepticia*).[5] In the case of a dowry of the first kind, the husband might retain what he had

[1] Tryfoninus in Dig., 23, 3, 75.
[2] Gaius, ii, 63. Paulus, ii, 21*b*.
[3] E.g. Juvenal, vi, 136–141. Martial, viii, 12.
[4] Apuleius *Apologia*, 523: Pleraque tamen rei familiaris in nomen uxoris callidissima fraude confert, etc.; id., 545, 546 proves further the power of the wife: ea condicione factam coniunctionem, si nullis a me susceptis liberis vita demigrasset, ut dos omnis, etc.—evidently the woman was dictating the disposal of her dowry.
[5] Ulpian, Tit., vi, 3, 4, and 5. Codex, v, 18, 4.

expended for his wife's funeral.[1]   The dowry was confiscated to the state if the woman was convicted of lèse majesté, violence against the state, or murder.[2]   If she suffered punishment involving loss of civil status under any other law which did not assess the penalty of confiscation, the husband acquired the dowry just as if she were dead. Banishment operated as no impediment; if the woman wished to leave her husband under these circumstances, her father could recover the dowry.[3]

A further confirmation of the power of the wife over her property is the law that prohibited gifts between husband and wife; obviously, a woman could not be said to have the power of making a gift if she had no right of property of her own. The object of the law mentioned was to prevent the husband and wife from receiving any lasting damage to his or her property by giving of it under the impulse of conjugal affection.[4]   This statute acted powerfully to prevent a husband from wheedling a wife out of her goods; and in case the latter happened to be of a grasping disposition the law was a protection to the husband and hence to the children, his heirs, for whose interests the Roman law constantly provided.

[1] Ulpian in Dig., xi, 7, 16; ibid., Papinian, 17; ibid., Julianus, 18.   Paulus, i, xxi, 11.

[2] Ulpian in Dig., 48, 20, 3.

[3] Ulpian in Dig., 48, 20, 5.

[4] Ulpian in Dig., 24 1, 1: Moribus apud nos receptum est, ne inter virum et uxorem donationes valerent. hoc autem receptum est, ne mutuo amore invicem spoliarentur, donationibus non temperantes, sed profusa erga se facilitate.

Gifts between husband and wife were nevertheless valid under certain conditions. It was permissible to make a present of clothing and to bestow various tokens of affection, such as ornaments. The husband could present his wife with enough money to rebuild a house of hers which had burned.[1] The Emperor Marcus Aurelius permitted a wife to give her husband the sum necessary to obtain public office or to become a senator or knight or to give public games.[2] A gift was also legal if made by the husband in apprehension that death might soon overtake him; if, for instance, he was very sick or was setting out to war, or to exile, or on a dangerous journey.[3] The point in all gifts was, that neither party should become richer by the donation.[4]

Some further considerations of the relation of husband and wife will aid in setting forth the high opinion which Roman law entertained of marriage and its constant effort to protect the wife as much as possible. A wife could not be held in a criminal action if she committed theft against her husband. The various statements of the jurists make the matter clear. Thus Paulus[5]: "A special action for the recovery of

[1] Paulus in Dig., 24, 1, 14.
[2] Gaius in Dig., 24, 1, 42; ibid., Licinius Rufus, 41; Ulpian, Tit. vii, 1.   Martial, vii, 64—et post hoc dominae munere factus eques.
[3] Paulus, ii, xxiii, 1.
[4] Cf. Paulus, ii, xxiii, 2.
[5] Paulus in Dig., 25, 2, 1.   Codex, v, 21, 2.

property removed [*rerum amotarum iudicium*] has been introduced against her who was a wife, because it has been decided that it is not possible to bring a criminal action for theft against her [*quia non placuit cum ea furti agere posse*]. Some —as Nerva Cassius—think she cannot even commit theft, on the ground that the partnership in life made her mistress, as it were. Others—like Sabinus and Proculus—hold that the wife can commit theft, just as a daughter may against her father, but that there can be no criminal action by established law." "As a mark of respect to the married state, an action involving disgrace for the wife is refused." [1] "Therefore she will be held for theft if she touches the same things after being divorced. So, too, if her slave commits theft, we can sue her on the charge. But it is possible to bring an action for theft even against a wife, if she has stolen from him whose heirs we are or before she married us; nevertheless, as a mark of respect we say that in each case a formal claim for restitution alone is admissible, but not an action for theft." [2] "If any one lends help or advice to a wife who is filching the property of her husband, he shall be held for theft. If he commits theft with her, he shall be held for theft, although the woman herself is not held." [3]

[1] Gaius in Dig., 25, 2, 2.
[2] Paulus in Dig., 25, 2, 3.
[3] Ulpian in Dig., 47, 2, 52. The respect shown for family relations may be seen also from the fact that a son could *complain—de facto matris queri*—if he believed that his mother had

A husband who did not avenge the murder of his wife lost all claims to her dowry, which was then confiscated to the state; this by order of the Emperor Severus.[1]

The laws on adultery are rather more lenient to the woman than to the man. In the first place, the Roman law insisted that it was unfair for a husband to demand chastity on the part of his wife if he himself was guilty of infidelity or did not set her an example of good conduct,[2]—a maxim which present day lawyers may reflect upon with profit. A father was permitted to put to death

---

brought in supposititious offspring to defraud him of some of his inheritance; but he was strictly forbidden to bring her into court with a public and criminal action—Macer in Dig., 48, 2, 11: *sed ream eam lege Cornelia facere permissum ei non est.*

[1] Ulpian in Dig., 48, 14, 27.

[2] Ulpian in Dig., 48, 5, 14 (13): Iudex adulterii ante oculos habere debet et inquirere, an maritus pudice vivens mulieri quoque bonos mores colendi auctor fuerit. periniquum enim videtur esse, ut pudicitiam vir ab uxore exigat, quam ipse non exhibeat. Cf. Seneca, *Ep.*, 94: Scis improbum esse qui ab uxore pudicitiam exigit, ipse alienarum corruptor uxorum. Scis ut illi nil cum adultero, sic nihil tibi esse debere cum pellice. Antoninus Pius gave a husband a bill for adultery against his wife "Provided it is established that by your life you give her an example of fidelity. It would be unjust that a husband should demand a fidelity which he does not himself keep"—quoted by St. Augustine, de Conj. Adult., ii, ch. 8. In view of these explicit statements it is difficult to see what the Church Father Lactantius meant by asserting (*de Vero Cultu*, 23): Non enim, sicut iuris publici ratio est, sola mulier adultera est, quae habet alium; maritus autem, etiamsi plures habeat, a crimine adulterii solutus est. Perhaps this deliberate distortion of the truth was another one of the libels against pagan Rome of which the pious Fathers are so fond "for the good of the Church."

his daughter and her paramour if she was still in
his power and if he caught her in the act at his
own house or that of his son-in-law; otherwise he
could not.[1] He must, however, put both man and
woman to death at once, when caught in the act;
to reserve punishment to a later date was unlawful.
The husband was not permitted to kill his wife;
he might kill her paramour if the latter was a man
of low estate, such as an actor, slave, or freedman, or had been convicted on some criminal charge involving loss of citizenship.[2] The
reason that the father was given the power
which was denied the husband was that the
latter's resentment would be more likely to blind
his power of judging dispassionately the merits
of the case.[3] If now the husband forgot himself
and slew his wife, he was banished for life if of
noble birth, and condemned to perpetual hard
labour if of more humble rank.[4] He must at once
divorce a wife guilty of adultery; otherwise he
was punished as a pander, and that meant loss
of citizenship.[5] Women convicted of adultery
were, when not put to death, punished by the
loss of half their dowry, a third part of their
other goods, and relegation to an island; guilty

[1] Papinian in Dig., 48, 5, 21 (20); ibid., Ulpian, 24 (23). Paulus,
ii, xxvi.
[2] Macer in Dig., 48, 5, 25 (24).
[3] Papinian in Dig., 48, 5, 23 (22).
[4] Papinian in Dig., 48, 5, 39 (38); ibid., Marcianus, 48, 8, 1.
[5] Paulus, ii, xxvi. Macer in Dig., 48, 5, 25 (24), ibid., Ulpian,
48, 5, 30 (29).

men suffered the loss of half of their possessions
and similar relegation to an island; but the guilty
parties were never confined in the same place.[1]
We have mention also in several writers of some
curious and vicious punishments that might be
inflicted on men guilty of adultery.[2]

Now, all this seems rigorous enough; but, as I
have already remarked, we must beware of im-
agining that a statute is enforced simply because
it stands in the code.   As a matter of fact, public
sentiment had grown so humane in the first three
centuries after Christ that it did not for a moment
tolerate that a father should kill his daughter,
no matter how guilty she was; and in all our
records of that period no instance occurs.   As to
husbands, we have repeated complaints in the
literature of the day that they had grown so
complaisant towards erring wives that they could
not be induced to prosecute them.[3]   A typical instance is related by Pliny.[4]   Pliny was summoned
by the Emperor Trajan to attend a council where,
among other cases, that of a certain Gallitta was
discussed.   She had married a military tribune
and had committed adultery with a common
captain (*centurio*).   Trajan sent the captain into

[1] Paulus, ii, xxvi.

[2] Juvenal, x. 317 ; quosdam moechos et mugilis intrat.   Cf.
Catullus, 15, 19.

[3] See, e.g., Capitolinus, *Anton. Pius*, 3.   Spartianus, *Sept.
Severus*, 18.   Pliny, *Panegyricus*, 83: multis illustribus dedecori
fuit aut inconsultius uxor assumpta aut retenta patientius, etc.

[4] Pliny, *Letters*. vi, 31.

exile. The husband took no measures against his wife, but went on living with her. Only by coercion was he finally induced to prosecute. Pliny informs us that the guilty woman had to be condemned, even against the will of her accuser.

A woman guilty of incest received no punishment, but the guilty man was deported to an island.[1] If the incest involved adultery, the woman was of course held on that charge.

We come now to a matter where the growing freedom of women reached its highest point—the **Divorce.** matter of divorce. Here again we have to note the progress of toleration and humanitarianism. In the early days of the Republic the family tie was rarely severed. Valerius Maximus tells us[2] of a quaint custom of the olden days, to the effect that "whenever any quarrel arose between husband and wife, they would proceed to the chapel of the goddess Viriplaca ["Reconciler of Husbands"], which is on the Palatine, and there they would mutually express their feelings; then, laying aside their anger, they returned home reconciled." During these days a woman could never herself take the initiative in divorce; the husband was all-powerful. The first divorce of which we have any record took place in the year 231 B.C., when Spurius Carvilius Ruga put away his wife for sterility. Public opinion censured him severely for it "because people thought

[1] Paulus, ii, xxvi, 15.
[2] Valerius Maximus, ii, 1, 6.

that not even the desire for children ought to have been preferred to conjugal fidelity and affection." [1] As the Empire extended and Rome became more worldly and corrupt, the reasons for divorce became more trivial. Sempronius Sophus divorced his wife because she had attended some public games without his knowledge. [2] Cicero, who was a lofty moralist—on paper,— put away his wife Terentia in order to marry a rich young ward and get her money if he could. Maecenas, the great prime-minister of Augustus, sent away and took back his wife repeatedly at caprice— perhaps he believed that variety is the spice of life. But during all this time the husband alone could annul marriage. [3]

Gradually, however, the status of women changed and they were given greater and greater liberty. Inasmuch as Roman marriage was a civil contract based on consent, strict justice had to allow that on this basis either party to the contract might annul the marriage at his or her pleasure. The result was that during the first three centuries after Christ the wife had absolute freedom to take the initiative and send her husband a divorce whenever and for whatever reason she wished.

[1] Aulus Gellius, xvii, 21, 44. Valerius Maximus, ii, 1, 4. Plutarch, *Roman Questions*, 14.

[2] Valerius Maximus, vi, 3, 12.

[3] "If you should catch your wife in adultery, you would put her to death with impunity; she, on her part, would not dare to touch you with her finger; and it is not right that she should"— Speech of Cato the Censor, quoted by Aulus Gellius, x, 23.

The proof of this fact is positively established not only from the statements of the jurists, but also from numberless accounts in the other writers of the day.[1] Divorce became, at least among the higher strata of society, extraordinarily frequent. That a lady of the Upper Four Hundred should have been content with only one husband was deemed worthy of special mention on her tomb; the word *univira* (a woman of one husband) may still be read on certain inscriptions. The satirists are fond of dwelling on the license allowed to women in the case of divorce. Martial, for instance,[2] says that one Theselina married ten husbands in one month. Still, allowing for the natural exaggeration of satirists, we are yet reasonably sure that divorce had reached great heights in the upper classes. Whether it was as bad among the middle classes is very improbable. There was one kind of marriage which, originally at least, did not admit of dissolution.[3] This was the solemn marriage by *confarreatio*, already described, which

---

[1] E. g., Marcellus in Dig., 24, 3, 38: Maevia Titio repudium misit, etc.; ibid., Africanus, 24, 3, 34: Titia divortium a Seio fecit, etc. Martial, x, 41: Mense novo Iani veterem, Proculeia, maritum Deseris, atque iubes res sibi habere suas. Apuleius, *Apologia*, 547: utramvis habens culpam mulier, quae aut tam intolerabilis fuit ut repudiaretur aut tam insolens ut repudiaret.

Novellae, 140, 1: Antiquitus quidem licebat sine periculo tales [i. e., those of incompatible temperament] ab invicem separari secundum communem voluntatem et consensum.

[2] Martial, vi, 7.

[3] Aulus Gellius, x, 15: Matrimonium flaminis nisi morte dirimi ius non est.

qualified the husband and wife for the special priesthood of Jupiter. Women soon grew to value their freedom too highly to enter it; as early as 23 A.D. the Senate had to relax some of the rigour of the old laws on the matter as a special inducement for women to consent to enter this union.[1]

We may now observe what became of the wife's property after divorce and what her rights were under such circumstances. If it was the husband who had taken the initiative and had sent his wife a divorce, and if the divorce was not the fault of the woman, she at once had an action in law for complete recovery of her dowry; on her own responsibility if she was *sui iuris*, otherwise with the help of her father.[2]   But even the woman still under guardianship could act by herself if her father was too sick or infirm or if she had no other agent to act for her.[3]   For the offence of adultery a husband had to pay back the dowry at once; for lesser guilt he might return it in instalments at intervals of six months.[4]   If, now, the divorce was clearly the fault of the woman, her husband could retain certain parts of the dowry in these proportions: for adultery, a sixth part for each of the children up to one half of the whole; for lighter offences, an eighth part; if the husband had

[1] Tacitus, *Annals*, iv, 16.
[2] Ulpian, vi, 6; id. in Dig., 24, 3, 2. Pauli fragmentum in Boethii commentario ad Topica, 2, 4, 19.
[3] Paulus in Dig. ii, 3, 41.
[4] Ulpian, vi, 13.

gone to expense or had incurred civil obligations for his wife's benefit or if she had removed any of his property, he could recover the amount.[1]

A year and six months must elapse after a divorce before the woman was allowed to marry again.[2] If at the time of the divorce she was pregnant, her husband was obliged to support her offspring, provided that within thirty days after the separation she informed him of her condition.[3] She could sue her former husband for damages if he insulted her.[4] Whether the children should stay with the mother or father was left to the discretion of the judge.[5]

The married woman had, as I have shown, complete disposal of her own property. Let us see next what rights those women had over their possessions who were widows or spinsters.

Property rights of widows and single women.

Roman Law constantly strove to protect the children and laid it down as a maxim that the property of their parents belonged to them.[6]

[1] Ulpian, vi, 9–17, and vii, 2–3.   Pauli frag. in Boethii comm. ad Top., ii, 4, 19.

[2] Ulpian, xiv: feminis lex Iulia a morte viri anni tribuit vacationem, a divortio sex mensum; lex autem Papia a morte viri biennii, a repudio anni et sex mensum.

[3] Ulpian in Dig., 25, 3, 1.   Paulus, ii, xxiv, 5.

[4] Ulpian in Dig., 25, 4, 8.

[5] Codex, v, 24, 1.

[6] Codex, vi, 60, 1: Res, quae ex matris successione fuerint ad filios devolutae, ita sint in parentum potestate, ut fruendi dumtaxat habeant facultatem, dominio videlicet earum ad liberos pertinente.

A widow could not therefore, except by special
permission from the emperor,[1] be the legal
guardian of her children, but must ask the court to
appoint one upon the death of her husband.[2]
This was to prevent possible mismanagement and
because "to undertake the legal defence of others
is the office of men."[3]   But she was permitted to
assume complete charge of her children's property
during their minority and enjoy the usufruct;
only she must render an account of the goods
when the children arrived at maturity.[4]   We
have many instances of women who managed their
children's patrimony and did it exceedingly well.
"You managed our patrimony in such wise," writes
Seneca to his mother,[5] "that you exerted yourself
as if it were yours and yet abstained from it as if
it belonged to others."[6]   Agricola, father-in-law of
Tacitus, had such confidence in his wife's business
ability that he made her co-heir with his daughter
and the Emperor Domitian.[7]   A mother could
get an injunction to restrain extravagance on

[1] Neratius in Dig., 26, 1, 18.

[2] Codex, v, 35, 1.

[3] Codex, ii, 12, 18: alienam suscipere defensionem virile officium est . . . filio itaque tuo, si pupillus est, tutorem pete.

[4] Ulpian, Tit. viii, 7a.   Paulus, i, 4, 4.

[5] ad Helviam matrem de consol., xiv, 3.

[6] Other instances of women trustees will be found in Apuleius,
Apologia 516; Paulus in Dig., iii, 5, 23 (24): avia nepotis sui
negotia gessit, etc.; ibid., Marcellus, 46, 3, 48: Titia cum
propter dotem bona mariti possideret, omnia pro domina egit,
reditus exegit, etc.

[7] Tacitus, Agricola, 43.

the part of her children.[1]   Women could not adopt.[2]

Married women, spinsters, and widows had as much freedom as men in disposing of property by will. If there were children, the Roman law put certain limitations on the testator's powers, whether man or woman. By the Falcidian Law no one was allowed to divert more than three fourths of his estate from his (or her) natural heirs.[3] But for any adequate cause a woman could disinherit her children completely; and there are many instances of this extant both in the Law Books and in the literature of the day.[4]

Single women had grown absolutely unshackled and even their guardians had become a mere formality, as the words of Gaius, already quoted (page 8) prove. That they had complete disposal of their property is proved furthermore by the numerous complaints in Roman authors about the sycophants who flattered and toadied the wealthy ladies with an eye to being remembered in their wills.[5] For it is evident that if these

[1] Frag. iur. Rom. Vat., 282.
[2] Ulpian, viii, 7a.
[3] Gaius, ii, 227. Digest, 35, 2.
[4] E.g. Pliny, Letters, v, 1. Codex, iii, 28, 19; id., iii, 28, 28. Cf. Codex, iii, 29, 1, and 29, 7; and Paulus in Dig., v, 2, 19. Note the extreme anxiety of the son of Prudentilla about her money as given by Apuleius, Apologia, 517. The estate of a mother who died intestate went to her children, not to her husband; the latter could only enjoy the interest until they arrived at maturity—Codex, vi, 60, 1; Modestinus in Dig., 38, 17, 4.
[5] E.g., Juvenal, iv, 18–21. Pliny, Letters, ii, 20.

women had not had the power freely to dispose of their own property, there would have been no point in paying them such assiduous court. The legal age of maturity was now twenty-five for both male and female.

Women engaged freely in all business pursuits. We find them in all kinds of retail trade and commerce,[1] as members of guilds,[2] in medicine,[3] innkeeping,[4] in vaudeville[5]; there were even female barbers[6] and charioteers.[7] Examples of women who toiled for a living with their own hands are indeed very old, as the widow, described by Homer, who worked for a scanty wage to support her fatherless children, or the wreathmaker, mentioned by Aristophanes.[8] But such was the case only with women of the lower classes; the lady of high birth acted through her agents.[9]

Women engaged in business pursuits.

[1] Digest, xiv, 1 and 3 and 8—on the actio exercitoria and institoria. Cf. Codex, iv, 25, 4: et si a muliere magister navis praepositus fuerit, etc. [2] CIL, xiv, 326.

[3] Martial, xi, 71. Apuleius, *Metam.*, v, 10. Soranus, i, 1, ch. 1 and 2. Galen, vii, 414 (cf. xiii, 341).

[4] E.g. Suetonius, *Nero*, 27.

[5] Carmina Priapea, 18 and 27. Ulpian, xiii, 1. The Roman drama had now degenerated into mere vaudeville, mostly lascivious dancing. Senators and their children were forbidden to marry any woman who had herself or whose father or mother had been on the stage. [6] Martial, ii, 17, 1.

[7] Petronius, *Sat.*, 45: Titus noster . . . habet et mulierem essedariam. This would not be strange, when we reflect that under Domitian noble ladies even fought in the arena.

[8] *Thesmophoriazusae*, 443–459.

[9] See Cicero, *pro Caecina*, 5, for an account of these business agents for women.

When so many women were engaged in business, occasions for lawsuits would naturally arise; we shall see next what power the woman had to sue. It was a standing maxim of the law that a woman by herself could not conduct a case in court.[1] She had to act through her agent, if she was independent, otherwise through her guardian. The supreme judge at Rome and the governor in a province assigned an attorney to those who had no agent or guardian.[2] But in this case again custom and the law were at variance. Various considerations will make it clear that women who sued had, in practice, complete disposal of the matter. I.—A woman who was still under the power of her father must, according to law, sue with him as her agent or appoint an agent to act with him. Nevertheless, a father could do nothing without the consent of his daughter.[3] Obviously, then, so far as the power of the father was concerned, a woman had practically the management of her suit. II.—The husband had no power. If he tried to browbeat her as to what to do, she could send him a divorce, a privilege which she had at her beck and call,

The right of women to sue.

[1] Paulus, ii, xi; id. in Dig., 16, 1, 1; Aulus Gellius, v, 19; Pomponius in Dig., 48, 2, 1: non est permissum mulieri publico iudicio quemquam reum facere.

[2] Ulpian in Dig., 1, 16, 9. Salvius Julianus, Pars Prima, vi: si non habebunt advocatum, ego dabo. Alexander Severus (222–235 A.D.) gave pensions to those advocates in the provinces who pleaded free of charge—Lampridius, *Alex. Severus*, 44.

[3] Cf. Paulus in Dig., 23, 3, 28. Codex, v, 13, 1, and 18, 1. Ulpian in Dig., iii, 3, 8.

as we have seen; and then she could force him to give her any guardian she wanted.[1] III.—That the authority of other guardians was in practice a mere formality, I have already proved (pp. 7 and 8).

From these considerations it is clear that the woman's wishes were supreme in the conduct of any suit. Moreover, the law expressly states that women may appoint whatever attorneys or agents they desire, without asking the consent of their legal guardians[2]; and thus they were at liberty to select a man who would manage things as they might direct. There were cases where even the strict letter of the law permitted women to lay an action on their own responsibility alone: if, when a suit for recovery of dowry was brought, the father was absent or hindered by infirmities[3]; if the woman sued or was sued to get or render an account of property managed in trust[4]; to avenge the death of a parent or children, or of patron or patroness and their children[5]; to lay bare any matter pertaining to the public grain supply[6]; and to disclose cases of treason.[7]

We read of many cases of women pleading

---

[1] Gaius, i, 137.

[2] Frag. iur. Rom. Vat., 325; id., 327 (from Papinian): mulieres quoque et sine tutoris auctoritate procuratorem facere posse.

[3] Ulpian in Dig., iii, 3, 8; ibid., Paulus, iii, 3, 41.

[4] Ulpian in Dig., iii, 5, 3.

[5] Pomponius in Dig., 48, 2, 1; ibid., Papinian, 48, 2, 2—who adds that she could also do so in a case regarding the will of a mother or father's freedman.

[6] Marcianus in Dig., 48, 2, 13.

[7] Papinian in Dig., 48, 4, 8.

publicly and bringing suit. Indeed, according to Juvenal—who is, however, a pessimist by profession—the ladies found legal proceedings so interesting that bringing suit became a passion with them as strong as it had once been among the Athenians.

Instances of women pleading in public and suing.

Thus Juvenal [1]: "There is almost no case in which a woman would n't bring suit. Manilia prosecutes, when she is n't a defendant. They draw up briefs quite by themselves, and are ready to cite principles and authorities to Celsus [a celebrated lawyer of that time]." Of pleading in public one of the celebrated instances was that of Hortensia, daughter of the great orator Quintus Hortensius, Cicero's rival. On an occasion when matrons had been burdened with heavy taxes and none of their husbands would fight the measure, Hortensia pleaded the case publicly with great success. All writers speak of her action and the eloquence of her speech with great admiration. [2] We hear also of a certain Gaia Afrania, wife of a Senator; she always conducted her case herself before the supreme judge, "not because there was any lack of lawyers," adds her respectable and scandalised historian, [3] "but because she had more than enough of impudence."

Quintilian mentions several cases of women

---

[1] Juvenal, vi, 242–245.

[2] Valerius Maximus, viii, 3, 3.   Appian, *B.C.*, iv, 32 ff.   Quintilian, i, 1, 6.

[3] Valerius Maximus, viii, 3, 2.

being sued [1]; Pliny tells how he acted as attorney
for some[2]; and the Law Books will supply any one
curious in the matter with abundant examples.[3]
A quotation from Pliny [4] will give an idea of the
kind of suit a woman might bring, and the great interest aroused thereby: "Attia Viriola, a woman of
illustrious birth and married to a former supreme
judge, was disinherited by her eighty-year-old
father within eleven days after he had brought
Attia a stepmother. Attia was trying to regain
her share of her father's estate. One hundred and
eighty jurors sat in judgment. The tribunal was
crowded, and from the higher part of the court
both men and women strained over the railings in
their eagerness to hear (which was difficult), and
to see (which was easy)."

There were many legal qualifications designed
to help women evade the strict letter of the law
when this, if enforced absolutely, would   *Partiality of*
work injustice. Ignorance of the law,   *the law to*
if there was no criminal offence involving   *women.*
good morals, was particularly accepted in the case
of women "on account of the weakness of the sex."[5]
A typical instance of the growth of the desire to
help women, protect them as much as possible,

[1] Quintilian, ix, 2, 20 and 34.
[2] E.g., Pliny, *Letters*, i, 5, and iv, 17.
[3] E.g., Huschke, pp. 796, 797, 803, 807, 809, 810, 856, 857, 858.
Or instances such as that mentioned in Digest, 48, 2, 18, where a
sister brings an action to prove her brother's will a forgery.
[4] Pliny, *Letters*, vi, 33.
[5] Paulus in Dig., 22, 6, 9.

and stretch the laws in their favour, may be taken from the senatorial decree known as the Senatus Consultum Velleianum.[1] This was an order forbidding females to become sureties or defendants for any one in a contract. But at the end of the first century of our era the Senate voted that the law be emended to help women and to give them special privileges in every class of contract. "We must praise the farsightedness of that illustrious order," comments the great jurist Ulpian,[2] "because it brought aid to women on account of the weakness of the sex, exposed, as it is, to many mishaps of this sort."

The rights of women to inherit under Roman law deserve some mention. Here again we may Rights of wo- note a steady growth of justice. Some men to inherit. general examples will make this clearer, before I treat of the specific powers of inheritance. I.—In the year 169 B.C. the Tribune Quintus Voconius Saxa had a law passed which restricted greatly the rights of women to inherit.[3] According to Dio[4] no woman was, by this statute, permitted to receive more than 25,000 sesterces—1250 dollars. In the second century after Christ, this law had fallen into complete desuetude.[5] II.—By

[1] Fully treated in Dig., 16, 1, and Paulus, ii, xi.

[2] Ulpian in Dig., 16, 1, 2.

[3] Aulus Gellius, xvii, 6. St. Augustine, de Civit. Dei, iii, 21: nam tunc, id est inter secundum et postremum bellum Carthaginiense, lata est etiam illa lex Voconia, ne quis heredem feminam faceret, nec unicam filiam.

[4] Dio, 56, 10.

[5] Aulus Gellius, xx, 1, 23. According to Dio, 56, 10, it was

the Falcidian Law, passed in the latter part of
the first century B.C., no citizen was allowed to
divert more than three fourths of his estate from
his natural heirs.[1] The Romans felt strongly
against any man who disinherited his children
without very good reason; the will of such a
parent was called *inofficiosum*, "made without
a proper feeling of duty," and the disinherited
children had an action at law to recover their
proper share.[2] A daughter was considered a
natural heir no less than a son and had equal
privileges in succession[3]; and so women were
bound to receive some inheritance at least.   III.—
It is a sad commentary on Christian rulers that for
many ages they allowed the crimes of the father
to be visited upon his children and by their bills
of attainder confiscated to the state the goods
of condemned offenders.   Now, the Roman law
stated positively that "the crime or punishment

Augustus who in the year 9 A.D. gave women permission to inherit any amount.

[1] Fully treated in Dig., 35, 2. Also in Gaius, ii, 227, and
Paulus, iii, viii, 1–3, and iv, 3, 3, and 5 and 6.

[2] Paulus, iv, Tit. v, 1. Cases in which "Complaints of Un-
dutiful Will" were the issue will be found, e.g., in Codex, iii,
28, 1 and 19 and 28; id., iii, 29, 1 and 7.

[3] Ulpian in Dig., 38, 16, 1: suos heredes accipere debemus
filios filias sive naturales sive adoptivos.   Instances of daughters
being left heiresses of whole estates may be found, e.g., in Dig.,
28, 2, 19: cum quidam filiam ex asse heredem scripsisset
filioque, quem in potestate habebat, decem legasset, etc.   Or
the example mentioned by Scaevola in Dig., 41, 9, 3: **Duae
filiae** intestato patri heres exstiterunt, etc.

of a father can inflict no stigma on his child." [1]   So far as the goods of the father were concerned, the property of three kinds of criminals escheated to the crown: (1) those who committed suicide while under indictment for some crime, [2] (2) forgers, [3] (3) those guilty of high treason. [4] Yet it seems reasonable to doubt whether these laws were very often carried out strictly to the letter. For example, the law did indeed hold that the estate of a party guilty of treason was confiscated to the state [5]; but even here it was expressly ordained that the goods of the condemned man's freedmen be reserved for his children. [6] Moreover, in actual practice we can find few instances where the law was executed in its literal severity even under the worst tyrants. It was Julius Caesar who first set the splendid example of allowing to the children of his dead foes full enjoyment of their patrimonies. [7] Succeeding

[1] Callistratus in Dig., 48, 19, 26: crimen vel poena paterna nullam maculam filio infligere potest. namque unusquisque ex suo admisso sorti subicitur nec alieni criminis successor constituitur; idque divi fratres Hierapolitanis rescripserunt. "Nothing is more unjust," writes Seneca (de Ira, ii, 34, 3), "than that any one should become the heir of the odium excited by his father."

[2] Paulus, v, xii, 1.

[3] Paulus, v, xii, 12.

[4] Ulpian in Dig., 48, 4, 11.

[5] Ulpian in Dig., 48, 4, 11.

[6] Hermogenianus in Dig., 48, 4, 9.

[7] Sulla had not only deprived the children of the proscribed of all their estates, but had also debarred them from aspiring to any political office—see Velleius Paterculus, ii, 28.

emperors followed the precedent.[1] Tyrants like Tiberius and Nero, strangely enough, in a majority of cases overruled the Senate when it proposed to confiscate the goods of those condemned for treason, and allowed the children a large part or all of the paternal estate.[2] Hadrian gave the children of proscribed offenders the twelfth part of their father's goods.[3] Antoninus Pius gave them all.[4] There was a strong public feeling against bills of attainder and this sentiment is voiced by all writers of the Empire. The law forbade wives to suffer any loss for any fault of their husbands.[5]

Since we have now noticed that women could inherit any amount, that they were bound to receive something under their fathers' wills, and that the guilt of their kin could inflict no prejudice upon them in the way of bills of attainder involving physical injury or civil status and, in practice, little loss so far as inheriting property

[1] For examples of the clemency of Augustus see Suetonius, *div. Aug.*, 33 and 51 and 67; Seneca, *de Ira*, iii, 23, 4 ff., and 40, 2; Velleius Paterculus, ii, 86, 87.

[2] For Tiberius see, e.g., Tacitus, *Annals*, iv—case of Silius; id., *Annals*, iii, 17, 18—case of Piso. For Nero, note Tacitus, *Annals*, xiii, 43—case of Publius Suilius. Clemency of Claudius mentioned in Dio, 60, 15, 16; of Vitellius in Tacitus, *Hist.*, ii, 62.

[3] Spartianus, *Had.*, 18.

[4] Capitolinus, *Anton. Pius*, 7. See also the anecdote of Aurelian in Vopiscus, *Aurelian*, 23.

[5] Codex, iv, 12, 2, rescript of Diocletian: ob maritorum culpam uxores inquietari leges vetant. proinde rationalis noster, si res quae a fisco occupatae sunt dominii tui esse probaveris, ius publicum sequetur.

was concerned, we may pass to a contemplation of the specific legal rights of inheritance of women.

If women were to be disinherited, it was sufficient to mention them in an aggregate; but males must be mentioned specifically.[1] If, however, they were disinherited in an aggregate (*inter ceteros*), some legacy had to be left them that they might not seem to have been passed over through forgetfulness.[2] I shall not concern myself particularly with testate succession, because here obviously the will of the testator could dispose as he wished, except in so far as he was limited by the Falcidian Law. The matter of intestate succession may well claim our attention; for therein we shall see what powers of inheritance were given the female sex. The general principles are explained by Gaius (iii, 1–38); and these principles followed, in the main, the law as laid down in the Twelve Tables (451 B.C.). According to these, the estates of those who died intestate belonged first of all to the children who were in the power of the deceased at the time of his death; there was no distinction of sex; the daughters were entitled to precisely the same amount as the sons.[3] If the children of the testator had died, the grandson or granddaughter *through the son* succeeded; or the great-grandson or great-

[1] Gaius, ii, 129 and 132.

[2] Gaius, ii, 132.

[3] Codex, iii, 36, 11: Inter filios ac filias bona intestatorum parentium pro virilibus portionibus aequo iure dividi oportere explorati iuris est.

granddaughter through the *grandson*. If a son and a daughter were alive, as well as grandsons and granddaughters through the *son*, they were all equally called to the estate. The estate was not divided per capita, but among families as a whole; for example, if of two sons one only was alive, but the other had left children, the testator's surviving son received one half of the patrimony and his grandchildren through his other son the other half, to be divided among them severally. If, then, there were six grandchildren, each received one twelfth of the estate.

Here the powers of women to inherit stopped. Beyond the tie of *consanguinitas*, that is, that of daughter to father, or granddaughter through a *son,* the female line must at once turn aside, and had no powers; the estate descended to the *agnati*, that is, male relatives on the father's side. Hence a mother was shut out by a brother of the deceased or by that brother's children. If there were no *agnati*, the goods were given to the *gentiles*, male relatives of the clan bearing the same name. In fact, under this régime we may say that of the female line the daughter alone was sure of inheriting something.

In the days of the Empire some attempts were made to be more just. It was enacted[1] that all the children should be called to the estate, whether they had been under the power of the testator at the time of his death or not; and female relatives

[1] Gaius, iii, 25-31.

were now allowed to come in for their share "in the third degree," that is, if there was neither a child or an agnate surviving. This was not much of an improvement; and the principle of agnate succession is the only point in which Roman law failed to give to women those equal rights which it allowed them in other cases.

There is no point on which Roman law laid more stress than that the children, both male and female, were to be constantly protected and must receive their legal share of their father's or mother's goods. After a husband's divorce or death his wife could, indeed, enjoy possession of the property and the usufruct; but the principal had to be conserved intact for the children until they arrived at maturity. In the same way a father was obliged to keep untouched for the children whatever had been left them by the mother on her decease [1]; and he must also leave them that part, at least, of his own property prescribed by the Falcidian Law. A case—and it was common enough in real life—such as that described by Dickens in *David Copperfield*, where, by the English law, a second husband acquired absolute right over his wife's property and shut out her son, would have been

Protection of property of children.

---

[1] See, e.g., Codex, vi, 60, 1: Res, quae ex matris successione fuerint ad filios devolutae, ita sint in parentum potestate, ut fruendi dumtaxat habeant facultatem, dominio videlicet eorum ad liberos pertinente.

impossible under Roman law. Neither husband
nor wife could succeed to one another's intestate
estate absolutely unless there were no children,
parents, or other relatives living.[1]

Rape of a woman was punished by death;
accessories to the crime merited the same penalty.[2]
Indecent exposure before a virgin met
with punishment out of course.[3]   Kid-
napping was penalised by hard labour in
Punishment of crimes against women.
the mines or by crucifixion in the case of those
of humble birth, and by confiscation of half the
goods and by perpetual exile in the case of a
noble.[4]   Temporary exile was visited upon those
guilty of abortion themselves[5]; if it was caused
through the agency of another, the agent, even
though he or she did so without evil intent, was
punished by hard labour in the mines, if of humble
birth, and by relegation to an island and confiscation of part of their goods, if of noble rank.[6]   If

[1] For all this, see Codex, v, 9, 5, and vi, 18, 1.

[2] Paulus, v, 4, 14, who adds that exile was the penalty if the
crime had not been completely carried out.   It would seem also
that ravished women had the option of deciding whether their
seducers should marry them or be put to death—see the *viti-
atarum electiones* as mentioned by Tacitus, *Dial. de Orat.*, 35.
According to Ruffus, 40, a soldier who did violence to a girl
had his nostrils cut off, besides being forced to give the injured
woman a third part of his goods: militi, qui puellae vim adtulerit
et stupraverit, nares abscinduntur, data puellae tertia militis
facultatum parte.

[3] Paulus, v, 4, 21.

[4] By the lex Fabia.   Paulus, v, 30 B.   Digest, 48, 15; 17, 2, 51.

[5] Ulpian in Dig., 48, 8, 8; ibid., Tryphoninus, 48, 19, 39.

[6] Paulus, v, 23, 14; id. in Dig., 48, 19, 38.

the victim died, the person who caused the abortion was put to death.[1]

The rights of women to an education were not questioned. That Sulpicia could publish amatory poems in honour of her husband and receive eulogies from writers like Martial[2] shows that she and ladies like her occupied somewhat the same position as Olympia Morata and Tarquinia Molza later in Italy during the Renaissance, or like some of the celebrated Frenchwomen, such as Madame de Staël. Seneca addresses a *Dialogue on Consolation* to one Marcia; such an idea would have made the hair of any Athenian gentleman in the time of Socrates stand on end. Aspasia was obliged to be a courtesan in order to become educated and to frequent cultivated society[3]; Sulpicia was a noble matron in good standing. The world had not stood still since Socrates had requested some one to take Xanthippe home, lest he be burdened by her sympathy in his last moments. Pains were taken that the Roman girl of wealth should have special tutors.[4] "Pompeius Saturninus recently read me some letters," writes Pliny[5] to one of his corre-

Rights of women to an education.

[1] Paulus, supra cit.

[2] Martial, x, 35, and x, 38.

[3] Sappho, Telesilla, and Corinna belong to an earlier period, when the Oriental idea of seclusion for women had not yet become firmly fixed in Greece. Women like Agallis of Corcyra, who wrote on grammar (Athenaeus, i, 25) and lived in a much later age, doubtless belonged to the *hetaerae* class.

[4] See, e.g., Pliny, *Letters*, v, 16.

[5] Pliny, *Letters*, i, 16.

spondents, "which he insisted had been written by his wife. I believed that Plautus or Terence was being read in prose. Whether they are really his wife's, as he maintains; or his own, which he denies; he deserves equal honour, either because he composes them, or because he has made his wife, whom he married when a mere girl, so learned and polished." The enthusiasm of the ladies for literature is attested by Persius.[1]

According to Juvenal, who, as an orthodox satirist, was not fond of the weaker sex, women sometimes became over-educated. He growls as follows[2]: "That woman is a worse nuisance than usual who, as soon as she goes to bed, praises Vergil; makes excuses for doomed Dido; pits bards against one another and compares them; and weighs Homer and Maro in the balance. Teachers of literature give way, professors are vanquished, the whole mob is hushed, and no lawyer or auctioneer will speak, nor any other woman." The prospect of a learned wife filled the orthodox Roman with peculiar horror.[3] No Roman woman ever became a public professor as did Hypatia or,

[1] Persius, i, 4–5: Ne mihi Polydamas et Troiades Labeonem praetulerint? "Are you afraid that Polydamas and the Trojan Ladies will prefer Labeo to me?" The *Trojan Ladies*, of course, stand for the aristocratic classes, Colonial Dames, so to speak, who were fond of tracing their descent back to Troy just as Americans like to discover that their ancestors came over in the *Mayflower*.

[2] Juvenal, vi, 434–440.

[3] Cf. Martial, ii, 90: sit mihi verna satur, sit non doctissima coniunx.

ages later, Bitisia Gozzadina, who, in the thirteenth
century, became doctor of canon and civil law at
the University of Bologna.

I have been speaking of women of the wealthier
classes; but the poor were not neglected. As far
back as the time of the Twelve Tables—450 B.C.
—parents of moderate means were accustomed to
club together and hire a schoolroom and a teacher
who would instruct the children, girls no less than
boys, in at least the proverbial three R's. Virginia
was on her way to such a school when she en-
countered the passionate gaze of Appius Claudius.
Such grammar schools, which boys and girls
attended together, flourished under the Empire as
they had under the Republic.[1] They were not
connected with the state, being supported by the
contributions of individual parents. To the end
we cannot say that there was a definite scheme
of public education for girls at the state's expense
as there was for boys.[2] Still, the emperors did
something. Trajan, Hadrian, Antoninus Pius,
Marcus Aurelius, and Alexander Severus, for
example, regularly supplied girls and boys with

[1] The famous verses of Martial:
    Quid tibi nobiscum, ludi scelerate magister?
    Invisum pueris virginibusque caput!
[2] Vespasian (69–79 A.D.) started free public education by ap-
pointing Quintilian Professor of Rhetoric subsidised by the state.
Succeeding emperors enlarged upon it; but especially Alexander
Severus (222–235 A.D.), who instituted salaries for teachers of
rhetoric, literature, medicine, mechanics, and architecture in
Rome and the provinces, and had poor boys attend the lectures
free of charge—see Lampridius, *Alex. Severus*, 44.

education at public expense[1]; under Trajan there were 5000 children so honoured. Public-spirited citizens were also accustomed to contribute liberally to the same cause; Pliny on one occasion[2] gave the equivalent of $25,000 for the support and instruction of indigent boys and girls.

It may not be out of place to speak briefly of the Vestal Virgins, the six priestesses of Vesta, who are the only instances in pagan antiquity of anything like the nuns of the Christians. The Vestals.
The Vestals took a vow of perpetual chastity.[3] They passed completely out of the power of their parents and became entirely independent. They could not receive the inheritance of any person who died intestate, and no one could become heir to a Vestal who died intestate. They were allowed to be witnesses in court in public trials, a privilege denied other women. Peculiar honour was accorded them and they were regularly appointed the custodians of the wills of the emperors.[4]

The position of women in slavery merits some attention, in view of the huge multitudes that

[1] Pliny, *Paneg.*, 26. Spartianus, *Hadrian*, 7, 8–9. Capitolinus, *Anton. Pius* 8; id. *M. Anton. Phil.* 11. Lampridius, *Alex. Severus*, 57.

[2] Pliny, *Letters*, vii, 18. The sum was 500,000 sesterces.

[3] Any infringement of this vow was punished by burial alive—for instances, see Suetonius, *Domitian*, 8; Herodian, iv, 6, 4; Pliny, *Letters*, iv, 11; Dio, 77, 16 (Xiphilin). Their paramours were beaten to death.

[4] A full account of the Vestals will be found in Aulus Gellius, i, 12.

were held in bondage. Roman law acknowledged no legal rights on the part of slaves.[1]

Female slaves. The master had absolute power of life
and death.[2] They were exposed to every
whim of master or mistress without redress.[3] If
some one other than their owner harmed them,
they might obtain satisfaction through their
master and for his benefit; but the penalty for the
aggressor was only pecuniary.[4] A slave's evidence
was never admitted except under torture.[5] If
a master was killed, every slave of his household
and even his freedmen and freedwomen were put to
torture, although the culprit may already have
been discovered, in order to ascertain the instigator
of the plot and his remotest accessories.[6]

The earlier history of Rome leaves no doubt
that before the Republic fell these laws were
carried out with inhuman severity. With the
growth of Rome into a world power and the consequent rise of humanitarianism[7] a strong public

[1] Quintilian, vii, 3, 27: ad servum nulla lex pertinet. On the
rare instances when a slave could inform against his master in
a public court, see Hermogenianus in Dig., v, 1, 53.

[2] Gaius, i, 52 ff.

[3] Gaius, iii, 222. Cf. Juvenal vi, 219–223, and 474–495.

[4] Gaius, iii, 222. Salvius Julianus, Pars Secunda, xv. Aulus
Gellius, xx, 1.

[5] Paulus, v, 16.

[6] Paulus, iii, v, 5 ff. Pliny, *Letters*, viii, 14. Tacitus, *Annals*,
xiii, 32.

[7] Valerius Maximus, vi, 8, in a chapter entitled *de fide ser-
vorum* speaks with great admiration of instances of fidelity on the
part of slaves. Seneca ate with his—*Epist.* 47, 13. Martial
laments the death of a favourite slave girl—v, 34 and 37. Dio

feeling against gratuitous cruelty towards slaves sprang up. This may be illustrated by an event which happened in the reign of Nero, in the year 58, when a riot ensued out of sympathy for some slaves who had been condemned *en masse* after their master had been assassinated by one of them.[1] Measures were gradually introduced for alleviating the hardships and cruelties of slavery. Claudius (41–54 A.D.) ordained[2] that since sick and infirm slaves were being exposed on an island in the Tiber sacred to Aesculapius, because their masters did not wish to bother about attending them, all those who were so exposed were to be set free if they recovered and never to be returned into the power of their masters; and if any owner preferred to put a slave to death rather than expose him, he was to be held for murder. Gentlemen began to speak with contempt of a master or mistress who maltreated slaves.[3] Hadrian (117–138 A.D.) modified the old laws to a remarkable degree: he forbade slaves to be put to death by their masters and commanded them to be tried by

---

(62, 27—Xiphilin) notes the heroic conduct of Epicharis, a freedwoman, who was included in a conspiracy against Nero; but she revealed none of its secrets, though tortured in every way by Tigellinus. The pages of Pliny are full of the spirit of kindliness to slaves.

[1] See Tacitus, *Annals*, xiv, 42 ff.
[2] Suetonius, *Claudius*, 25. Dio, 60, 29 (Xiphilin).
[3] See, e.g., Seneca, *de Clem.*, i, 18, 1 and 2—especially the anecdote of Vedius Pollio (mentioned also by Dio, 54, 23). The interesting letter of Pliny, viii, 16; and cf. iii, 14, and v, 19. Juvenal, vi, 219–223.

regularly appointed judges; he brought it about
that a slave, whether male or female, was not to be
sold to a slave-dealer or trainer for public shows
without due cause; he did away with *ergastula*
or workhouses, in which slaves guilty of offences
were forced to work off their penalties in chains
and were confined to filthy dungeons; and he
modified the law previously existing to the extent
that if a master was killed in his own house, the
inquisition by torture could not be extended to
the whole household, but to those only who, by
proximity to the deed, could have noticed it.[1]
Gaius observes[2] that for slaves to be in complete
subjection to masters who have power of life and
death is an institution common to all nations.
"But at this time," he continues, "it is permitted
neither to Roman citizens nor any other men who
are under the sway of the Roman people to vent
their wrath against slaves beyond measure and
without reason. In fact, by a decree of the
sainted Antoninus (138–161 A.D.) a master who
without cause kills his slave is ordered to be held
no less than he who kills another's slave.[3] An
excessive severity on the part of masters is also
checked by a constitution of the same prince.
On being consulted by certain governors about
those slaves who rush for refuge to the shrines of

[1] Spartianus, *Hadrian*, 18.
[2] Gaius, i, 52ff. Cf. Ulpian in Dig., 1, 12, 1 and 8.
[3] The punishment for this was pecuniary damages equal to
twice the highest value of a slave during the year in which he
was killed.

the gods or the statues of emperors, he ordered
that if the cruelty of masters seemed intolerable
they should be compelled to sell their slaves."
Severus ordained that the city prefect should
prevent slaves from being prostituted.[1]   Aurelian
gave his slaves who had transgressed to be heard
according to the laws by public judges.[2]   Tacitus
procured a decree that slaves were not to be put
to inquisitorial torture in a case affecting a master's
life, not even if the charge was high treason.[3]   So
much for the laws that mitigated slavery under
the Empire.   They were not ideal; but they would
in more respects than one compare favourably
with the similar legislation that was in force, prior
to the Civil War, in the American Slave States.

SOURCES

I.   Iurisprudentiae Anteiustinianae quae Supersunt. ed. Ph.
Eduardus Huschke. Lipsiae (Teubner), 1886 (fifth edition).

II.   Codex Iustinianus. Recensuit Paulus Krueger. Berolini
apud Weidmannos, 1877.

Corpus Iuris Civilis: Institutiones recognovit Paulus
Krueger; Digesta recognovit Theodorus Mommsen.   Berolini
apud Weidmannos, 1882.

Novellae: Corpus Iuris Civilis. Volumen Tertium recognovit
Rudolfus Schoell; Opus Schoellii morte interceptum absolvit
G. Kroll.   Berolini apud Weidmannos, 1895.

III.   The Fragments of the Perpetual Edict of Salvius Julianus.   Edited by Bryan Walker.   Cambridge University
Press, 1877.

---

[1] Ulpian in Dig., i, 12, 8: hoc quoque officium praefecto urbi
a divo Severo datum est, ut mancipia tueatur ne prostituantur.

[2] Vopiscus, *Aurelian*, 49.

[3] Vopiscus, *Tacitus*, 9.

IV. Pomponii de Origine Iuris Fragmentum: recognovit
Fridericus Osannus. Gissae, apud Io. Rickerum, 1848.

V. Corpus Inscriptionum Latinarum, Consilio et Auctoritate
Academiae Litterarum Regiae Borussicae editum. Berolini
apud Georgium Reimerum (begun in 1863).

VI. Valerii Maximi Factorum et Dictorum Memorabilium
Libri Novem: cum Iulii Paridis et Ianvarii Nepotiani Epitomis:
iterum recensuit Carolus Kempf. Lipsiae (Teubner), 1888.

VII. Cassii Dionis Cocceiani Rerum Romanarum libri
octaginta: ab Immanuele Bekkero Recogniti. Lipsiae, apud
Weidmannos, 1849.

VIII. C. Suetoni Tranquilli quae Supersunt Omnia: recensuit Carolus L. Roth. Lipsiae (Teubner), 1898.

IX. A. Persii Flacci, D. Iunii Iuvenalis, Sulpiciae Saturae;
recognovit Otto Iahn. Editio altera curam agente Francisco
Buecheler. Berolini, apud Weidmannos, 1886.

X. Eutropi Breviarium ab Urbe Condita: recognovit Franciscus Ruehl. Lipsiae (Teubner), 1897.

XI. Herodiani ab Excessu Divi Marci libri octo: ab Immanuele Bekkero recogniti. Lipsiae (Teubner), 1855.

XII. A. Gellii Noctium Atticarum libri XX: edidit Carolus
Hosius. Lipsiae (Teubner), 1903.

XIII. Petronii Saturae et Liber Priapeorum: quartum edidit
Franciscus Buecheler: adiectae sunt Varronis et Senecae Saturae
similesque Reliquiae. Berolini, apud Weidmannos, 1904.

XIV. M. Valerii Martialis Epigrammaton libri: recognovit
Walther Gilbert. Lipsiae (Teubner), 1896.

XV. Cornelii Taciti Libri qui Supersunt: quartum recognovit
Carolus Halm. Lipsiae (Teubner), 1901.

XVI. C. Vellei Paterculi ex Historiae Romanae libris duobus
quae supersunt: edidit Carolus Halm. Lipsiae (Teubner), 1876.

XVII. L. Annaei Senecae Opera quae Supersunt: recognovit
Fridericus Haase. Lipsiae (Teubner), 1898.

XVIII. Athenaei Naucratitae Deipnosophistarum libri XV:
recensuit Georgius Kaibel. Lipsiae (Teubner), 1887.

XIX. Lucii Apulei Metamorphoseon libri XI. Apologia et
Florida. Recensuit J. van der Vliet. Lipsiae (Teubner), 1897.

XX. C. Plini Caecili Secundi Epistularum libri novem.
Epistularum ad Traianum liber. Panegyricus. Recognovit
C. F. W. Mueller. Lipsiae (Teubner), 1903.

XXI. Scriptores Historiae Augustae: edidit Hermannus Peter. Lipsiae (Teubner), 1888.

XXII. M. Fabii Quintiliani Institutionis Oratoriae libri XII: recensuit Eduardus Bonnell. Lipsiae (Teubner), 1905.

XXIII. Marci Antonini Commentariorum libri XII: iterum recensuit Ioannes Stich. Lipsiae (Teubner), 1903.

XXIV. C. Plinii Secundi Naturalis Historiae libri XXXVII: recognovit Ludovicus Ianus. Lipsiae (Teubner), 1854.

XXV. XII Panegyrici Latini: recensuit Aemilius Baehrens. Lipsiae (Teubner), 1874.

XXVI. Plutarchi Scripta Moralia, Graece et Latine: Parisiis, editore Ambrosio F. Didot, 1841.

Plutarchi Vitae Parallelae: iterum recognovit Carolus Sintennis. Lipsiae (Teubner), 1884.

XXVII. Ammiani Marcellini Rerum Gestarum libri qui supersunt: recensuit V. Gardthausen. Lipsiae (Teubner), 1875.

XXVIII. Poetae Latini Minores: recensuit Aemilius Baehrens. Lipsiae (Teubner), 1883.

CHAPTER II

MEANWHILE a new world force, destined to overthrow the old order of things, was growing slowly to maturity and spreading out its might until eventually it fought its way to pre-eminence. I have traced the rights of women under the régime of pagan Rome; I shall inquire next into the position of women under Christianity. We must first note the attitude of the early Christians towards women in general; for that attitude will naturally be reflected in any laws made after the Church has become supreme and is combined with and directs the State. That will demand a special chapter on Canon Law; but in the present chapter I propose to show how women were regarded by the Christians in the centuries which were the formative period of the Church.

The direct words of Christ so far as they relate to women and as we have them in the Gospels concern themselves wholly to bring about purity in the relation of the sexes. "Ye have heard that it was said, Thou shalt not commit adultery; but I say unto you, that every one that looketh on a woman to lust after her hath committed adultery with her already in his heart.''[1] His commands on the subject of divorce are positive and un-equivocal: "It was said also, Whosoever shall put away his wife, let him give her a writing of divorce-ment; but I say unto you, that every one that putteth away his wife, saving for the cause of fornication, maketh her an adultress; and whoso-ever shall marry her when she is put away, com-mitteth adultery."[2] Christ was content to lay down great ethical principles, not minute regula-tions. Of any inferiority on the part of women he says nothing, nor does be concern himself with giving any directions about their social or legal rights. He blessed the marriage at Cana; and to the woman taken in adultery he showed his usual clemency. For the rest, his relations with women have an atmosphere of rare sympathy, gentleness, and charm.

But as soon as we leave the Gospels and read the Apostles we are in a different sphere. The Apostles were for the most part men of humble position, and their whole lives were directed by inherited beliefs which were distinctly Jewish and Oriental or Greek; not Western. In the Orient woman has from the dawn of history to the present day occupied a position exceedingly low. Indeed, in Mohammedan countries she is regarded merely

[1] *Matthew* 5, 27 ff.
[2] *Matthew* 5, 31 ff.; id. 19, 3 ff. *Mark* 10, 2–12. *Luke* 16, 18.

as a tool for the man's sensual passions and she
is not allowed to have even a soul. In Greece
women were confined to their houses, were uneducated, and had few public rights and less moral
latitude; their husbands had unlimited license.[1]
The Jewish ideal is by no means a lofty one and
cannot for a moment compare with the honour accorded the Roman matron under the Empire. According to *Genesis* a woman is the cause of all the
woes of mankind. *Ecclesiasticus* declares that the
badness of men is better than the goodness of
women.[2]   In *Leviticus*[3] we read that the period of
purification customary after the birth of a child is
to be twice as long in the case of a female as in a

---

[1] Plutarch lived in the second century A.D.; but he has inherited
the Greek point of view and advises a wife to bear with meekness the infidelities of the husband—see *Praecep. Coniug.*, 16.
His words are often curiously similar to those of the Apostles,
e.g., *Coniug. Praecep.*, 33: "The husband shall rule the wife not
as if master of a chattel, but as the soul does the body." Id.
37: "Wives who are sensible will be silent when their husbands
are angry and vent their passion; when their husbands are
silent, then let them speak to them and mollify them." However, like the Apostles, he enjoins upon husbands to honour their
wives; his essay on the "Virtues of Women"—γυναικῶν ἀρεταί—
is an affectionate tribute to their worth.

Some of the respectable Puritan gentlemen at Rome also
held that a wife be content to be a humble admirer of her husband (e.g., Pliny, *Paneg.*, 83, hoc efficiebat, quod mariti minores
erant . . . nam uxori sufficit obsequii gloria, etc.). But
Roman law insisted that what was morally right for the man
was equally so for the woman; just as it compelled a husband
himself to observe chastity, if he expected it from his wife.

[2] *Ecclesiasticus* 42, 14.

[3] *Leviticus* xii, 1–5.

male.   The inferiority of women was strongly felt;
and this conception would be doubly operative on
men of humble station who never travelled, who
had received little education, and whose ideas were
naturally bounded by the horizon of their native
localities.   We are to remember also that the East
is the home of asceticism, a conviction alien to
the Western mind.   There is no parallel in Western
Europe to St. Simeon Stylites.

We would, therefore, expect to find in the teachings of the Apostles an expression of Jewish, i.e.,
Eastern ideals on the subject of women; and we do
so find them.   Following the express commands of
Christ, they exhorted to sexual purity and reiter-
ated his injunctions on the matter of divorce.
They went much farther and began to legislate on
more minute details.   Paul allows second marriages
to women [1]; but thinks it better for a widow to
remain as she is. [2]   It is better to marry than to
burn; yet would he prefer that men and women
should remain in celibacy. [3]   The power of the
father to arrange a marriage for his daughter was,
under Roman law, limited by her consent; but
the words of Paul make it clear that it was now to
be a Christian precept that a father could determine
on his own responsibility whether his daughter
should remain a virgin. [4]   Wives are to be in subjection to their husbands, and "let the wife see that

[1] *Romans* 7, 2–4.
[2] *Corinthians* i, 7, 39.
[3] *Corinthians* i, 7, 1 ff.
[4] *Corinthians* i, 7, 37.

she fear her husband."[1]   Woman is the weaker
vessel[2]; she is to be silent in church; if she desires
to learn anything, she should ask her husband
at home.[3]   Furthermore: "I permit not a woman
to teach, nor to have dominion over a man,
but to be in quietness. For Adam was first
formed, then Eve; and Adam was not beguiled,
but the woman being beguiled hath fallen into
transgression; but she shall be saved through
childbearing, if they continue in faith and love
and sanctification with sobriety."[4]   The apparel
of women also evoked legislation from the Apostles.
Women were to pray with their heads veiled "for
the man is not of the woman, but the woman for
the man."[5]   Jewels, precious metal, and costly
garments were unbecoming the modest woman.[6]

In this early stage of Christianity we may already distinguish three conceptions that were quite
foreign to the Roman jurist: I. The inferiority
and weakness of women was evident from the
time of Eve and it was an act of God that punished
all womankind for Eve's transgression. Woman
had been man's evil genius. II. She was to be
submissive to father or husband and not bring
her will in opposition to theirs. III. She must
not be prominent in public, she must consider her

---

[1] *Ephesians* 5, 22 and 33.
[2] *Peter* i, 3, 7.
[3] *Corinthians* i, 14, 34.
[4] *Timothy* i, 2, 12–15.
[5] *Corinthians* i, 11, 8.
[6] *Timothy* i, 2, 9. *Peter* i, 3.

conduct and apparel minutely, and she was exhorted to remain a virgin, as being thus in a more exalted position. At the same time insistence was placed on the fact that a virgin, wife, and widow must be given due honour and respect, must be provided for, and allowed her share in taking part in those interests of the community which were considered her sphere.

If, now, we examine the writings of the Church Fathers, we shall see these ideas elaborated with all the vehemence of religious zeal.

The general opinions of the Fathers regarding women present a curious mixture. They are fond of descanting on the fact that woman is responsible for all the woes of mankind and that her very presence is dangerous. At the same time they pay glowing tribute to women in particular. St. Jerome held that women were naturally weaker, physically and morally, than men.[1] The same saint proves that all evils spring from women[2]; and in another passage he opines that marriage is indeed a lottery and the vices of women are too great to make it worth while.[3] "The sex is

[1] Abelard, *Ep.*, 9, in vol. 178, p. 325, of Migne: Beatus Hieronymus . . . tanto magis necessarium amorem huius studii (i.e. the Scriptures) censuit, quanto eas naturaliter infirmiores et carne debiliores esse conspexit. Cf. St. Paul of Nolan, *Letters*, 23, § 135—Migne 61, p. 273: Hi enim (i.e. evil spirits) petulantius infirmiora vasa pertentant, sicut non Adam, sed Evam coluber aggressus est.

[2] Adversus Iovianum, i, 48—Migne, vol. 23, p. 278.

[3] Adversus Iovianum, i, 28—Migne, vol. 23, pp. 249–250: Qui enim ducit uxorem, in ambiguo est, utrum odiosam an ama-

practiced in deceiving," observes St. Maximus.[1]
St. Augustine disputes subtly whether woman is
the image of God as well as man. He says no,
and proves it thus[2]: The Apostle commands
that a man should not veil his head, because he
is the image of God; but the woman must veil hers,
according to the same Apostle; therefore the
woman is not the image of God. "For this
reason, again," continues the Saint, "the Apostle
says 'A woman is not permitted to teach, nor
to have dominion over her husband.'" Bishop
Marbodius calls woman a "pleasant evil, at once
a honeycomb and a poison" and indicts the sex,[3]

bilem ducat. Si odiosam duxerit, ferri non potest. Si amabilem,
amor illius inferno et arenti terrae et incendio comparatur.
He quotes the Old Testament, especially *Pr.* 30, 16, to support
his views.

[1] S. Maximi Episcopi Taurinensis—Homilia 53, 1—Migne,
vol. 57, p. 350.

[2] Augustinus: *Quaest. ex vet. Test.*, 21: an mulier imago Dei sit
. . . unde et Apostolus, Vir quidem, inquit, non debet
velare caput, cum sit imago et gloria Dei; mulier autem, inquit,
velet caput. Quare? Quia non est imago Dei. Unde denuo dicit
Apostolus: Mulieri autem docere non permittitur, neque dominari
in virum. Migne, vol. 35, p. 2228.

[3] Migne, vol. 171, pp. 1698–1699:

> Femina dulce malum, pariter favus atque venenum,
> Melle linens gladium cor confodit et sapientum.
> Quis suasit primo vetitum gustare parenti?
> Femina. Quis patrem natas vitiare coegit?
> Femina. Quis fortem spoliatum crine peremit?
> Femina. Quis iusti sacrum caput ense recidit?
> Femina.—etc., ad lib.

However, in another poem he acknowledges that there is
nothing more beautiful than a good woman:

something on the order of Juvenal or Jonathan
Swift, by citing the cases of Eve, the daughters of
Lot, Delilah, Herodias, Clytemnestra, and Progne.
The way in which women were regarded as at once
a blessing and a curse is well illustrated also in a
distich of Sedulius: "A woman alone has been
responsible for opening the gates of death; a
woman alone has been the cause of a return to
life." [1]

That women should be in subjection, in accordance with the dictum of Paul, the Church Fathers
assert emphatically. "How can it be said of a
woman that she is the image of God," exclaims
St. Augustine, [2] "when it is evident that she is
subject to the rule of her husband and has no
authority! Why, she can not teach, nor be a
witness, nor give security, nor act in court; how
much the more can she not govern!" Women are
commanded again and again not to perform any
of the functions of men and to yield a ready

In cunctis quae dante Deo concessa videntur
Usibus humanis, nil pulchrius esse putamus,
Nil melius muliere bona, etc.

[1] Migne, vol. 80, p. 307. The sentiment is more fully developed in another poem—Migne, vol. 80, p. 307:

Femina causa fuit humanae perditionis;
    Qua reparatur homo, femina causa fuit.
Femina causa fuit cur homo ruit a paradiso;
    Qua redit ad vitam, femina causa fuit.
Femina prima parens exosa, maligna, superba;
    Femina virgo parens casta, benigna, pia.

[2] *Quaest. ex vet. Test.*, 45: Migne, vol. 35, p. 2244.

and unquestioning obedience to their husbands.[1]
The Fathers also insist that marriage without a
paternal parent's consent is fornication.[2]

Marriage was looked upon as a necessary evil,
permitted, indeed, as a concession to the weakness of mankind, but to be avoided if possible.
"Celibacy is to be preferred to marriage," says
St. Augustine.[3] "Celibacy is the life of the
angels," remarks St. Ambrose.[4] "Celibacy is a
spiritual kind of marriage," according to St.
Optatus.[5] "Happy he," says Tertullian,[6] "who
lives like Paul!" The same saint paints a lugubri-
ous picture of marriage and the "bitter pleasure of
children" (*liberorum amarissima voluptate*) who
are burdens and just as likely as not will turn out
criminals. "Why did the Lord cry woe unto those
that are pregnant and give suck, unless it was to
call attention to the fact that children will be a

[1] E.g., Tertullian, *de virg. vel.*, 9. St. Paul of Nolan, letter
23, § 135—Migne, 61, p. 273. Id., letter 26, vol. 61, p. 732
of Migne. Cf. Augustine, letter 262, § 5—Migne, 33, p.
1079.

[2] Basilius, *ad Amphil.*, c. 42: Matrimonia sine iis, qui potestatem
habent, fornicationes sunt.

Ambrose says: Honorantur parentes Rebeccae muneribus,
consulitur puella non de sponsalibus, illa enim expectat iudicium
parentum; non est enim virginalis pudoris eligere maritum.

[3] Virginitas praeferenda coniugio—August., vol. 44, p. 142 of
Migne. The Council of Trent, eleven centuries later, in its
twenty-fourth session, re-echoed this sentiment and anathem-
atised any one who should deny it.

[4] Migne, vol. 16, p. 342.

[5] Id., 11, p. 1074.

[6] Tertullian *ad uxorem*, i, 3.

hindrance on the day of judgment?"[1] When such views were entertained of marriage, it need not seem remarkable that Tertullian and St. Paul of Nolan, like Tolstoy to-day, discovered the blessings of a celibate life after they were married, and ran away from their wives.[2] Jerome finds marriage useful chiefly because it produces virgins.[3]

As for second marriages, the Montanist and the Novatian sects condemned them absolutely, on the ground that if God has removed a wife or husband he has thereby signified his will to end the marrying of the parties; Tertullian calls second marriage a species of prostitution.[4] Jerome expresses the more tolerant and orthodox view: "What then? Do we condemn second marriages? Not at all; but we praise single ones. Do we cast the twice-married from the Church? Far from it; but we exhort the once-married to continence. In Noah's ark there were not only clean, but also unclean animals."[5]

[1] Id. ad uxorem, i, 5. See also Gregory of Nyassa, de Virg., iii, on the evils of matrimony.

[2] v. Tertullian, ad uxorem. For Paul of Nolan, see Migne, vol. 61, p. 22.

[3] Laudo nuptias, laudo coniugium, sed quia mihi virgines generant.

[4] Ad uxorem, i, 7 and 9: non aliud dicendum erit secundum matrimonium quam species stupri.

[5] Jerome, Epist., 123. See also id., Epistola de viduitate servanda, Migne 22, p. 550, and the Epist. de monogamia, Migne, 22, p. 1046. Ambrose, de viduis liber unus, Migne, 16, p. 234. Cf. Alanus de Insulis in Migne, vol. 210, p. 194: Vidua ad secundas nuptias non transeat.

As the Fathers were very well aware of the subtle influence of dress on the sexual passions, we have a vast number of minute regulations directing virgins, matrons, and widows to be clothed simply and without ornament; virgins were to be veiled. [1] Tertullian, with that keen logic of which the Church has always been proud in her sons, argues that inasmuch as God has not made crimson or green sheep it does not behoove women to wear colours that He has not produced in animals naturally. [2] St. Augustine forbids nuns to bathe more than once a month, unless under extreme necessity. [3]

As soon as the Church begins to exercise an influence upon law, we shall expect to see the legal position of women changed in accordance with certain general principles outlined above, viz: I. That inasmuch as Adam was formed before Eve and as women are the weaker vessels, they should confine themselves to those duties only which society has, from time immemorial, assigned

[1] See, e.g., St. Cyprian, *de habitu virginum*. Tertullian, *de virginibus velandis* and *de cultu feminarum*. Treatises on the way widows should dress were written, among others, by St. Paul of Nolan, *Epist.* 23, §§ 133–135—Migne 61; Augustine, St. Fulgentius Rusp., St. Paulinus Aquil., and St. Petrus Damianus.

[2] *De cultu feminarum*, i, 8.

[3] Lavacrum etiam corporum ususque balneorum non sit assiduus, sed eo quo solet intervallo temporis tribuatur, hoc est, semel in mense. Nisi infirmitatis necessitas cogat, corpus saepius non lavandum — Augustine, *de monialibus*, Migne, vol. 33, page 963.

them as their peculiar sphere. II. They should be meek, and not oppose father or husband; and to these they should go for advice on all matters. III. All license, such as the Roman woman's right of taking the initiative in a divorce, must never be tolerated. IV. They should never transgress the bounds of strictest decorum in conduct and dress, lest they seduce men; and they must never be conspicuous in public or attempt to perform public functions. V. They are to be given due honour and are to be cared for properly.

The legal rights of women would be affected, moreover, by a difference in the spirit of the law. The Roman jurist derived his whole sanction from reason and never allowed religious considerations, as such, to influence him when legislating on women. He recognised that laws are not immutable, but must be changed to fit the growth of equity and tolerance. No previous authority was valid to him if reason suggested that the authority's dictum had outlived its usefulness and must be adapted to larger ideas. It never occurred to him to make the inferiority of woman an act of God. On the other hand, the Church referred everything to one unchanging authoritative source, the Gospels and the writings of the Apostles; faith and authority took the place of reason; and any attempt to question the injunctions of the Bible was regarded as an act of impiety, to be punished accordingly. And as the various regulations about women had now a divine sanction, the permanence of these convictions was doubly assured.

SOURCES

I.   The Bible.
II.   Patrologia Latina: edidit J. P. Migne. Parisiis. 221 volumes (finished 1864).

/

CHAPTER III

CHRISTIANITY became the state religion
under Constantine, who issued the Edict of
Milan, giving toleration to the Christians, in
the year 313. The emperors from Constantine
through Justinian (527–565) modified the various
laws pertaining to the rights of women in various
ways. To the enactments of Justinian, who caused
the whole body of the Roman law to be collected,
I intend to give special attention. We must not,
as yet, expect to find the strict views of the Church
Fathers carried out in any severe degree. On
the contrary the old Roman law was still so
powerful that it was for the most part beyond the
control of ecclesiasts. Justinian was an ardent
admirer of it and could not escape from its prevailing spirit. Canon law had not yet developed.
When the old Roman civilisation in Italy has
succumbed completely to its barbarian conquerors;
when the East has been definitely sundered from
the West; when the Church has risen supreme,
has won temporal power, and has developed
canon law into a force equal to the civil law,—

then finally we shall expect to see the legal rights of women changed in accordance with two new world forces—the Roman Catholic Church and the Germanic nations.   I shall now discuss legislation having to do with my subject under the Christian emperors from Constantine (306–337) through the reign of Justinian (527–565).

The power of husband and wife to divorce at will and for any cause, which we have seen obtained **Divorce:** under the old Roman law, was confined **rescript of** to certain causes only by Theodosius and **Theodosius and** Valentinian (449 A.D.).   These emperors **Valentinian.** asserted vigorously that [1] the dissolution of the marriage tie should be made more difficult, especially out of regard to the children. Pursuant to this idea the power of divorce was given for the following reasons alone: adultery, murder, treason, sacrilege, robbery; unchaste conduct of a husband with a woman not his wife and vice-versa; if a wife attended public games without her husband's permission; and extreme physical violence of either party.   A woman who sent her husband a bill of divorce for any other reason forfeited her dowry and all ante-nuptial gifts and could not marry again for five years, under penalty of losing all civil rights.   Her property accrued to her husband to be kept in trust for the children.

Justinian made more minute regulations on the subject of divorce.   To the valid causes for

[1] Codex, v, 17, 8 contains this rescript in full.

divorce as laid down by Theodosius and Valentinian he added impotence; if a separation was obtained on this ground, the husband might Justinian on
retain ante-nuptial gifts.[1]   Abortion divorce.
committed by the wife or bathing with other men
than her husband or inveigling other men to be her
paramours—these offences on the part of the wife
gave her husband the right of divorce.[2]   Captivity
of either party for a prolonged period of time was
always a valid reason.   Justinian added also[3]
that a man who dismissed his wife without any of
the legal causes mentioned above existing or who
was himself guilty of any of these offences must
give to his wife one fourth of his property up to
a sum not to exceed one hundred *librae* of gold,
if he owned property worth four hundred *librae*
or more; if he had less, one fourth of all he possessed
was forfeit.   The same penalties held for the wife
who presumed to dismiss her husband without the
offences legally recognised existing.   The forfeited
money was at the free disposal of the blameless
party if there were no children; these being extant,
the property must be preserved intact for their
inheritance and merely the usufruct could be
enjoyed by the trustees.   A woman who secured
a divorce through a fault of her husband had
always to wait at least a year before marrying
again *propter seminis confusionem.*[4]

[1] Codex, v, 17, 10.
[2] Codex, v, 17, 11.
[3] Id.
[4] Novellae, 22, 18.

Justin, the nephew and successor of Justinian, reaffirmed the right to divorce by mutual consent, thus abrogating the laws of his pre-decessors.[1] Justinian had ordained that if husband and wife separated by mutual consent, they were to be forced to spend the rest of their lives in a convent and forfeit to it one third of their goods.[2] Justin, then, made the pious efforts of his uncle naught. Nothing can more clearly illustrate than his decree how small a power the Church still possessed to mould the tenor of the law; for such a thing as divorce by mutual consent, without any necessary reason, was a serious misdemeanour in the eyes of the Church Fathers, who passed upon it their severest censures.

Justin re-vokes decrees of Justinian.

On the subject of adultery Justinian enacted that if the husband was the guilty party, the dowry and marriage donations must be given his wife; but the rest of his property accrued to his relatives, both in ascending and descending lines, to the third degree; these failing, his

Adultery.

---

[1] Novellae, 140, 1: Antiquitus quidem licebat sine periculo tales (i. e., those of incompatible temperament) ab invicem separari secundum communem voluntatem et consensum hoc agentes, sicut et plurimae tunc leges extarent hoc dicentes et *bona gratia* sic procedentem solutionem nuptiarum patria vocitantes voce. Postea vero divae memoriae nostro patri . . . . legem sancivit prohibens cum consensu coniugia solvi. . . . Haec igitur aliena nostris iudicantes temporibus in praesenti sacram constituimus legem, per quam sancimus licere ut antiquitus consensu coniugum solutiones nuptiarum fieri.

[2] Novellae, 134, 11.

goods were confiscated to the royal purse.[1] A
woman guilty of adultery was at once sent to a
monastery. After a space of two years her husband could take her back again, if he so wished,
without prejudice. If he did not so desire, or if
he died, the woman was shorn and forced to spend
the rest of her life in a nunnery; two thirds of her
property were given to her relatives in descending
line, the other third to the monastery; if there were
no descendants, ascendants got one third and
the monastery two thirds; relatives failing, the
monastery took all; and in all cases goods inserted
in the dowry contract were to be kept for the
husband.[2]

The legislation of the earlier Christian emperors
on second marriages reflects the various Second mar-
feelings of the Church Fathers on the   riages.
subject. Under the old law, people could marry
as often as they wished without any penalties.[3]
But we have seen that among some of the Church-
men second marriages were held in peculiar ab-
horrence, and third nuptials were regarded as a
hideous sin; while the orthodox clergy, like St.
Augustine and St. Jerome, permitted second and
third marriages, but damned them with faint
praise and urged Christians to be content with

[1] Novellae, 134, 10.
[2] Novellae, 134, 10.
[3] Novellae, 22 (praefatio): Antiquitas equidem non satis
aliquid de prioribus aut secundis perscrutabatur nuptiis, sed
licebat et patribus et matribus et ad plures venire nuptias et
lucro nullo privari, et causa erat in simplicitate confusa.

one venture. Public opinion, custom, and the influence of the old Roman law were too powerful to allow Christian monarchs to become fanatical on the subject [1]; but certain stricter regulations were introduced by the pious Gratian,

Valentinian, and Theodosius, in the

Strict laws of Gratian, Valentinian, and Theodosius. years 380, 381, and 382. [2] As under the old laws, any widow who married

again before the legal time of mourning —a year—had expired, became infamous and lost both cast and all claims to the goods of her deceased husband. She was furthermore not permitted to give a second husband more than one third of her property nor leave him more than one third by will; and she could receive no intestate succession beyond the third degree. A woman who proceeded to a second marriage after the legal period of mourning, must make over at once to the children of the first marriage all the property which her former husband had given or left to her. As to her own personal property, she was allowed to possess it and enjoy the income while she lived, but not to alienate it or leave it by will to any one except the children of the first marriage. As I have before remarked, Roman law constantly had the interest of the children at heart. [3] If

---

[1] The language of some of them is pretty strong, however— matre iam secundis nuptiis *funestata*—Codex, v, 9, 3 (Gratian, Valentinian, Theodosius).

[2] For these see Codex, v, 9, 1 and 2 and 3.

[3] Cf. Codex, v, 9, 4. Nos enim hac lege id praecipue custodi-

there was no issue of the first marriage, then the woman had free control. A mother acquired full right—as the old Senatus consultum Tertullianum had decreed—to the property of a son or daughter who died childless [1]; but if she married a second time, and her son or daughter died without leaving children or grandchildren, she was expelled from all succession and distant relatives acquired the property. [2]

Justinian changed these enactments to a pronounced degree. "We are not making laws that are too bitter against women who marry a second time," he remarks, [3] "and we do not want to lead them, in consequence of such action, to the harsh necessity, unworthy of our age, of abstaining from a chaste second marriage and descending to illegitimate connections." He ordained, therefore, that the law mentioned above be annulled and that mothers should have absolutely unrestricted rights of inheritance to a deceased child's property along with the latter's brothers and sisters; and second marriage was

Justinian moderates these laws to a great degree.

---

endum esse decrevimus, ut ex quocumque coniugio suscepti filii patrum suorum sponsalicias retineant facultates.

[1] Codex, vi, 56, 5.

[2] Novellae, ii, 3: ex absurditate legis, licet praemoriantur filii omnes, non relinquentes filios aut nepotes, nihilominus supplicium manet, et non succedit eis mater, sed expellitur ab eorum inhumane successione . . . sed succedunt quidem illis aliqui ex longa cognatione.

[3] Novellae, ii, 3.

never to create any prejudice.[1]   In the earlier part
of his reign Justinian also forbade husband or
wife to leave one another property under the
stipulation that the surviving partner must not
marry again[2]; but later, when his zeal for reform
had become more pronounced and fanatical, he
revoked this and gave the conditioned party the
option either of enjoying the property by remaining
unmarried or of forfeiting it by a second union.[3]

Constantine ordained,[4] in the year 336, that
if an engagement was broken by the death
Breaking of of one of the contracting parties and
engagements. if the *osculum*[5] had taken place, half
of whatever donations had been given was
to be handed over to the surviving party and
half to the heirs of the deceased; but if the
solemn *osculum* had not yet taken place, all
gifts went to the heirs of the deceased.   There
was also a law that if either party broke the engagement to enter monastic life, the man who did so
lost all that he had given by way of earnest
money for the marriage contract (*arrarum nomine*);
if it was the woman who took the initiative, she
was compelled to return twice the amount of any
sums she had received.   This was changed by

[1] Novellae ii, 3.

[2] Codex, vi, 40, 2 and 3.

[3] Novellae, 22, 44: unde sancimus, si quis prohibuerit ad aliud
venire matrimonium, etc.

[4] Codex, v, 3, 16.

[5] The *osculum* was a sort of "donation on account of
marriage" made on the day of the formal engagement.

Justinian, who enacted that those who broke an engagement to enter monastic life should merely return or receive whatever donations had been made.[1] Constantine and his successors abrogated the old time Julian laws, which had inflicted certain penalties—such as limited rights of inheritance—on men and women who did not marry.[2]

I have already pointed out that gifts between husband and wife were illegal and I have explained the reasons. Justinian allowed the husband to make donations to his wife, in such wise, however, that all chance of intent to defraud might be absent.[3] He ordained also that if husband or wife left the married state to embrace a celibate life, each party was to keep his or her own property as per marriage contract or as each would legitimately in the case of the other's death.[4] If any one, after vowing the monastic life, returned to the world, his or her

Changes in the law of gifts.

[1] Codex, i, 3, 54 (56).
[2] Codex, viii, 57 (58), 1 and 2. Cf. Codex, viii, 58 (59), 1 and 2.
[3] Codex, v, 3, 10.
[4] Codex, i, 3, 54 (56). Gregory of Tours informs us that according to the Council of Nicaea—325 A.D.—a wife who left her husband, to whom she was happily married, to enter a nunnery incurred excommunication. He means probably: if she went without her husband's consent. Greg. 9, 33: Tunc ego accedens ad monasterium canonum Nicaenorum decreta relegi, in quibus continetur: quia si quae reliquerit virum et thorum, in quo bene vexit, spreverit, dicens quia non sit ei portio in illa caelestis regni gloria qui fuerit coniugio copulatus, anathema sit. (Note of editor: Videtur esse canon 14 concilii Grangensis, quod concilium veteres Nicaeno subiungere solebant; idque indicat titulus in veteribus scriptis.)

goods were forfeit to the monastery which he or
she had left.[1]

The consent of the father or, if he was dead, of
near relatives was emphatically declared necessary
Various en- by the Christian emperors for a marriage
actments on and the woman had practically no will
marriage. of her own although, if several suitors
were proposed to her, she might be requested to
name which one she preferred.[2]   Marriage with
a Jew was treated as adultery.[3]   Women who
belonged to heretical sects were to have no
privileges.[4]   Justinus and Justinian abrogated the
old law which forbade senators to marry freedwomen or any woman who had herself or whose
parents had followed the stage.   Actresses were
now permitted, on giving up their profession, to
claim all the rights of other free women; and a
senator could marry such or even a freedwoman
without prejudice.[5]

Under the old law, as we have seen, a son and a
daughter had equal rights to intestate succession;
Changes in but beyond the relationship of daughter
the laws of in- to father or sister to brother women had
heritance. no rights to intestate succession unless
there were no agnates, that is, male relatives on
the father's side.   Thus, an aunt would not be
called to the estate of a nephew who died childless,

[1] Codex, i, 3, 54 (56).
[2] Codex, v, 4, 20, and 5, 18.
[3] Codex, i, 9, 6.
[4] Novellae, cix, 1.
[5] Codex, v, 4, 23 and 28.

but the uncle was regularly admitted. So, too, a nephew was admitted to the intestate succession of an uncle, who died without issue, but the niece was shut out. All this was changed by Justinian, who gave women the same rights of inheritance as men under such conditions.[1] If the children were unorthodox, they were to have absolutely no share of either parent's goods.[2]

The Christian emperors permitted widows to be guardians over their children if they **Women as** promised on oath not to marry again **guardians.** and gave security against fraud.[3] Justinian forbade women to act by themselves in **In suits.** any legal matters.[4]

Arcadius and Honorius (397 A.D.) enacted some particularly savage bills of attainder, which were in painful contrast to the clemency **Bills of** of their pagan predecessors. Those **attainder.** guilty of high treason were decapitated and their goods escheated to the crown. "To the sons of such a man [i.e., one condemned for high treason]," write these amiable Christians,[5] "we allow their lives out of special royal mercy—for they ought really to be put to death along with their fathers— but they are to receive no inheritances. Let them be paupers forever; let the infamy of their father ever follow them; they may never aspire to office;

[1] Codex, vi, 58, 14.
[2] Codex, i, 5, 19.
[3] Codex, v, 35, 2 and 3.
[4] Codex, ii, 55, 6.
[5] Codex, ix, 8, 5.

in their lasting poverty let death be a relief and
life a punishment. Finally, any one who tries to
intercede for these with us is also to be infamous."[1]
However, to the daughters of the condemned these
emperors graciously granted one fourth of their
mother's but not any of their father's goods.   In
the case of crimes other than high treason the
children or grandchildren were allowed one half of
the estate.[2]   Constantine decreed that a wife's
property was not to be affected by the condemnation of her husband.[3]

Ravishers of women, even of slaves and freedwomen, were punished by Justinian with death;
Rape.   but in the case of freeborn women only
did the property of the guilty man and
his abettors become forfeit to the outraged victim.
A woman no longer had the privilege of demand-
ing her assailant in marriage.[4]

SOURCES

Roman Law as cited in Chapter I, especially the *Novellae* of
Justinian.

---

[1] This law was evidently lasting, for it is quoted with approval
by Pope Innocent III, in the year 1199—see Friedberg, *Corpus
Iuris Canonici*, vol. ii, p. 782.

[2] Codex, ix, 49, 10.

[3] Codex, v, 16, 24.

[4] For all these enactments see Codex, i, 3, 53 (54), and ix, 13.

CHAPTER IV

WOMEN AMONG THE GERMANIC PEOPLES

A SECOND world force had now come into its own. The new power was the Germanic peoples, those wandering tribes who, after shattering the Roman Empire, were destined to form the modern nations of Europe and to find in Christianity the religion most admirably adapted to fill their spiritual needs and shape their ideals. In the year 476 the barbarian Odoacer ascended the throne of the Caesars. He still pretended to govern by virtue of the authority delegated to him by Zeno, emperor at Constantinople; but the rupture between East and West was becoming final and after the reign of Justinian (527–565) it was practically complete. Henceforth the eastern empire had little or nothing to do with western Europe and subsisted as an independent monarchy until Constantinople was taken by the Turks in 1453. I shall not concern myself with it any longer.

In western Europe, then, new races with new ideals were forming the nations that to-day are England, Germany, France, Spain, Italy, and Austria. It is interesting to note what some of these barbarians thought about women and what place they assigned them.

Our earliest authorities on the subject are Julius Caesar and Tacitus. Caesar informs us [1] **Julius Caesar's** that among the Gauls marriage was a **account.** well recognized institution. The husband contributed of his own goods the same amount that his wife brought by way of dowry; the combined property and its income were enjoyed on equal terms by husband and wife. If husband or wife died, all the property became the possession of the surviving partner. Yet the husband had full power of life and death over his wife as over his children; and if, upon the decease of a noble, there were suspicions regarding the manner of his death, his wife was put to inquisitorial torture and was burnt at the stake when adjudged guilty of murder. Among the Germans women seem to have been held in somewhat greater respect. German matrons were esteemed as prophetesses and no battle was entered upon unless they had first consulted the lots and given assurance that the fight would be successful. [2] As for the British, who were not a Germanic people, Caesar says that they practiced polygamy and near relatives were accustomed to have wives in common. [3]

Tacitus wrote a century and a half after Julius

[1] *de Bell. Gall.*, vi, 19.
[2] Id., i, 50.
[3] Id., v, 14.

Caesar, when the tribes had become better known to the Romans; hence we get from him more detailed information. From him we The account learn that both the Sitones—a people of Tacitus. of northern Germany—and the British often bestowed the royal power on women, a circumstance which aroused the strong contempt of Tacitus, who was in this respect of a conservative mind.[1] The Romans had, indeed, good reason to remember with sorrow the valiant Boadicea, queen of the Britons.[2] Regarding the Germans Tacitus wrote a whole book in which he idealises that nation as a contrast to the lax morality of civilised Rome, much as Rousseau in the eighteenth century extolled the virtues of savages in a state of nature. What Tacitus says in regard to lofty morals we shall do well to take with a pinch of salt; but we may with more safety trust his accuracy when he depicts national customs. From Tacitus we learn that the Germans believed something divine resided in women[3]; hence their respect for them as prophetesses.[4] One Velaeda by her

[1] *Agricola*, 16. *Germania*, 45: Suionibus Sitonum gentes continuantur. Cetera similes, uno differunt, quod femina dominatur; in tantum non modo a libertate, sed etiam a servitute degenerant. No woman ever reigned alone as queen of the Roman Empire until 450 A.D., when Pulcheria, sister of Theodosius II, ascended the throne of the East; but she soon took the senator Marcian in marriage and made him king.

[2] *Agricola*, 16.

[3] *Germania*, 8.

[4] Procopius, *de bello Vandalico*, ii, 8, observes the same thing among the Maurousians, or Moors, in northern Africa: ἄνδρα γὰρ

soothsaying ruled the tribe of Bructeri completely [1]
and was regarded as a goddess, [2] as were many
others. [3] The German warrior fought his best
that he might protect and please his wife. [4] The
standard of conjugal fidelity was strict [5]; men were
content with one wife, although high nobles were
sometimes allowed several wives as an increase
to the family prestige. [6] The dowry was brought
not by the wife to the husband, but to the wife
by the husband—evidently a survival of the
custom of wife purchase; but the wife was accustomed to present her husband with arms and the
accoutrements of war. [7] She was reminded that
she took her husband for better and worse, to be
a faithful partner in joy and sorrow until death. [8]
A woman guilty of adultery was shorn and her
husband drove her naked through the village
with blows. [9]

We see, then, that by no means all of these
barbarian nations had the same standards in
regard to women. Of written laws there were

μαντεύεσθαι ἐν τῷ ἔθνει τούτῳ οὐ θέμις, ἀλλὰ γυναῖκες σφίσι κάτοχοι
ἐκ δή τινος ἱερουργίας γινόμεναι προλέγουσι τὰ ἐσόμενα, τῶν πάλαι
χρηστηρίων οὐδενὸς ἧσσον.

[1] Tacitus, *Hist.*, iv, 61, and v, 24.
[2] Id., *Germania*, 8.
[3] Ibid., 8.
[4] Ibid., 7.
[5] Ibid., 17.
[6] Ibid.
[7] Ibid., 18.
[8] Ibid., 18 and 19.
[9] Ibid., 19.

none as yet. But contact with the civilisation of Rome had its effect; and when Goths, Burgundians, Franks, and Lombards had founded new states on the ruins of the western Roman Empire, the national laws of the Germanic tribes began to be collected and put into writing at the close of the fifth century. Between the fifth and the ninth centuries we get the Visigothic, Burgundian, Salic, Ripuarian, Alemannic, Lombardian, Bavarian, Frisian, Saxon, and Thuringian law books. They are written in medieval Latin and are not elaborated on a scientific basis. Three distinct influences are to be seen in them: (1) native race customs, ideals, and traditions; (2) Christianity; (3) the Roman civil law, which was felt more or less in all, but especially in the case of the Visigoths; as was natural, since this people had been brought into closest touch with Rome. Inasmuch as the barbarians allowed all peoples conquered by them to be tried under their own laws, the old Roman civil law was still potent in all its strength in cases affecting a Roman. Let us endeavour to glean what we can from the barbarian codes on the matter of women's rights.

The woman was always to be under guardianship among the Germanic peoples and could never be independent under any conditions. Perhaps we should rather call the power (*mundium*) wielded by father, brother, husband, or other male relative a protectorate; for in those early days among rude peoples any legal action might involve fighting to prove the merits of one's case, and the woman would therefore constantly need a champion to assert her rights in the lists. Thus the woman was under the perpetual guardianship of a male relative and must do nothing without his consent, under penalty of losing her property.[1] Her guardian arranged her marriage for her as he wished, provided only that he chose a free man for her husband[2]; if the woman, whether virgin or widow, married without his consent, she lost all power to inherit the goods of her relatives[3]; and her husband was forced to pay to her kin a recompense amounting to 600 *solidi* among the Saxons, 186 among the Burgundians.[4]

[1] Liutprand, i, 5: Si filiae aut sorores contra voluntatem patris aut fratris egerint, potestatem habet pater aut frater iudicandi res suas quomodo aut qualiter voluerit.

[2] Leges Liutprandi, vi, 119: si quis filiam suam aut sororem alii sponsare voluerit, habeat potestatem dandi cui voluerit, libero tamen homini.   Lex Wisigothorum, iii, 1, 7 and 8.

[3] Leges Liutprandi, vi, 119.   Lex Angliorum et Werinorum, x, 2: si libera femina sine voluntate patris aut tutoris cuilibet nupserit, perdat omnem substantiam quam habuit vel habere debuit.   Reply of a bishop quoted by Gregory of Tours, 9, 33: quia sine consilio parentum eam coniugio copulasti, non erit uxor tua.   But the law of the Visigoths (iii, 1, 8, and 2, 8) merely deprived her of succession to the estate of her parents.

[4] Lex Saxonum, vi, 2: Si autem sine voluntate parentum, puella tamen consentiente, ducta fuerit (uxorem ducturus) bis ccc solidos parentibus eius componat.   Lex Burgundionum: *Add.*, 14. cf. Edictum Rotharis, 188: si puella libera aut vidua sine voluntate parentum ad maritum ambulaverit, liberum tamen, tunc maritus, qui eam acceperit uxorem, componat pro anagrip solidos XX et propter faidam alios XX.

The feeling of caste was very strong; a woman must not marry below her station.[1] By a law of the Visigoths she who tried to marry her own slave was to be burned alive[2]; **Marriage.** if she attempted it with another's bondman, she merited one hundred lashes.[3] The dowry was a fixed institution as among the Romans; but the bridegroom regularly paid a large sum to the father or guardian of the woman. This *wittemon* was regarded as the price paid for the parental authority (*mundium*) and amounted among the Saxons to 300 *solidi*.[4] As a matter of fact this custom practically amounted to the intended husband giving the dowry to his future wife. The husband was also allowed to present his wife with a donation (*morgengabe*) on the morning after the

[1] By a law of the Alemanni (*Tit.*, 57), if two sisters were heiresses to a father's estate and one married a vassal (*colonus*) of the King or Church and the other became the wife of a free man equal to her in rank, the latter only was allowed to hold her father's land, although the rest of the goods were divided equally.

[2] Lex Wisigothorum, iii, 2, 2.

[3] Ibid., iii, 2, 3.

[4] Lex Saxonum, vi, 1: uxorem ducturus CCC solidos det parentibus eius. See also the lex Burgundionum, 66, 1 and 2 and 3. In the case of a widow who married again the gift of the husband was called *reiphe* or *reippus* and very solemn ceremonies belonged to the giving of it according to the Salic law, *Tit.*, 47: si, ut fieri adsolet, homo moriens viduam dimiserit et eam quis in coniugium voluerit accipere, antequam eam accipiat Tunginus aut Centenarius Mallum indicent, et in ipso Mallo scutum habere debet, et tres homines vel caussas mandare. Et tunc ille, qui viduam accipere vult, cum tribus testibus qui adprobare debent, tres solidos aeque pensantes, et denarium habere debet, etc.

wedding; the amount was limited by King Liutprand to not more than one fourth of all his goods. [1]
Breaking an engagement after the solemn betrothal had been entered into was a serious
business. The Visigoths refused to allow one party
to break an engagement without the consent of
the other; and if a woman, being already engaged,
went over to another man without her parent's
or fiancé's leave, both she and the man who took
her were handed over as slaves to the original
fiancé. [2] The other barbarians were content to
inflict a money fine for breach of promise. [3]

The woman on marrying passed into the power
of her husband "according to the Sacred Scriptures," and the husband thereupon acquired the lordship of all her property. [4]
The law still protected the wife in some ways.
The Visigoths gave the father the right of demand-
ing and preserving for his daughter her dowry. [5]
The Ripuarians ordained that whatever the hus-

Power of the husband.

[1] Leges Liutprandi, ii, 1.

[2] Lex Wisigothorum, iii, 1, 2 and 3, and iii, 6, 3.

[3] E.g., 62 *solidi* by the Salic law, *Tit.*, 70. See also Lex
Baiuvariorum, *Tit.*, vii, 15 and 16 and 17. Lex Alemannorum,
52, 1; 53; 54.

[4] Lex Burgundionum, *Add. primum*, xiii: quaecunque mulier
Burgundia vel Romana voluntate sua ad maritum ambulaverit,
iubemus ut maritus ipse de facultate ipsius mulieris, sicut in
eam habet potestatem, ita et de rebus suis habeat.

Lex Wisigothorum, iv, 2, 15: Vir qui uxorem suam secundum
sacram scripturam habet in potestate, similiter et in servis suis
potestatem habebit, et omnia quae cum servis uxoris suae vel
suis in expeditione acquisivit, in sua potestate permaneant.

[5] Lex Wisigothorum, iii, Tit. 1, 6.

band had given his wife by written agreement must remain inviolate. [1] King Liutprand made the presence of two or three of the woman's male relatives necessary at any sale involving her goods, to see to it that her consent to the sale had not been forced. [2]

On the subject of divorce the regulations of the several peoples are various; but the commands of the New Testament are alike strongly felt in all; and we may expect to find divorce limited by severe restrictions. [3] The Burgundians allowed it only for adultery or grave crimes, such as violating tombs. If a wife presumed to dismiss her husband for any other cause, she was put to death (*necetur in luto*); to a husband who sent his wife a divorce without these specific reasons existing the law was more indulgent, allowing him to preserve his life by paying to his injured wife twice the amount that he had originally given her parents for her, and twelve *solidi* in addition; and in case he attempted to prove her guilty of one of the charges mentioned above and she was adjudged innocent, he forfeited all his goods to her and was forced to leave his home. [4] The Visigoths

Divorce.

---

[1] Lex Ripuariorum, 37, 1.

[2] Leges Liutprandi, iv, 4.

[3] That is, for the common people. Kings have always had a little way of doing as they pleased. See the anecdote of King Cusupald in Paulus' *Hist. Langobard*, i, 21: secunda autem (sc. filia Wacchonis) dicta est Walderada, quae sociata est Cusupald, alio regi Francorum, quam ipse odio habens uni ex suis, qui dicebatur Garipald, in coniugium tradidit.

[4] For all this see Lex Burgundionum, 34, 1-4.

were equally strict; the husband who dismissed his wife on insufficient legal grounds lost all power over her and must return all her goods; his own must be preserved for the children; if there were none, the wife acquired his property. A woman who married a divorced man while his first wife was living, was condemned for adultery and accordingly handed over to the first wife to be disposed of as the latter wished; exile, stripes, and slavery were the lot of a man who took another wife while his first partner was still alive. [1] The Alemanni and the Bavarians, who were more remote from Italy and hence from the Church, were influenced more by their own customs and allowed a pecuniary recompense to take the place of the harsher enactments. [2]

Adultery was not only a legal cause for divorce, but also a grave crime. All the barbarian peoples are agreed in so regarding it, but their

Adultery.

penalties vary according as they were more or less affected by proximity to Italy, where the power of the Church was naturally strongest. The Ripuarians, the Bavarians, and the Alemanni preferred a money fine ranging from fifty to two hundred *solidi*. [3] Among the Visigoths the guilty party was usually bound over in servitude to the injured person to be disposed of as the latter

[1] For all these, see Lex Wisigothorum, iii, 6, 1 and 2.

[2] Capitula Addita ad Legem Alemannorum, 30. Lex Baiu-variorum, vii, 14.

[3] Lex Ripuariorum, *Tit.*, 35. Lex Baiuvariorum, vii. Lex Alemannorum, 51, 1.

wished.[1] Sometimes the law was harsher to women than to men; thus, according to a decree of Liutprand,[2] a husband who told his wife to commit adultery or who did so himself paid a mulct of fifty *solidi* to the wife's male relatives; but if the wife consented to or hid the deed, she was put to death. The laws all agree that the killing of adulterers taken in the act could not be regarded as murder.

It is always to be remembered that although the statutes were severe enough, yet during this period, as indeed throughout all history, they were defied with impunity. Charlemagne, for example, the most Christian monarch, had a large number of concubines and divorced a wife who did not please him; yet his biographer Einhard, pious monk as he was, has no word of censure for his monarch's irregularities[3]; and policy prevented the Church from thundering at a king who so valiantly crushed the heretics, her enemies. Bishop Gregory of Tours tells us without a hint of being shocked that Clothacharius, King of the Franks, had many concubines.[4] Con-

The Church indulgent toward kings.

[1] Lex Wisigothorum, iii, 6, 1 and 2, and iii, 4, 1.

[2] Leges Liutprandi, vi, 130.

[3] Einhard, *Vita Kar. Mag.*, 17: Deinde cum matris hortatu filiam Desiderii regis Langobardorum duxisset uxorem, incertum qua de causa, post annum eam repudiavit et Hildigardam de gente Suaborum praecipuae nobilitatis feminam in matrimonium duxit. . . . Habuit et alias tres filias . . . duas de Fastrada uxore . . . tertiam de concubina quadam . . . defuncta Fastrada . . . tres habuit concubinas.

[4] Gregory of Tours, 4, 3.

cubinage was, in fact, the regular thing.[1] But neither in that age, nor later in the case of Louis XIV, nor in our own day in the case of Leopold of Belgium has the Church had a word of reproach for monarchs who broke with impunity moral laws on which she claims always to have insisted without compromise.

In accordance with the commands of Scripture neither the divorced man nor the divorced woman could marry again during the lifetime of the other party. To do so was to commit adultery, for which the usual penalties went into effect.

Remarriage.

A woman's property would consist of any or all of these:

Property rights and powers.

I. Her share of the property of parents or brothers and sisters.

II. Her dowry and whatever nuptial donations (*morgengabe*) her husband had given her, and whatever she had earned together with her husband.

There could be no account of single women's property or disposal of what they earned, because in the half-civilised state of things which then obtained there was no such thing as women engaging in business; indeed, not even men of any pretension did so; war was their work. The unmarried woman was content to sit by the fire

---

[1] The concubines of Theodoric—Jordanes, *de orig. acti busque Get.*, 58.   Huga, king of the Franks, had a filium quem ex concubina genuit—Widukind, *Res Gest. Sax.*, i, 9.

and spin under the guardianship and support of a
male relative. Often she would enter a convent.

I shall first discuss the laws of inheritance as
affecting women, in order to note what property
she was allowed to acquire. In this connection
it is well to bear in mind a difference between
Roman and Germanic law. The former viewed
an inheritance as consisting always of a totality
of all goods, whether of money, land, movables,
cattle, dress, or what not. But among the
Germanic peoples land, money, ornaments, and the
like were regarded as so many distinct articles of
inheritance, to some of which women might have
legal claims of succession, but not necessarily to
all. This is most emphatically shown in the case
of land. Of all the barbarian peoples, the Ripuarians alone allowed women the right to succeed
to land.¹ Among other nations a daughter or
sister or mother, whoever happened to be the
nearest heir, would get the money, slaves, etc.,
but the nearest *male* kin would get the land.²
Only if male kin were lacking to the fifth degree
—an improbable contingency—did alodial inheritance "pass from the lance to the spindle."³

¹ Lex Ripuariorum, *Tit.*, 48. Lex Angliorum et Werinorum,
vi—*de alodibus*, 1: hereditatem defuncti filius, non filia susci-
piat. Salic Law, *Tit.*, 62: *de alodis*, 6: de terra vero Salica in
mulierem nulla portio hereditatis transit, sed hoc virilis sexus
adquirat, hoc est, filii in ipsa hereditate succedunt. Lex Saxonum, vii, 1: Pater aut mater defuncti filio, non filiae hereditatem relinquit.

² Cf. Lex Angliorum et Werinorum, vi: *de alodibus*.

³ Ibid., vi, 8: post quintam autem (*sc.* generationem) filia ex

In respect to all other things a daughter was co-heir with a son to the estate of a father or mother. According to the Salic and Ripuarian law this would be one order of succession [1]:

 I. Children of the deceased.

 II. These failing, surviving mother or father of deceased.

 III. These failing, brother or sister of deceased.

 IV. These failing, sister of mother of deceased.

 V. These failing, sister of father of deceased.

 VI. These failing, male relatives on father's side.

It will be observed that in such a succession these laws are more partial to women relatives than the Roman law; an aunt, for example, is called before an uncle. An uncle would certainly exclude an aunt under the Roman law; but most of the Germanic codes allowed them an equal succession. [2] Nevertheless, when women did inherit under the former, they acquired the land also. Moreover, the woman among the Germanic nations must always be under guardianship; and whereas under the Empire the power of the guardian was in practice reduced to nullity, as I have shown, among the barbarians it was extremely powerful, because to assert one's rights often involved fighting in the lists to determine the judgment

---

toto, sive de patris sive de matris parte, in hereditatem succedat, et tunc demum hereditas ad fusum a lancea transeat.

 [2] Lex Salica, *Tit.*, 62.   Lex Ripuariorum, *Tit.*, 56.

 [3] Cf. Lex Wisigothorum, iv, 2, 7 and 9.

of God. It was a settled conviction among the Germanic peoples that God would give the victory to the rightful claimant. As women could not fight, a champion or guardian was a necessity. This was not true in Roman courts, which preferred to settle litigation by juristic reasoning and believed, like Napoleon, that God, when appealed to in a fight, was generally on the side of the party who had the better artillery.

Children inherited not only the estate but also the friendships and enmities of their fathers, which it was their duty to take up. Hereditary feuds were a usual thing. [1] King Liutprand ordained, [2] however, that if a daughter alone survived, the feud was to be brought to an end and an agreement effected.

Some of the nations seem to have provided that children must not be disinherited except for very strong reasons; for example, the law of the Visigoths [3] forbids more than one third of their estate being alienated by mother or father, grandmother or grandfather. The Alemanni permitted a free man to leave all his property to the Church and his heirs had no redress [4]; but the Bavarians compelled him before entering monastic life to distribute among his children their proportionate parts. [5]

[1] Tacitus, *Germania*, 21.
[2] Legis Liutprandi, ii, 7.
[3] Lex Wisigothorum, iv, 5, 1.
[4] Lex Alemannorum, *Tit.*, i.
[5] Lex Baiuvariorum, *Tit.*, i.

We may pass now to the property rights of the married woman. The relation of her husband

Property of the married woman.

to the dowry I have already explained. The dowry was conceived as being ultimately for the children; only when there were no children, grandchildren, or great-grandchildren did the woman have licence to dispose of the dowry as she wished: this was the law among the Visigoths.[1] The dowry, then, was to revert to the children or grandchildren at the death of the wife; if there were none such, to the parents or relatives who had given her in marriage; these failing, it escheated to the Crown—so according to Rotharis.[2] By the laws of the Visigoths[3] when the wife died, her husband continued in charge of the property; but, as under the Roman law, he had to preserve it entire for the children, though he might enjoy the usufruct. When a son or daughter married, their father must at once give them their share of their mother's goods, although he could still receive the income of one third of the portion. If son or daughter did not marry, they received one half their share on becoming twenty years of age; their father might claim the interest of the other half while he lived; but at his death he must leave it to them. When a woman left no children, her father or nearest male kin usually demanded the dowry back.[4]

[1] Lex Wisigothorum, iv, 2, 20.
[2] Edictum Rotharis, i, 121.   [3] Lex Wisigothorum, iv, 2, 13.
[4] Cf. Capitula addita ad legem Alemannorum, 29. Lex Saxonum, viii, 2.

When the husband died, his estate did not go to his wife, but to his children or other relatives.[1] If, however, any property had been earned by the joint labour of husband and wife, the latter had a right to one half among the Westfalians; to one third among the Ripuarians; to nothing among the Ostfalians.[2] Children remained in the power of their mother if she so desired and provided she remained a widow. A mother usually had the enjoyment of her dowry until her death, when she must leave it to her children or to the donor or nearest relative.[3] If the husband died without issue, some nations allowed the wife a certain succession to her husband's goods, provided that she did not marry again. Thus, the Burgundians gave her under such conditions one third of her husband's estate to be left to his heirs, however, at her death.[4] The Bavarians, too, under the same conditions allowed her one half of her husband's goods[5] and even if there was issue, granted her the right to the interest of as much as one child received.[6]

A widow who married again lost the privilege

---

[1] Cf. lex Wisigothorum, iv, 2, 11: maritus et uxor tunc sibi hereditario iure succedant, quando mulla affinitas usque ad septimum gradum de propinquis eorum vel parentibus inveniri poterit. See also Lex Burgundionum, 14, 1.

[2] Lex Saxonum, ix. Lex Ripuariorum, 37, 2.

[3] Lex Saxonum, viii. Lex Wisigothorum, iv, 3, 3. Lex Burgundionum 85, 1, and 62, 1.

[4] Lex Burgundionum, 42, 1; 62, 1; 74, 1.

[5] Lex Baiuvariorum, xiv, 9, 1.

[6] Ibid., xiv, 6.

of guardianship over her children, who thereupon passed to a male relative of the first husband. As to the dowry of the prior union the woman must make it over at once to her children according to some laws or, according to others, might receive the usufruct during life and leave it to the children of the first marriage at her death. Any right to the property of her first husband she of course lost. [1] When there was no issue of the first marriage then the dowry and nuptial donations could usually follow her to a second union.

Criminal law among these half civilised nations could not but be a crude affair. Their **Criminal law pertaining to women.** civilisation was in a state of flux, and immediate practical convenience was the only guide. They were content to fix the penalties for such outrages as murder, rape, insult, assault, and the like in money; the Visigoths alone were more stringent in a case of rape, adding 200 lashes and slavery to the ravisher of a free woman who had accomplished his purpose. [2] Some enactments which may well strike us as peculiar deserve notice. For example, among the Saxons the theft of a horse or an ox or anything worth three *solidi* merited death; but murder was atoned for by pecuniary damages. [3] Among

---

[1] For all this, see Lex Burgundionum, 24 and 62 and 74. Lex Wisigothorum, iv, Tit. 3. Lex Baiuvariorum, 14. Lex Alemannorum, 55 and 56.

[2] Lex Wisigothorum, iii, 3, 1.

[3] Lex Saxonum, iv. In the early days when the Great West of the United States was just being opened up and when society

the Burgundians, if a man stole horses or cattle
and his wife did not at once disclose the deed,
she and her children who were over fourteen were
bound over in slavery to the outraged party "because it hath often been ascertained, that these
women are the confederates of their husbands in
crime."[1]

The most minute regulations prevailed on the
subject of injury to women.   Under the Salic law[2]
for instance, if a free man struck a free women on
the fingers or hand, he had to pay fifteen *solidi;*
if he struck her arm, thirty *solidi;* if above her
elbow, thirty-five *solidi;* if he hit her breast, forty-
five *solidi.* The penalties for murdering a free
woman were also elaborated on the basis of her
value to the state as a bearer of children. By the
same Salic law[3] injury to a pregnant woman
resulting in her death merited a fine of seven
hundred *solidi;* but two hundred was deemed
sufficient for murder of one after her time
for bearing children had passed. Similarly, for
killing a free woman after she had begun to
have children the transgressor paid six hundred
solidi; but for murdering an unmarried freeborn girl only two hundred. The murder
of a free women was punished usually by a fine

there was in a very crude state, a horse thief was regularly hanged;
but murder was hardly a fault.

[1] Lex Burgundionum, 47, 1 and 2.   The guilty man was put
to death.

[2] Lex Salica, *Tit.*, 23.

[3] Id., *Tit.*, 28.

(*wergeld*) equal to twice the amount demanded
for a free man "because," as the law of the Bavarians has it, [1] "a woman can not defend herself
with arms. But if, in the boldness of her heart
(per audaciam cordis sui), she shall have resisted
and fought like a man, there shall not be a double
penalty, but only the recompense usual for a man
[160 *solidi*]." Fines were not paid to the state,
but to the injuried parties or, if these did not
survive, to the nearest kin. If the fine could not
be paid, then might death be meted to the guilty. [2]

Another peculiar feature of the Germanic law
was the appeal to God to decide a moot point by
various ordeals. For example, by the laws of the
Angles and Werini, if a woman was accused of
murdering her husband, she would ask a male
relative to assert her innocence by a solemn oath [3]
or, if necessary, by fighting for her as her champion
in the lists. God was supposed to give the victory
to the champion who defended an innocent party.

[1] Lex Baiuvariorum, *Tit.*, xiii, 2.

[2] Cf. lex Salica, *Tit.*, 61—a very curious account of formalities
to be observed in such a case.

[3] It was deemed sufficient for a male relative, say, the father,
to assert the innocence of the woman under solemn oath: for
it was thought that he would be unwilling to do this if he knew
the woman was guilty and so incur eternal Hell-fire as a punishment for perjury. An example of this solemn ceremony is
told interestingly by Gregory of Tours, 5, 33. A woman at
Paris was charged by her husband's relatives with adultery and
was demanded to be put to death. Her father took a solemn
oath that she was innocent. Far from being content with this,
the husband's kin began a fight and the matter ended in a whole-
sale butchery at the church of St. Dionysius.

If she could find no champion, she was permitted to walk barefoot over nine red-hot ploughshares [1]; and if she was innocent, God would not, of course, allow her to suffer any injury in the act.

Perhaps a word on the status of women in slavery among the Germanic nations will not be out of place. The new nations looked **Women in** upon a slave as a chattel, much as the **slavery.** Romans did. If a wrong was done a slave woman, her master received a recompense from the aggressor, but she did not, for to hold property was denied her. But we may well believe that the great value which the Church put on chastity and conjugal fidelity rendered the slave woman less exposed to the brutal passions of her lord than had been the case under the Empire. Thus, by a law of King Liutprand, a master who committed adultery with the wife of a slave was compelled to free both [2]; and the Visigoths [3] inflicted fifty lashes and a fine of twenty *solidi* upon the man who used violence to another man's slave woman.

On comparing the position of women under Roman law and under the Germanic nations, as we have observed them thus far, we should note first of all that under the latter women benefited chiefly by the insistence of the Church on the value

[1] Lex Angliorum et Werinorum, xiv: aut si campionem non habuerit, ipsa ad novem vomeres ignitos examinanda mittatur.

[2] Leges Liutprandi, vi, 140.

[3] Lex Wisigothorum, iii, 4, 16.

of chastity in both sexes. That in those days the passions of men were difficult to restrain in practice does not invalidate the real service done the world by the ideal that was insisted upon,[1] an ideal which was certainly not held in pagan antiquity except by a few great minds. Although the social position of woman was thus improved, the character of the age and the sentiments of the Bible which I have already quoted made her status far inferior to her condition under Roman law so far as her legal rights were concerned. In a period[2] when the assertion of one's rights constantly demanded fighting, the woman was forced to rely on the male to champion her; the Church, in accordance with the dicta of the Apostles, encouraged and indeed commanded her to confine herself to the duties of the household, to leave legal matters to men, and to be guided by their advice; and thus she was prevented from asserting herself out of regard for the strong public opinion on the subject, which was quite alien to the sentiments of the old Roman law. Henceforward also we are to have law based on old customs and *theology*,[3] not on practical convenience or scientific reasoning.

[1] See the interesting story of the girl who slew Duke Amalo, as narrated by Gregory of Tours, 9, 27.

[2] The bloody nature of the times is depicted naïvely by Gregory, Bishop of Tours, who wrote the history of the Franks. See, e.g., the stories of Ingeltrudis, Rigunthis, Waddo, Amalo, etc., in Book 9. Gregory was born in 539.

[3] *Corpus Iuris Canonici* (Friedberg), vol. i, p. i, *Distinctio Prima :* ius naturae est quod in lege et *evangelio* continetur.

SOURCES

I. Corpus Iuris Germanici Antiqui: edidit Ferd. Walter. Berolini—impensis G. Reimeri, 1824. 3 vols.

II. C. Iulii Caesaris Commentarii de Bello Gallico: recognovit Geo. Long. Novi Eboraci apud Harperos Fratres. 1883.

III. Cornelii Taciti libri qui supersunt: quartum recognovit Carolus Halm. Lipsiae (Teubner), 1901.

IV. Sancti Georgii Florentii Gregorii, Episcopi Turonensis, Historiae Ecclesiasticae Francorum libri decem: edidit J. Guadet et N. R. Taranne. Parisiis, apud Julium Renouard et Socios, 1838.

V. Iordanis de Origine Actibusque Getorum: edidit Alfred Holder. Freiburg und Tübingen; Verlagsbuchhandlung von J. C. B. Mohr.

VI. Widukindi Rerum Gestarum Saxonicarum libri tres. Accedit libellus de Origine Gentis Suevorum. Editio quarta: post Georgium Waitz recognovit Karolus A. Kehr. Hannoverae et Lipsiae Impensis Bibliopolii Hahniani, 1904.

VII. Procopii Caesariensis opera omnia: recognovit Jacobus Haury. Lipsiae. (Teubner). 1905.

VIII. Einhardi Vita Karoli Magni. Editio quinta. Post G. H. Pertz recensuit G. Waitz. Hannoverae et Lipsiae, 1905.

IX. Pauli Historia Langobardorum: edidit Georg Waitz. Hannoverae, impensis Bibliopolii Hahniani, 1878.

CHAPTER V

DIGRESSION ON THE LATER HISTORY OF
ROMAN LAW

WITH Charlemagne, who was crowned Emperor by the Pope in the year 800, began the definite union of Church and State and the Church's temporal power. Henceforth for seven centuries, until the Reformation, we shall have to reckon with canon law as a supreme force in determining the question of the position of women. A brief survey of the later history of the old Roman Law will not be out of place in order to note what influence, if any, it continued to exert down the ages.

The body of the Roman law, compiled by order of Justinian (527–565 A.D.), was intended primarily for the eastern empire; but when, in the year 535, the Emperor conquered the western Goths, who then ruled Italy, he ordered his laws taught in the school of jurisprudence at Rome and practiced in the courts. I have already remarked that the barbarians who overran Italy allowed the vanquished the right to be judged in most cases by their own code. But the splendid fabric of the Roman law was too elaborate a system to win the attentive study of a rude people; the Church had its own canons, the people their own ancestral customs; and until the twelfth century no development of the Roman Civil Code took place. Finally, during the twelfth century, the great school at Bologna renewed the study with vigour, and Italy at the present day derives the basic principles of its civil law from the Corpus of Justinian. Practically the same story holds true of France,[1] of Spain, and of the Netherlands, all of whom have been influenced particularly by the great jurists of the sixteenth century who were simply carrying further the torch that had been lit so enthusiastically at Bologna in the twelfth century.

As to Germany,[2] when that unhappy country had been separated from France and Italy after the Treaty of Verdun in 843, Carlovingian law and the ancient German law books fell into disuse. The law again rested on unwritten customs, on the decisions of the judges and their assessors, and on agreements of the interested parties (feudal services and tenures). Not till the twelfth and thirteenth centuries was any record made of the rules of law which had arisen; many laws of cities on various matters and in various provinces were recorded by public authority; and thus

[1] French customary law began to be written in the thirteenth century and was greatly affected by the Roman law.

[2] The succeeding paragraphs are a summary of the account by the learned Professor Mackeldey, who has investigated Roman law with the most minute diligence.

originated the so-called law books of the Middle
Ages, the private labours of experienced men, who
set forth the legal principles which were recognised
in all Germany, or at least in certain parts of it.
There were no law schools as yet, and scientific
compilation of German law was not even thought
of. After the University of Bologna had revived
the study of Roman law in Italy, the Italian
universities attracted the German youth, who on
their return would labour to introduce what they
had learned. Their efforts were seconded by the
clergy, through the close connection with canon
law which was in force in Germany. German
emperors and territorial lords also favoured Roman
law because they saw how well suited it was to
absolutism; they liked to engage jurists trained
in Italy, especially if they were doctors of both
canon and Roman law. Nor did the German
people object. From the fourteenth century
many schools of jurisprudence were established
on Italian models.

At present, the law of Justinian has only such
force as is received by usage or as it has acquired by
recognition. I. The Roman law forms in Germany the principal law in some branches, that is,
it is in so far its basis that the German law is
only an addition or modification of it. In other
branches it is only supplementary, that is, it is
merely subsidiary to the German law. II. Only
the glossed parts and passages of Justinian's
law collection have binding force in Germany.

III. Only those glossed passages are binding which contain the latest rule of law. Consequently the historical materials contained in them, though always of great importance for discovering the latest law, have not binding force. IV. Those precepts of the Roman law which relate to Roman manners and institutions unknown in Germany are inapplicable here, though glossed. V. The Roman law has but slight application to such objects and transactions as were unknown to the Romans and are of purely Germanic origin. VI. With the limitations above enumerated the Roman law has been adopted as a whole and not in detached parts.

In England Roman law has had practically no effect. In the year 1149 a Lombard jurist, Vacarius, lectured on it at Oxford; but there were no results. Canon law is, of course, a force to be reckoned with in Britain as on the Continent.

Before we enter the question of women's rights during the Middle Ages, we must take a general survey of the character of that period; for obviously we cannot understand its legislation without some idea of the background of social, political, and intellectual life. In the first place, then, the Church was everywhere triumphant and its ideals governed legislation completely on such matters as marriage. The civil law of Rome, as drawn up first by the epitomisers and later studied more carefully at Bologna, served to indicate general principles in cases to which canon law did not apply; but there was little jurisdiction in which the powers ecclesiastical could not contrive to take a hand. At the same time Germanic ideals and customs continued a powerful force. For a long time after the partition of the vast empire of Charlemagne government was in a state of chaos and transition from which eventually the various distinct states arose. A struggle between kings and nobles for supremacy dragged along for many generations; and as during that contest each feudal lord was master in his own domain, there was no consistent code of laws for all countries or, indeed, for the same country. Yet the character of the age determined in a general way the spirit that dictated all laws. Society rested on a military and aristocratic basis, and when the ability to wield arms is essential to maintain one's rights, the position of women will be affected by that fact. Beginning with the twelfth century city life began to exert a political influence; and this, again, did not fail to have an effect on the status of women. Of any participation of women in intellectual life there could be no question until the Renaissance, although we do meet here and there with isolated exceptions, a few ladies of high degree like Roswitha of Gandersheim and Hadwig, Duchess of Swabia, niece of Otto the Great, and Heloise. The learning was exclusively scholastic, and from any share in that women were barred. When people are kept in ignorance, there is less inducement for them to believe that they have any rights or to assert them if they do think so.

We shall do well to bear in mind, in noting the laws relative to women, that theory is one thing and practice quite another.   Hence, although the doctrines of the Church on various matters touching the female sex were characterised by the greatest purity, we shall see that in practice they were not strictly executed.   Religion does in fact play a less considerable part in regulating the daily acts of men than theologians are inclined to believe.   If anything proves this, it is the history of that foulest stain on Christian nations—prostitution.   We might expect that since the Roman Catholic Church insists so on chastity the level of this virtue would certainly be higher in countries which are almost exclusively Catholic, like Spain and Italy, than in Protestant lands; but no one who has ever travelled in Spain or Italy fails to recognise that the conduct of men is as lamentably low in these as in England, Germany, or the United States.

With this brief introduction I shall proceed next to explain the position of women under the canon law, a code which affected all countries of Europe equally until the Reformation; and in connection with this I shall give some idea of the attitude of the Roman Catholic Church towards women and women's rights at the present day.

CHAPTER VI

THE CANON LAW AND THE ATTITUDE OF THE
ROMAN CATHOLIC CHURCH

THE canon law reaffirms woman's subjection to man in no uncertain terms. The wife must The canon law reaffirms the subjection of women. be submissive and obedient to her husband.[1] She must never, under penalty of excommunication, cut off her hair, because "God has given it to her as a veil and as a sign of her subjection."[2] A woman who assumed men's garments was accursed[3]; it will be remembered that the breaking of this law was one of the charges which brought Joan of Arc to the stake. However learned and holy, woman

[1] Augustine quoted by Gratian, *Causa*, 33, *Quaest.* 5, chapters 12–16—Friedberg, i, pp. 1254, 1255. Ambrose and Jerome on the same matter, ibid., *c.* 15 and 17, Friedberg, i, p. 1255. Gratian, *Causa* 30, *Quaest.* 5, *c.* 7—Friedberg, i, p. 1106: Feminae dum maritantur, ideo velantur, ut noverint se semper viris suis subditas esse et humiles.

[2] Gratian, *Distinctio*, 30, *c.* 2—Friedberg, i, p. 107: Quecumque mulier, religioni iudicans convenire, comam sibi amputaverit quam Deus ad velamen eius et ad memoriam subiectionis illi dedit, tanquam resolvens ius subiectionis, anathema sit. Cf. Gratian, *Causa*, 15, *Quaest.* 3—Friedberg, i, p. 750.

[3] Gratian, *Dist.*, 30, *c.* 6, Friedberg, i, p. 108. See also *Deuteronomy* xxii, 5.

must never presume to teach men publicly.[1]
She was not allowed to bring a criminal action
except in cases of high treason or to avenge the
death of near relatives.[2] Parents could dedicate
a daughter to God while she was yet an infant;
and this parental vow bound her to the nunnery
when she was mature, whether she was willing or
not.[3] Virgins or widows who had once consecrated
themselves to God might not marry under pain of
excommunication.[4] Parents could not prevent a
daughter from taking vows, if she so wished, after
she had attained the age of twelve.[5]

The most important effect of the canon law
was on marriage, which was now a sac- *Women and*
rament and had its sanction not in *marriage under*
the laws of men, but in the express de- *canon law.*

[1] Gratian, *Dist.*, 23, *c.* 29—Friedberg, i, p. 86: Mulier, quamvis
docta et sancta, viros in conventu docere non praesumat.

[2] Id., *Causa*, 15, *Quaest.* 3—Friedberg, i, p. 750.

[3] Id., *Causa*, 20, *Quaest.* 1, *c.* 2—Friedberg, i, pp. 843–844,
quoting Gregory to Augustine, the Bishop of the Angles: Ad-
didistis adhuc, quod si pater vel mater filium filiamve intra septa
monasterii in infantiae annis sub regulari tradiderunt disciplina,
utrum liceat eis, postquam ad pubertatis inoleverint annos,
egredi, et matrimonio copulari. Hoc omnino devitamus, quia
nefas est ut oblatis a parentibus Deo filiis voluptatis frena re-
laxentur. Id., *c.* 4—Fried., i, p. 844: quoting Isidore—quicumque
a parentibus propriis in monasterio fuerit delegatus, noverit se
ibi perpetuo mansurum. Nam Anna Samuel puerum suum
natum et ablactatum Deo pietate obtulit. Id., *c.* 7—Fried., i,
pp. 844–845.

[4] Gratian, *Dist.*, 27, *c.* 4 et 9, and *Dist.*, 28, *c.* 12—Friedberg, i,
pp. 99 and 104. Id., *Causa*, 27, *Quaest.* 1, *c.* 1 and 7—Friedberg,
i, pp. 1047 and 1050.

[5] Gratian, *Causa*, 20, *Quaest.* 2, *c.* 2—Friedberg, i, pp. 847–848.

crees of God. Hence even engagements acquired
a sacred character unknown to the Roman law;
and when a betrothal had once been entered into,
it could be broken only in case one or both
of the contracting parties desired to enter a
monastery.[1] Free consent of both man and
woman was necessary for matrimony.[2] There
must also be a dowry and a public ceremony.[3]
The legitimate wife is thus defined[4]: "A chaste
virgin, betrothed in chastity, dowered according to
law, given to her betrothed by her parents, and
received from the hands of the bridesmaids [*a
paranimphis accipienda*]; she is to be taken
according to the laws and the Gospel and the
marriage ceremony must be public; all the days
of her life—unless by consent for brief periods to

[1] Cf. Council of Trent, Session 24, "On the Sacrament of
Matrimony," *Canon* 6: "If anyone shall say that matrimony
contracted but not consummated is not dissolved by the solemn
profession of religion by one of the parties married: let him be
anathema."

Gratian, *Causa*, 27, *Quaest.* ii, *c.* 28—Fried., i, p. 1071. Id., *c.*
46, 47, 50, 51—Fried., i, pp. 1076, 1077, 1078.

[2] Gratian, *Causa*, 30, *Quaest.* 2—Fried., i, p. 1100: Ubi non est
consensus utriusque, non est coniugium. Ergo qui pueris dant
puellas in cunabulis et e converso, nihil faciunt, nisi uterque
puerorum postquam venerit ad tempus discretionis consentiat,
etiamsi pater et mater hoc fecerint et voluerint. Id. *Causa*, 31,
Quaest. 2—Fried., i, 1112–1114: sine libera voluntate nulla est
copulanda alicui.

[3] Gratian, *Causa*, 30, *Quaest.* 5, *c.* 6—Friedberg, i, p. 1106: Nul-
lum sine dote fiat coniugium; iuxta possibilitatem fiat dos, nec
sine publicis nuptiis quisquam nubere vel uxorem ducere praesumat.

[4] Gratian, *Causa*, 30, *Quaest.* 5, *c.* 4—Friedberg, i, p. 1105.

devote to worship—she is never to be separated
from her husband; for the cause of adultery she is
to be dismissed, but while she lives her husband
may marry no other." The blessing of the priest
was necessary. About every form connected with
the marriage service the Church threw its halo of
mystery and symbol to emphasise the sacred
character of the union. Thus[1]: "Women are
veiled during the marriage ceremony for this
reason, that they may know they are lowly and
in subjection to their husbands. . . . A ring is
given by the bridegroom to his betrothed either
as a sign of mutual love or rather that their hearts
may be bound together by this pledge. For this
reason, too, the ring is worn on the fourth finger,
because there is a certain vein in that finger which
they say reaches to the heart."

Clandestine marriages were forbidden,[2] but the
Church always presumed everything it could in
favour of marriage and its indissolubility.   Clandestine
Thus, Gratian remarks[3]: "Clandestine   marriages.
marriages are, to be sure, contrary to law; nevertheless, they can not be dissolved." The reason
for forbidding them was perfectly reasonable:
one party might change his or her mind and there
would be no positive proof that a marriage had
taken place, so that a grave injury might be inflicted on an innocent partner by an unscrupulous

---

[1] Gratian, *Causa*, 30, *Quaest.* 5, *c.* 7—Friedberg, i, p. 1106
[2] Id., *c.* 1—Friedberg, i, p. 1104.
[3] Id., *c.* 8—Friedberg, i, p. 1107.

one who desired to dissolve the union.[1]   Yet the
marriage by consent alone without any of the
ceremonies or the blessing of the priest was
perfectly valid, though not "according to law"
(*legitimum*), and could not be dissolved.[2]   Not
until the great Council of Trent in 1563 was this
changed.   At that time all marriages were declared invalid unless they had been contracted in
the presence of a priest and two or three witnesses.[3]

The Church is seen in its fairest light in its
provisions to protect the wife from sexual brutality

Protection to on the part of her husband, and it
women.   deserves high praise for its stand on
such matters.[4]   Various other laws show the same
regard for the interests of women.   A man who was
entering priestly office could not cast off his wife
and leave her destitute, but must provide living
and raiment for her.[5]   Neither husband nor wife
could embrace the celibate life nor devote themselves to continence without the consent of the
other.[6]   A man who cohabited with a woman as his

---

[1] Gratian, *Causa*, 30, *Quaest.* 5, *c.* 9—Friedberg, i, p. 1107.

[2] Gratian, *Causa*, 28, *Quaest.* i,*c.* 17—Friedberg, i, p. 1089: illo-
rum vero coniugia, qui contemptis omnibus illis solempnitatibus
solo affectu aliquam sibi in coniugem copulant, huiuscemodi
coniugium non legitimum, sed ratum tantummodo esse creditur.

[3] Sessio xxiv, cap. i—De Reformatione Matrimonii.

[4] See Gratian, *Dist.*, v, *c.* 4—Friedberg, i, p. 8, e. g., . . .
ita ut morte lex sacra feriat, si quis vir ad menstruam mulierem
accedat.

[5] Gratian, *Dist.*, 31, *c.* 11—Friedberg, i, p. 114.

[6] Gratian, *Causa*, 27, *Quaest.* 2, *c.* 18–22, and 24–26—Friedberg i, pp. 1067–1070.

concubine, even though she was of servile condition or questionable character, could not dismiss her and marry another saving for adultery.[1] Slaves were now allowed to contract marriages and masters were not permitted to dissolve them.[2]

It has always been and still is the boast of the Roman Catholic Church that it has been the supreme protector of women on account of its stand on divorce. Says Cardinal Gibbons[3]: "Christian wives and mothers, what gratitude you owe to the Catholic Church for the honorable position you now hold in society! If you are no longer regarded as the slave, but the equal, of your husbands; if you are no longer the toy of his caprice, and liable to be discarded at any moment; but if you are recognised as the mistress and queen of your household, you owe your emancipation to the Church. You are especially indebted for your liberty to the Popes who rose up in all the majesty of their spiritual power to vindicate the rights of injured wives against the lustful tyranny of their husbands." In view of such a claim I may be justified in entering a somewhat more detailed account of this subject.

Divorce.

On the subject of divorce the Roman Catholic Church took the decided position which it continues to maintain at the present day. Marriage when

---

[1] Gratian, *Dist.*, 34, *c.* 4—Friedberg, i, p. 126. Id., *Causa*, 29, *Quaest.* 1—Friedberg, i, p. 1092. Id., *Causa*, 29, *Quaest.* 2, *c.* 2.

[2] Id., *Causa*, 29, *Quaest.* 2, *c.* 1 and 8.

[3] "Divorce," by James Cardinal Gibbons, in the *Century*, May, 1909.

entered upon under all the conditions demanded by the Church for a valid union is indissoluble.[1] A separation "from bed and board" (*quoad thorum seu quoad cohabitationem*) is allowed for various causes, such as excessive cruelty, for a determinate or an indeterminate period; but there is no absolute divorce even for adultery. For this cause a separation may, indeed, take place, but the bond of matrimony is not dissolved thereby and neither the innocent nor the guilty party may marry again during the lifetime of the other partner.

All this seems very rigorous. It is true that the Roman Catholic Church does not permit "divorce." But it allows fourteen cases where a marriage can be declared absolutely null and void, as if it had never existed; and in these cases the man or woman may marry again. To say that the Roman Church does not allow divorce is, therefore, playing upon words. The instruments used to render its strict theory ineffective are "diriment impediments" and "dispensations."

By the doctrine of "diriment impediments" the Pope or a duly constituted representative can declare that a marriage has been null and void from the very beginning because of some impediment defined in the canon law. Canon IV of the twenty-fourth session of the Council of Trent

[1] For this and what immediately follows see *Session* 24 of the Council of Trent "On the Sacrament of Matrimony" and also the Catholic Encyclopedia under "Divorce."

anathematises anyone who shall say that the
Church cannot constitute impediments dissolving
marriage, or that she has erred in constituting
them. The impediments which can annul marriage are described in the official Catholic Encyclopedia, vol. vii, pages 697–698. Among them are
impuberty and impotency. Then there is "dis-
parity of worship," which renders void the marriage of a Christian—that is, a Roman Catholic,
with an infidel,—that is, one who is unbaptised.
Marriage of a Roman Catholic with a baptised non-
Catholic constitutes a "relative" impediment and
needs a special dispensation and provisoes, such as
a guarantee to bring up the children in the Roman
faith to give it validity. Another impediment is
based on the presumption of want of consent,
"the nullity being caused by a defect of consent."
"This defect," says the Catholic Encyclopedia,
"may arise from the intellect or the will; hence
we have two classes. Arising from the intellect
we have: insanity; and total ignorance, even if in
confuso of what marriage is (this ignorance, however, is not presumed to exist after the age of
puberty has been reached); and lastly error, where
the consent is not given to what was not intended.
Arising from the will, a defect of consent may be
caused through deceit or dissimulation, when one
expresses exteriorly a consent that does not really
exist; or from constraint imposed by an unjust
external force, which causes the consent not to be
free." Consanguinity and affinity are diriment

impediments. Consanguinity "prohibits all marriages in the direct ascending or descending line in infinitum, and in the collateral line to the fourth degree or fourth generation." Affinity "establishes a bond of relationship between each of the married parties and the blood relations of the other, and forbids marriage between them to the fourth degree. Such is the case when the marriage springs from conjugal relations; but as canon law considers affinity to spring also from illicit intercourse, there is an illicit affinity which annuls marriage to the second degree only." Then there is "spiritual relationship"; for example, the marriage of one who stood as sponsor in confirmation with a parent of the child is null and void.

Under the canon law, even more resources are open for the man who is tired of his wife; by the doctrine, namely, of "spiritual fornication." Adultery is, of course, recognised as the cause that admits a separation. But the canon law remarks that idolatry and all harmful superstition —by which is meant any doctrine that does not agree with that of the Church—is fornication; that avarice is also idolatry and hence fornication; that in fact no vice can be separated from idolatry and hence all vices can be classed as fornication; so that if a husband only tried a little bit, he could without much trouble find some "vice" in his wife that would entitle him to a separation.[1]

---

[1] Gratian, *Causa* 28, *Quaest.* i, *c.* 5—Friedberg, i, pp. 1080–1081. Licite dimittitur uxor que virum suum cogere querit ad malum.

When all these fail, recourse can be had to a dispensation. The Church reserves the right to give dispensations for all impediments. Canon III of the twenty-fourth session of Trent says: "If anyone shall say, that only those degrees of consanguinity and affinity which are set down in *Leviticus* [xviii, 6 ff.] can hinder matrimony from being contracted, and dissolve it when contracted; and that the Church can not dispense in some of those degrees, or ordain that others may hinder and dissolve it; let him be anathema."

The minute and far-fetched subtleties which the Roman Church has employed in the interpretation of these relationships make escape from the marital tie feasible for the man who is eager to disencumber himself of his life's partner. The man of limited means will have a hard time of it. The great and wealthy have been able at all periods, by working one or more of these doctrines, to reduce the theory of the Roman Church to nullity in practice. Napoleon had his marriage to Josephine annulled on the ground that he had never intended to enter into a religious marriage with

---

Idolatria, quam secuntur infideles, et quelibet noxia superstitio fornicatio est. Dominus autem permisit causa fornicationis uxorem dimitti. Sed quia dimisit et non iussit, dedit Apostolo locum monendi, ut qui voluerit non dimittat uxorem infidelem, quo sic fortassis possit fidelis fieri. Si infidelitas fornicatio est, et idolatria infidelitas, et avaritia idolatria, non est dubitandum et avaritiam fornicationem esse. Quis ergo iam quamlibet illicitam concupiscentiam potest recte a fornicationis genere separare, si avaritia fornicatio est?

her, although the day before the ceremony he had
had the union secretly blessed by Cardinal Fesch.
On the basis of this avowed lack of intent, his
marriage with Josephine was declared null and
void, and he was free to marry Louisa. A plea
along the same lines is being worked by the Count
de Castellane now. Louis XII, having fallen in
love with Anne of Brittany, suddenly discovered
that his wife was his fourth cousin, that she was
deformed, and that her father had been his god-
father; and for this the Pope gave him a dispensation and his legitimate wife was sent away.
The Pope did not thunder against Louis XIV for
committing adultery with women like Louise de
la Vallière and Madame de Montespan. It is
certainly true that in the case of Philip Augustus
of France and Henry VIII of England the Pope
did protect injured wives; but both these monarchs
were questioning the Vatican's autocracy. The
matrimonial relations of John of England, Philip's
contemporary, were more corrupt than those of
the French king; but, while the Pope chastised
John for his defiance of his political autonomy, he
did not excommunicate him on any ground of
morality. The statement of Cardinal Gibbons
is not entirely in accordance with history; he
does not take all facts into consideration, as is also
true of his complacent assumption that outside
of the Roman Church no economic forces and no
individuals have had any effect in elevating the
moral and economic status of women.

Questions such as those of inheritance belong
properly to civil law; but the canon law claimed
to be heard in any case into which any
spiritual interest could be foisted. Thus   *Inheritance*
in the year 1199 Innocent III enacted that children of heretics be deprived of all their offending
parents' goods "since in many cases even according to divine decree children are punished in this
world on account of their parents."[1]

The attitude of the Roman Catholic Church
towards women's rights at the present day is
practically the same as it has been for
eighteen centuries. It still insists on the   *General atti-
subjection of the woman to the man, and   *tude towards
it is bitterly hostile to woman suffrage.   *women at the
                                                  present day
This position is so well illustrated by an article
of the Rev. David Barry in the Roman Catholic
paper, the Dublin *Irish Ecclesiastical Review*, that
I cannot do better than quote some of it. "It
seems plain enough," he says, "that allowing
women the right of suffrage is incompatible with
the high Catholic ideal of the unity of domestic
life. Even those who do not hold the high and
rigid ideal of the unity of the family that the
Catholic Church clings to must recognise some
authority in the family, as in every other society.

[1] Friedberg, ii, pp. 782 and 783: Quum enim secundum legiti-
mas sanctiones, etc.

Lea, in his *History of Confession and Indulgences*, ii, p. 87,
quotes Zanchini, *Tract. de Haeret., cap.* 33, to the effect that
goods of a heretic were confiscated and disabilities inflicted on
two generations of descendants.

Is this authority the conjoint privilege of husband and wife? If so, which of them is to yield, if a difference of opinion arises? Surely the most uncompromising suffragette must admit that the wife ought to give way in such a case. That is to say, every one will admit that the wife's domestic authority is subordinate to that of her husband. But is she to be accorded an autonomy in outside affairs that is denied her in the home? Her authority is subject to her husband's in domestic matters—her special sphere; is it to be considered co-ordinate with his in regulating the affairs of the State? Furthermore, there is an argument that applies universally, even in the case of those women who are not subject to the care and protection of a husband, and even, I do not hesitate to say, where the matters to be decided on would come specially within their cognisance, and where their judgment would, therefore, be more reliable than that of men. It is this, that in the noise and turmoil of party politics, or in the narrow, but rancorous arena of local factions, it must needs fare ill with what may be called the passive virtues of humility, patience, meekness, forbearance, and self-repression. These are looked on by the Church as the special prerogative and endowment of the female soul. . . . But these virtues would soon become sullied and tarnished in the dust and turmoil of a contested election; and their absence would soon be disagreeably in evidence in the character of women, who are, at the same time, almost constitutionally debarred from pre-eminence in the more robust virtues for which the soul of man is specially adapted."

Cardinal Gibbons, in a letter to the National League for the Civic Education of Women—an anti-suffrage organisation—said that "woman suffrage, if realised, would be the death-blow of domestic life and happiness" (Nov. 2, 1909).

Rev. William Humphrey, S. J., in his *Christian Marriage*, chap. 16, remarks that woman is "the subordinate equal of man"—whatever that means.

A few Roman Catholic prelates, like Cardinal Moran, have advocated equal suffrage, but they are in the minority. The Pope has not yet definitely stated the position of the Church; individual Catholics are free to take any side they wish, as it is not a matter of faith; but the tendency of Roman Catholicism is against votes for women.

SOURCES

I. Corpus Iuris Canonici: recognovit Aemilius Friedberg. Lipsiae (Tauchnitz) Pars Prior, 1879. Pars Secunda, 1881.

II. Sacrosanctum Concilium Tridentinum, additis Declarationibus Cardinalium, Concilii Interpretum, ex ultima recognitione Joannis Gallemart, etc. Coloniae Agrippinae, apud Franciscum Metternich, Bibliopolam. MDCCXXVII.

III. The Catholic Encyclopedia. New York, Robert Appleton Company. (Published with the *Imprimatur* of Archbishop Farley.)

IV. Various articles by Catholic prelates, due references to which are given as they occur.

CHAPTER VII

SINCE I have now given a brief summary of the canon law, which until the Reformation marked the general principles that guided the laws of all Europe on the subject of women, I propose next to consider more particularly the history of women's rights in England; for the institutions of England, being the basis of our own, will necessarily be more pertinent to us than those of Continental countries, to which I shall not devote more than a passing comment here and there. My inquiry will naturally fall into certain well-defined parts. The status of the unmarried woman is different from that of her married sister and will, accordingly, demand separate consideration. The rights of women, again, are to be viewed both from the legal and the social standpoint. Their legal rights include those of a private nature, such as the disposal of property, and public rights, such as suffrage, sitting on a jury, or holding office. Under social rights are included the right to an education, to earn a living, and the like. Let us glance first at the history of the legal rights of single women.

From very early times the law has continued to put the single woman of mature age on practically a par with men so far as private rights are concerned. She could hold land, make a will or contract, could sue and be sued, all of her own initiative; she needed no guardian. She could herself, if a widow, be guardian of her own children. In the case of inheritance, however, women have to within extremely recent times been treated less generously than men. The male sex has been preferred in an in- ^{Single women: Pollock and Maitland i, pp. 482-485.} ^{Pollock and Maitland, ii, 260-313. Blackstone, ii, ch. 14.} inheritance; males excluded females of equal degree; or, in the words of Blackstone: "In collateral inheritances the male stock shall be preferred to the female; that is, kindred derived from the blood of the male ancestors, however remote, shall be admitted before those from the blood of the female, however near; unless where the lands have, in fact, descended from a female. Thus the relations on the father's side are admitted *in infinitum* before those on the mother's side are admitted at all." Blackstone justly remarks that this harsh enactment of the laws of England was quite unknown to the Roman law "wherein brethren and sisters were allowed to succeed to equal portions of the inheritance." As an example, suppose we look for the heir of John Stiles, deceased. The order of succession would be:

I. The eldest son, Matthew Stiles, or his issue.

II. If his line is extinct, then Gilbert Stiles

and the other sons, respectively, in order of birth, or their issue.

III.   In default of these, all the daughters together, Margarite and Charlotte Stiles, or their issue.

IV.   On the failure of the descendants of John Stiles himself, the issue of Geoffrey and Lucy Stiles, his parents, is called in, viz.: first, Francis Stiles, the eldest brother of the whole blood, or his issue.

V.   Then Oliver Stiles, and the other whole brothers, respectively, in order of birth, or their issue.

VI.   Then the sisters of the whole blood all together, Bridget and Alice Stiles, or their issue.

And so on.   It will be noted that females of equal degree inherited together; and that a daughter excluded a brother of the dead man. Men themselves, if younger sons, have suffered what seems to us a grave injustice in the prevalence of the right of primogeniture, whereby, if there are two or more males in equal degree, the eldest only can inherit.   This law might work for the benefit of certain females; thus, the daughter, granddaughter, or great-granddaughter of an eldest son will succeed before the younger son.

To public rights, such as sitting on a jury [1] or

[1] If a woman sentenced to execution declared she was pregnant, a jury of twelve matrons could be appointed on a writ *de ventre inspiciendo* to determine the truth of the matter; for she could not be executed if the infant was alive in the womb. The same jury determined the case of a widow who feigned her-

holding offices of state, women never were admitted; that is a question that has become prominent only in the twentieth century and will demand consideration in its proper place.

Unlike the Roman law, English law allows parents to disinherit children completely, if they so desire, without being under any compulsion to leave them a part of their goods. **Power of parents.** As to legal power over children, the mother, as such, is entitled to none, says Blackstone,[1] but only to reverence and respect. Now, however, by the statute 2 and 3 Vict., c. 54, commonly called *Talfourd's Act*, an order may be made on petition to the court of chancery giving mothers access to their children and, if such children are within the age of seven years, for delivery of them to their mother until they attain that age. But no woman who has been convicted of adultery is entitled to the benefit of the act. The father has legal power up to the time when his children come of age; then it ceases. Until that time, his consent is necessary to a valid marriage; he may receive the profit of a child's estate, but only as guardian or trustee, and must render an account when the child attains his majority; and he may have the benefit of his children's labour while they live with him.

---

self with child in order to exclude the next heir and when she was suspected of trying to palm off a supposititious birth. But from all other jury duties women have always been excluded "on account of the weakness of the sex"—*propter defectum sexus.*

[1] Blackstone, i, ch. 16.

We are ready now to observe the status of women in marriage. The question of their legal rights in this relation offers the most illuminating insight into their conditions in the various epochs of history. Matrimony is a state over which the Church has always asserted special jurisdiction. By the middle of the twelfth century it was law in England that to it belonged this prerogative. The ecclesiastical court, for example, pronounced in a given case whether there had been a valid marriage or not; the temporal court took this decision as one of the bases for determining a matter of inheritance, whether a woman was entitled to dower, and the like. The general precepts laid down by canon law in the case of a wife have already been noted. These rules need now to be supplemented by an account of the position of women in marriage under the common law.

Under the older common law the husband was very much lord of all he surveyed and even more. An old enactment thus describes a husband's duty [1]: "He shall treat and *govern* the aforesaid A well and decently, and shall not inflict nor cause to be inflicted any injury upon the aforesaid A except in so far as he may lawfully

Husband and wife. Pollock and Maitland, ii, 399-436. Blackstone, i, ch 15. Bryce, pp. 818-830.

[1] Reg. Brev. Orig., f. 89: quod ipse praefatam A bene et honeste tractabit et gubernabit, ac damnum vel malum aliquod eidem A de corpore suo, aliter quam ad virum suum ex causa regiminis et castigationis uxoris suae licite et rationabiliter pertinet, non faciet nec fieri procurabit.

and reasonably do so in accordance with *the right of a husband to correct and chastise his wife.*" Blackstone, who wrote in 1763, has this to say on the husband's power to chastise his wife: "The husband also, by the old law, might give his wife moderate correction. For, as he is to answer for her misbehaviour, the law thought it reasonable to intrust him with this power of restraining her, by domestic chastisement, in the same moderation that a man is allowed to correct his apprentices or children, for whom the master or parent is also liable in some cases to answer. But this power of correction was confined within reasonable bounds, and the husband was prohibited from using any violence to his wife *aliter quam ad virum, ex causa regiminis et castigationis uxoris suae, licite et rationabiliter pertinet.* [1] The civil law gave the husband the same, or a larger, authority over his wife; allowing him for some misdemeanours *flagellis et fustibus acriter verberare uxorem* [to give his wife a severe beating with whips and clubs]; for others, only *modicam castigationem adhibere* [to apply moderate correction]. But with us in the politer reign of Charles the Second, this power of correction began to be doubted; and a wife may now have security of the peace against her husband, or, in return, a husband against his wife. Yet the lower rank of people, who were always fond of the old common law, still claim and

[1] " Except in so far as he may lawfully and reasonably do so in order to correct and chastise his wife."

exert their ancient privilege; and the courts of law will still permit a husband to restrain a wife of her liberty, in case of any gross misbehaviour." Doubtless what Mr. Weller, Sr., describes as the "amiable weakness" of wife-beating was not necessarily confined to the "lower rank." For instance, some of the courtly gentlemen of the reign of Queen Anne were probably not averse to exercising their old-time prerogative. Says Sir Richard Steele (*Spectator*, 479): "I can not deny but there are Perverse Jades that fall to Men's Lots, with whom it requires more than common Proficiency in Philosophy to be able to live. When these are joined to men of warm Spirits, without Temper or Learning, they are frequently corrected with Stripes; but one of our famous Lawyers is of opinion, That this ought to be used sparingly." The law was, indeed, even worse than might appear from the words of Blackstone. The wife who feared unreasonable violence could, to be sure, bind her husband to keep the peace; but she had no action against him. A husband who killed his wife was guilty of murder, but the wife who slew her husband was adjudged guilty of petty treason; and whereas the man would be merely drawn and hanged, the woman, until the reign of George III, was drawn and burnt alive. [1]

[1] The learned commentator Christian adds a few more cases where formerly the criminal law was harshly prejudiced against women. Thus: "By the Common Law, all women were denied

The right of a husband to restrain a wife's liberty may not be said to have become completely obsolete until the case of *Reg. v. Jackson* in 1891.[1] Wife-beating is still a flagrantly common offence in England.

Turning now to the question of the wife's property in marriage, we shall be forced to believe that Blackstone was an optimist of unusual magnitude when he wrote that the female sex was "so great a favourite of the laws of England." Not to weary the reader by minute details, I cannot do better than give Messrs. Pollock and Maitland's excellent summary of the final shape taken by the common law— a glaring piece of injustice, worthy of careful reading, and in complete accord with Apostolic injunctions: "I. In the lands of which the wife is tenant in fee, whether they belonged to her at the date of the marriage or came to her during the marriage, the husband has an estate which will endure during the marriage, and this he can alienate without her concurrence. If a child is born of the marriage, thenceforth the husband as 'tenant by courtesy' has an estate which will

Wife's property in marriage.

---

the benefit of clergy; and till the *3 and 4 W. and M., c. 9* [*William and Mary*] they received sentence of death and might have been executed for the first offence in simple larceny, bigamy, manslaughter, etc., however learned they were, merely because their sex precluded the possibility of their taking holy orders; though a man who could read was for the same crime subject only to burning in the hand and a few months' imprisonment."

[1] 1 Q. B. p. 671—in the Court of Appeal.

endure for the whole of his life, and this he can alienate without the wife's concurrence. The husband by himself has no greater power of alienation than is here stated; he cannot confer an estate which will endure after the end of the marriage or (as the case may be) after his own death. The wife has during the marriage no power to alienate her land without her husband's concurrence. The only process by which the fee can be alienated is a *fine* to which both husband and wife are parties and to which she gives her assent after a separate examination.

" II.   A widow is entitled to enjoy for her life under the name of dower one third of any land of which the husband was seised in fee at any time during the marriage. The result of this is that during the marriage the husband cannot alienate his own land so as to bar his wife's right of dower, unless this is done with her concurrence, and her concurrence is ineffectual unless the conveyance is made by *fine*." [This inconvenience for an unscrupulous husband was evaded in modern conveyancy by a device of extreme ingenuity finally perfected only in the eighteenth century. Professor James Bryce remarks (p. 820): "As this right (i.e., the right of dower) interfered with the husband's power of freely disposing of his own land, the lawyers at once set about to find means of evading it, and found these partly in legal processes by which the wife, her consent being ascertained by the courts, parted with her right, partly by an ingenious device whereby lands could be conveyed to a husband without the right of dower attaching to them, partly by giving the wife a so-called jointure which barred her claim."]

"III.   Our law institutes no community, even of movables, between husband and wife.   Whatever movables the wife has at the date of the marriage become the husband's, and the husband is entitled to take possession of and thereby to make his own whatever movables she becomes entitled to during the marriage, and without her concurrence he can sue for all debts that are due her. On his death, however, she becomes entitled to all movables and debts that are outstanding, or (as the phrase goes) have not been 'reduced into possession.'   What the husband gets possession of is simply his; he can freely dispose of it *inter vivos* or by will.   In the main, for this purpose as for other purposes, a 'term of years' is treated as a chattel, but under an exceptional rule the husband, though he can alienate his wife's 'chattel real' *inter vivos*, cannot dispose of it by his will.   If he has not alienated it *inter vivos*, it will be hers if she survives him.   If he survives her, he is entitled to her 'chattels real' and is also entitled to be made the administrator of her estate.   In that capacity he has a right to whatever movables or debts have not yet been 'reduced into possession' and, when the debts have been paid, he keeps these goods as his own.   If she dies in his lifetime, she can have no other intestate successor.   Without his consent she can make no will, and any consent that he may have given is revocable at any time before the will is proved.

"IV. Our common law—but we have seen that this rule is not very old—assured no share of the husband's personality to the widow. He can, even by his will, give all of it away from her except her necessary clothes, and with that exception his creditors can take all of it. A further exception, of which there is not much to be read, is made of jewels, trinkets, and ornaments of the person, under the name of paraphernalia. The husband may sell or give these away in his lifetime, and even after his death they may be taken for his debts; but he cannot give them away by will. If the husband dies during the wife's life and dies intestate she is entitled to a third, or, if there be no living descendant of the husband, to one half of his personality [but see the note of Bryce, above]. But this is a case of pure intestate succession; she only has a share of what is left after payment of her husband's debts.

"V. During the marriage the husband is in effect liable to the whole extent of his property for debts incurred or wrongs committed by his wife before the marriage, also for wrongs committed during the marriage. The action is against him and her as co-defendants. If the marriage is dissolved by his death, she is liable, his estate is not. If the marriage is dissolved by her death, he is liable as her administrator, but only to the extent of the property which he takes in that character." [Mr. Ashton, in his very interesting book, p. 31, quotes a peculiar note from a Parish Register in the reign of Queen Anne to this effect: "John Bridmore and Anne Sellwood, both of Chiltern all Saints, were married October 17, 1714. The aforesaid Anne Sellwood was married in her Smock, without any clothes or headgier on." "This is not uncommon," remarks Mr. Ashton, "the object being, according to a vulgar error, to exempt the husband from the payment of any debts his wife may have contracted in her ante-nuptial condition. This error seems to have been founded on a misconception of the law, as it is laid down 'the husband is liable for the wife's debts, because he acquires an absolute interest in the personal estate of his wife.' An unlearned person from this might conclude, and not un-reasonably, that if his wife had no estate whatever he could not incur any liability."]

"VI. During the marriage the wife cannot contract on her own behalf. She can contract as her husband's agent and has a certain power of pledging his credit in the purchase of necessaries. At the end of the Middle Ages it is very doubtful how far this power is to be explained by an 'implied agency.' The tendency of more recent times has been to allow her no power that cannot be thus explained, except in the exceptional case of desertion."

A perusal of these laws shows that they are

immensely inferior to the Roman law, which not only gave the wife full control of her property, but protected her from coercion and bullying on the part of the husband. The amendment of these injustices has been very recent indeed. Successive statutes in 1870, 1874, and 1882 [1] finally abrogated the law which gave the husband full ownership of his wife's property by the mere act of marriage. Beginning with the year 1857, too, enlightenment in England had progressed to such a remarkable degree that certain acts were passed forbidding a husband to seize his wife's earnings and neglect her [2]; and she was actually allowed to keep her own wages after the desertion of her lord. Before that time he might desert his wife repeatedly, and return from time to time to take away her earnings and sell everything she had acquired. An act in 1886 (49 *and* 50 *Vict.*, *c.* 52) gave magistrates the power to order a husband to pay his wife a weekly sum, not exceeding two pounds, for her support and that of the children if it appeared to the magistrates that the deserting husband had

[1] *Married Women's Property Act*, 45 and 46 V., c. 75—Aug. 18, 1882.

[2] Note this incident, from the *Westminister Review*, October, 1856: "A lady whose husband had been unsuccessful in business established herself as a milliner in Manchester. After some years of toil she realised sufficient for the family to live upon comfortably, the husband having done nothing meanwhile. They lived for a time in easy circumstances after she gave up business and then the husband died, *bequeathing all his wife's earnings to his own illegitimate children.* At the age of 62 she was compelled, in order to gain her bread, to return to business."

the means of maintaining her, but was unwilling
to do so. Still, the husband can at any time
terminate his desertion and force his wife to take
him back on penalty of losing all rights to such
maintenance. There was frantic opposition to
all of these revolutionary enactments and many
prophets arose crying woe; but the acts finally
passed and England still lives.

Until the Reformation divorce was regulated
by the canon law in accordance with the principles
which I have explained. After the   Divorce.
Reformation the matter at once assumed   Authorities
                                          as above;
a different aspect because all Protestants and Howard,
agreed in denying that marriage is a   ii, 3-117.
sacrament. Scotland in this as in other respects
has been more liberal than England; as early as
1573 desertion as well as adultery had become
grounds for divorce. But in England the force of
the canon law continued. In Blackstone's day
there were still, as under the canon law, only
two kinds of separation. Complete dissolution
of the marriage tie (*a vinculo matrimonii*) took
place only on a declaration of the Ecclesiastical
Court that on account of some canonical impediment, like consanguinity, the marriage was
null and void from the beginning. Separation
"from bed and board" (*a mensa et thoro*) simply
gave the parties permission no longer to live
together and was allowed for adultery or some
other grave offences, like intolerable cruelty or
a chronic disease. However, some time before

Blackstone's day it had become the habit to get a dissolution of marriage *a vinculo matrimonii* for adultery by Act of Parliament; but the legal process was so tedious, minute, and expensive that only the very rich could afford the luxury.[1] In the case of a separation *a mensa et thoro* alimony was allowed the wife for her support out of her husband's estate at the discretion of the ecclesiastical judges.

The initiative in divorce by Act of Parliament was usually taken by the husband; not until 1801 did a woman have the temerity so to assert her rights. The fact is, ever since the dawn of history society has, with its usual double standard of morality for men and women, insisted that while the husband must never tolerate infidelity on the part of the wife, the wife should bear with meekness the adulteries of her husband. Plutarch in his *Conjugal Precepts* so advises a wife; and this pious frame of mind has continued down the centuries to the present day. Devout old Jeremy Taylor in his *Holy Living*—a book which is read by few, but praised by many—thus counsels the suffering wife[2]: "But if, after all the fair deportments and innocent chaste compliances, the husband be morose and ungentle, let the wife discourse thus: 'If, while I do my duty, my husband neglects me, what will he do if I neglect him?' And if she thinks to be separated by reason of her

---

[1] For a full account of the elaborate machinery see Chitty's note to Blackstone, vol. i, p. 441, of Sharswood's edition.

[2] *Holy Living, ch.* 3, *section* 1: *Rules for Married Persons.*

husband's unchaste life, let her consider that the man will be incurably ruined, and her rivals could wish nothing more than that they might possess him alone." Dr. Samuel Johnson ably seconded the holy Jeremy's advice by declaring that there is a boundless difference between the infidelity of the man and that of the woman. In the husband's case "the man imposes no bastards upon his wife." Therefore, "wise married women don't trouble themselves about infidelity in their husbands." [1] Until very recent times not only men but also women have been unanimous in counselling abject submission to and humble adoration of the husband. A single example out of hundreds will serve excellently as a pattern. In 1821 a "Lady of Distinction" writes to a "Relation Shortly after Her Marriage" as follows [2]: "The most perfect and implicit faith in the superiority of a husband's judgment, and the most absolute obedience to his desires, is not only the conduct that will insure the greatest success, but will give the most entire satisfaction. It will take from you a thousand cares, which would have answered to no purpose; it will relieve you from a weight of thought that would be very painful, and in no way profitable. . . . It has its origin in reason,

[1] Boswell, vii, 288. Perhaps if the venerable Samuel had had the statistics of venereal disease given by adulterous husbands to wives and children he might not have been so sure of his contention.

[2] Quoted by Professor Thomas in the *American Magazine*, July, 1909.

in justice, in nature, and in the law of God. . . .
I have told you how you may, and how people
who are married do, get a likeness of countenance;
and in that I have done it. You will understand
me, that by often looking at your husband's face,
by smiling on the occasions on which he does, by
frowning on those things which make him frown,
and by viewing all things in the light in which you
perceive he does, you will acquire that likeness of
countenance which it is an honour to possess, because it is a testimony of love. . . . When your
temper and your thoughts are formed upon those
of your husband, according to the plan which I have
laid down, you will perceive that you have no will,
no pleasure, but what is also his. This is the
character the wife of prudence would be apt to
assume; she would make herself the mirror, to show,
unaltered, and without aggravation, diminution,
or distortion, the thoughts, the sentiments, and
the resolutions of her husband. She would have
no particular design, no opinion, no thought, no
passion, no approbation, no dislike, but what
should be conformable to his own judgment. . . .
I would have her judgment seem the reflecting
mirror to his determination; and her form the
shadow of his body, conforming itself to his
several positions, and following it in all its movements. . . . I would not have you silent; nay,
when trifles are the subject, talk as much as any
of them; but distinguish when the discourse turns
upon things of importance."

It is not strange, therefore, that no woman protested publicly against a husband's infidelity until 1801.   Up to 1840 there were but three cases of a woman's taking the initiative in divorce, namely, in 1801, 1831, and 1840; and in each case the man's adultery was aggravated by other offences.   In two other suits the Lords rejected the petition of the wife, although the misconduct of the husband was clearly proved.   But redress was still by the elaborate machinery of Act of Parliament and hence a luxury only for the wealthy until 1857, when a special Court for Divorce and Matrimonial Causes was established. [1] Nevertheless, the law as it stands to-day is not of a character to excite admiration or to prove the existence of the proverbial "British Fair Play." A husband can obtain a divorce upon proof of his wife's infidelity; but the wife can get it only by proving, in addition to the husband's adultery, either that it was aggravated by bigamy or incest or that it was accompanied by cruelty or by two years' desertion.   Misconduct by the husband bars him from obtaining a divorce.   The court is empowered to regulate at its discretion the property rights of divorced people and the custody of the children. [2]   All attempts have failed to make the law recognise that the misconduct of the husband shall be regarded equally as culpable as the wife's.

[1] See 20 *and* 21 *V.*, *c.* 85—Aug. 28, 1857.
[2] See 7 *Edw.*, *c.* 12—Aug. 9, 1907—Matrimonial Causes Act, which also gives the court discretion in alimony.

We may pause a moment to glance at the provisions made by the criminal law for protecting women. The offence that most closely

Rape and the age of legal consent. touches women is rape. The punishment of this in Blackstone's day was death [1]; but in the next century the death penalty was repealed and transportation for life substituted. [2] The saddest blot on a presumably Christian civilisation connected with this matter is the so-called "age of legal consent." Under the older Common Law this was *ten* or *twelve;* in 1885 it was *thirteen*, at which period a girl was supposed to be at an age to know what she was doing. But in the year 1885 Mr. Stead told the London public very plainly those hideous truths about crimes against young girls which everybody knew very well had been going on for centuries, but which no one ever before had dared to assert. The result was that Parliament raised the "age of legal consent" to *sixteen*, where it now stands. [3]

[1] Blackstone, iv, ch. 15.

[2] 4 *and* 5 *V.*, *c.* 56, *s.* 3.

[3] The Criminal Law Amendment Act, 1885, 48 *and* 49 *V. c.* 69, section 5: "Any person who (1) unlawfully and carnally knows or attempts to have unlawful carnal knowledge of any girl being of or above the age of thirteen years and under the age of sixteen, or (2) unlawfully and carnally knows or attempts to have carnal knowledge of any female idiot or imbecile woman or girl under circumstances which do not amount to rape, but which prove that the offender knew at the time of the commission of the offence that the woman or girl was an idiot or imbecile, shall be guilty of a misdemeanour, and being convicted thereof shall be liable at the discretion of the Court to be imprisoned for any term not exceeding two years, with or without hard labour."

The idea that any girl of this age is sufficiently mature to know what she is doing by consenting to the lust of scoundrels is a fine commentary on the acuteness of the legal intellect and the high moral convictions of legislators.

The rights of women to a higher education is distinctly a movement of the last half of the nineteenth century. It is true that throughout history there are many examples of remarkably well-educated women— **Women's rights to an education.** Lady Jane Grey, for example, or Queen Elizabeth, or Olympia Morata, in Italy, she who in the golden period of the Renaissance became a professor at sixteen and wrote dialogues in Greek after the manner of Plato. But on looking closely into these instances we shall find first that these ladies were of noble rank and only thanks to their lofty position had access to knowledge; and secondly that they stand out as isolated cases—the great masses of women never dreamed beyond the traditional Kleider, Küche, Kinder, and Kirche. That an elementary education, consisting of reading, writing, and simple arithmetic, was offered them freely by hospital, monastery, and the like schools even as early as Chaucer—this we know; nevertheless, beyond that they were not supposed to aspire. So very recently, indeed, have women

---

Section 4: "Any one who unlawfully and carnally knows any girl under the age of thirteen shall be guilty of felony, and being convicted thereof shall be liable to be kept in penal servitude for life." Any one who merely attempts it can be imprisoned for any term not exceeding two years, with or without hard labour.

secured the rights to a higher education that
many thousands to-day can easily recall the
intensely bitter attacks which were directed
against colleges like Wellesley and Bryn Mawr in
their inception. Until the middle of the nineteenth century the whole education—what there
was of it—of a girl was arranged primarily with a
view to capture a husband and, once having him
secure, to be his loving slave, to dwell with adoring
rapture on his superior learning, and to be humbly
grateful if her liege deigned from time to time to
throw his spouse some scraps of knowledge which
might be safely administered without danger of
making her think for herself. These facts no one
can well deny; but a few instances of prevalent
opinion, in addition to those which I have already
quoted, will afford the amusement of concrete
examples.

Mrs. Chapone, in the eighteenth century,
advised her niece to avoid the study of classics
and science lest she "excite envy in one sex and
jealousy in the other." Lady Mary Wortley
Montagu laments thus: "There is hardly a
creature in the world more despicable and more
liable to universal ridicule than a learned woman,"
and "folly is reckoned so much our proper sphere,
we are sooner pardoned any excesses of that than
the least pretensions to reading and good sense."
Pursuant to the prevailing sentiment on the
education of women, the subjects which they
studied and the books which they were allowed

to read were carefully regulated. As to their reading, it was confined to romantic tales whereof the exceeding insipidity could not awaken any symptom of intelligence. Lyly dedicated his *Euphues* to the "Ladies and Gentlewomen of England" and Sidney's *Arcadia* owed its vast success to its female readers.

The subjects studied followed the orthodox views. Beginning with the reign of Queen Anne boarding-schools for girls became very numerous. At these schools "young Gentlewomen" were "soberly educated" and "taught all sorts of learning fit for young Gentlewomen." The "learning fit for young Gentlewomen" comprised "the Needle, Dancing, and the French tongue; a little Music on the Harpsichord or Spinet, to read, write, and cast accounts in a small way." Dancing was the all-important study, since this was the surest route to their Promised Land, matrimony. The study of French consisted in learning parrot-like a modicum of that language pronounced according to the fancy of the speaker. As, however, the young beau probably did not know any more himself, the end justified the means. Studies like history, when pursued, were taken in homœopathic doses from small compendiums; and it was adequate to know that Charlemagne lived somewhere in Europe about a thousand or so years ago. Yet even this was rather advanced work and exposed the woman to be damned by the report that she was educated. Ability to cook was not despised and pastry schools were not uncommon. Thus in the time of Queen Anne appears this: "To all Young Ladies: at Edw. Kidder's Pastry School in little Lincoln's Inn Fields are taught all Sorts of Pastry and Cookery, Dutch hollow works, and Butter Works," etc.

At last in the first decades of the nineteenth century the civilised world began slowly to take some thought of women's higher education and to wake up to the fact that because a certain system has been in vogue since created man does not necessarily mean that it is the right one; a very heretical and revolutionary idea, which has always been and still is ably opposed by that great host of people who have steadily maintained that when men and women once begin to think for themselves society must inevitably run to ruin. In 1843 there was established a certain Governesses' Benevolent Institution. This was in its inception a society to afford relief to governesses, i.e., women engaged in tutoring, who might be temporarily in straits, and to raise annuities for those who were past doing work. Obviously this would suggest the question of what a competent governess was; and this in turn led to the demand for a diploma as a warrant of efficiency. That called attention to the extreme ignorance of the members of the profession; and it was soon felt that classes of instruction were needed. A sum of money was accordingly collected in 1846 and given the Institution for that purpose. Some eminent

professors of King's College volunteered to lecture;
and so, on a small scale to be sure, began what
is now Queen's College, the first college for women
in England, incorporated by Royal Charter in
1853. In 1849 Bedford College for women had
been founded in London through the unselfish
labours of Mrs. Reid; but it did not receive its
charter until 1869. Within a decade Cheltenham,
Girton, Newnham, and other colleges for women
had arisen. Eight of the ten men's universities
of Great Britain now allow examinations and
degrees to women also; Oxford and Cambridge
do not.

Since then women's right to any higher education which they may wish to embrace has been
permanently assured. As early as 1868 **Women in the**
Edinburgh opened its courses in phar- **professions.**
macy to women. In 1895 there were already
264 duly qualified female physicians in Great
Britain. In many schools they are allowed to
study with men, as at the College of Physicians
and Surgeons at Edinburgh; there are four medical
schools for women only. We find women now
actively engaged in agriculture, apiculture, poultry-
keeping, horticulture; in library work and index-
ing; in stenography; in all trades and professions.
The year 1893 witnessed the first appointment of
women as factory inspectors, two being chosen
that year in London and in Glasgow. Notting-
ham had chosen women as sanitary inspectors in
1892. Thus in about two decades woman has

advanced farther than in the combined ages which preceded. Before these very modern movements we may say that the stage was the only profession which had offered them any opportunity of earning their living in a dignified way. It seems that a Mrs. Coleman, in 1656, was the first female to act on the stage in England; before that, all female parts had been taken by boys or young men. A Mrs. Sanderson played Desdemona in 1660 at the Clare Market Theatre. In 1661, as we may see from Pepys' *Diary* (Feb. 12, 1661), an actress was still a novelty; but within a few decades there were already many famous ones.

We have seen that now woman has obtained practically all rights on a par with men. There are still grave injustices, as in divorce; but the battle is substantially won. One right still remains for her to win, the right, namely, to vote, not merely on issues such as education—this privilege she has had for some time—but on all political questions; and connected with this is the right to hold political office. We may fittingly close this chapter by a review of the history of the agitation for woman suffrage.

Woman suffrage in England.

In the year 1797 Charles Fox remarked: "It has never been suggested in all the theories and projects of the most absurd speculation, that it would be advisable to extend the elective suffrage to the female sex." Yet five years before Mary Wollstonecraft had published her *Vindication of*

the Rights of Women. Presently the writings of
Harriet Martineau upon political economy proved
that women could really think on politics.

We may say that the general public first began
to think seriously on the matter after the epoch-
making Reform Act of 1832. This celebrated
measure admitted £10 householders to the right
to vote and carefully excluded females; yet it
marked a new era in the awakening of civic
consciousness: women had taken active part in the
attendant campaigns; and the very fact that
"male persons" needed now to be so specifically
designated in the bill, whereas hitherto "persons"
and "freeholders" had been deemed sufficient,
attests the recognition of a new factor in
political life.

In 1865 John Stuart Mill was elected to Parliament. That able thinker had written on *The
Subjection of Women* and was ready to champion
their rights. A petition was prepared under the
direction of women like Mrs. Bodichon and Miss
Davies; and in 1867 Mill proposed in Parliament
that the word *man* be omitted from the People's
Bill and *person* substituted. The amendment
was rejected, 196 to 83.

Nevertheless, the agitation was continued. The
next year constitutional lawyers like Mr. Chis-
holm Anstey decided that women might be legally entitled to vote; and 5000 of them applied
to be registered. In a test case brought before the
Court of Common Pleas the verdict was adverse,

on the ground that it was contrary to usage for
women to vote. The fight went on. Mr. Jacob
Bright in 1870 introduced a "Bill to Remove the
Electoral Disabilities of Women" and lost. In
1884 Mr. William Woodall tried again; he lost
also, largely through the efforts of Gladstone; and
the same statesman was instrumental in killing
another bill in 1892, when Mr. A. J. Balfour urged
its passage.

At the present day women in England cannot
vote on great questions of universal state policy
nor can they hold great offices of state. Yet their
gains have been enormous, as I shall next de-
monstrate; and in this connection I shall also
glance briefly at their vast strides in the colonies.

In 1850 Ontario gave all women school suffrage.
In 1867 New South Wales gave them municipal
suffrage. In 1869 England granted municipal
suffrage to single women and widows; Victoria
gave it to all women, married or single. In
England in 1870 the Education Act, by which
school boards were created, gave women the
same rights as men, both as regards electing and
being elected. In 1871 West Australia gave them
municipal suffrage; in 1878 New Zealand gave
school suffrage. In 1880 South Australia gave
municipal suffrage. In 1881 widows and single
women obtained municipal suffrage in Scotland
and Parliamentary suffrage on the Isle of Man.
Municipal suffrage was given by Ontario and
Tasmania in 1884 and by New Zealand and New

Brunswick in 1886; by Nova Scotia and Manitoba in 1887. In 1888 England gave women county suffrage and British Columbia and the North-West Territory gave them municipal suffrage. In 1889 county suffrage was given the women of Scotland and municipal suffrage to single women and widows in the Province of Quebec. In 1893 New Zealand gave full suffrage. In 1894 parish and district suffrage was given in England to women married and single, with power to elect and to be elected to parish and district councils. In 1895 South Australia gave full state suffrage to all women. In 1898 the women of Ireland were given the right to vote for all officers except members of Parliament. In 1900 West Australia granted full state suffrage to all. In 1902 full national suffrage was given all the women in federated Australia and full state suffrage to those of New South Wales. In 1903 Tasmania gave full state suffrage; in 1905 Queensland did the same; in 1908 Victoria followed. In 1907 England made women eligible as mayors, aldermen, and county and town councillors. In London, for example, at the present time women can vote for the 28 borough councils and 31 boards of guardians of the London City Council; they can also be themselves elected to these; be members of the central unemployed body or of the 23 district committees, and can be co-opted to all other bodies, like the local pension committees. Women can be aldermen of the Council; and there is nothing to prevent one from holding even the office of chairman.

At the present moment the cause of woman suffrage in England is being furthered chiefly by two organizations which differ in methods. The National Union of Women's Suffrage Societies has adopted the "constitutional" or peaceful policy; but the National Women's Social and Political Union is "militant" and coercive.

SOURCES

I.   The English Statutes. Published by Authority during the Various Reigns.

II.   Studies in History and Jurisprudence: by James Bryce. Oxford University Press, 1901. Pages 782-859 on "Marriage and Divorce."

III.   History of English Law: by Frederick Pollock and Frederic Maitland. 2 vols. Cambridge University Press, 1898—second edition.

IV.   Commentaries on the Laws of England: by Sir William Blackstone. With notes selected from the editions of Archbold, Christian, Coleridge, etc., and additional notes by George Sharswood, of the University of Pennsylvania. 2 vols. Philadelphia, 1860—Childs and Peterson, 602 Arch Street.

V.   A History of Matrimonial Institutions, chiefly in England and the United States: by George Elliott Howard. 4 vols. The University of Chicago Press, 1904.

VI.   Social England: edited by H. D. Traill. 6 vols. G. P. Putnam's Sons, 1901.

VII.   Social Life in the Reign of Queen Anne, taken from original sources: by John Ashton. London, Chatto and Windus, 1897.

VIII.   The Renaissance of Girls' Education in England: by Alice Zimmern. London, A. D. Innes and Co., 1898.

IX.   Progress in Women's Education in the British Empire:

edited by the Countess of Warwick. Being the Report of the Education Section, Victorian Era Exhibition, 1897. Longmans, Green, & Co., 1898.

X.   Current Literature from the Earliest Times to the Present Day, references to which are noted as they occur.

CHAPTER VIII

WOMEN'S RIGHTS IN THE UNITED STATES

IT has been my aim, in this short history of the growth of women's rights, to depict for the most part the strictly legal aspect of the matter; but from time to time I have interposed some typical illustration of public opinion, in order to bring into greater prominence the ferment that was going on or the misery which existed behind the scenes. A history of legal processes might otherwise, from the coldness of the laws, give few hints of the conflicts of human passion which combined to set those processes in motion. Before I present the history of the progress of women's rights in the United States, I shall place before the reader some extracts which are typical and truly representative of the opposition which from the beginning of the agitation to the present day has voiced itself in all ranks of life. Let the reader bear carefully in mind that from 1837 to the beginning of the twentieth century such abuse as that which I shall quote as typical was hurled from ten thousand throats of men and women unceasingly; that Mrs. Stanton, Miss Anthony, and Mrs. Gage were hissed, insulted, and offered physical violence by mobs in New York [1] and Boston to an extent inconceivable in this age; and that the marvellously unselfish labour of such women as these whom I have mentioned and of men like Wendell Phillips is alone responsible for the improvement in the legal status of women, which I propose to trace in detail. Some expressions of the popular attitude follow:

From a speech of the Rev. Knox-Little at the Church of St. Clements in Philadelphia in 1880: "God made himself to be born of a woman to sanctify the virtue of endurance; loving submission is an attribute of a woman; men are logical, but women, lacking this quality, have an intricacy of thought. There are those who think women can be taught logic; this is a mistake. They can never by any power of education arrive at the same mental status as that enjoyed by men, but they have a quickness of apprehension, which is usually called leaping at conclusions, that is astonishing. There, then, we have distinctive traits of a woman, namely, endurance, loving submission, and quickness of apprehension. Wifehood is the crowning glory of a woman. In it she is bound for all time. To her husband she owes the duty of unqualified obedience. There is no crime which a man can commit which justifies his wife in leaving him or

Examples of opposition to women's rights.

[1] See, for example, the account in the *New York Tribune*, Sept. 8, 9, and 12, 1853, of what happened at the Women's Rights Convention at that time.

applying for that monstrous thing, divorce. It is
her duty to subject herself to him always, and no
crime that he can commit can justify her lack
of obedience. If he be a bad or wicked man, she
may gently remonstrate with him, but refuse him
never. Let divorce be anathema; curse it; curse
this accursed thing, divorce; curse it, curse it!
Think of the blessedness of having children. I am
the father of many children and there have been
those who have ventured to pity me. 'Keep your
pity for yourself,' I have replied, 'they never cost
me a single pang.' In this matter let woman
exercise that endurance and loving submission
which, with intricacy of thought, are their only
characteristics."

From the Philadelphia *Public Ledger and Daily
Transcript*, July 20, 1848: "Our Philadelphia ladies
not only possess beauty, but they are celebrated
for discretion, modesty, and unfeigned diffidence,
as well as wit, vivacity, and good nature. Who
ever heard of a Philadelphia lady setting up for a
reformer or standing out for woman's rights, or as-
sisting to *man* the election grounds [*sic*], raise a regi-
ment, command a legion, or address a jury? Our
ladies glow with a higher ambition. They soar to
rule the hearts of their worshippers, and secure
obedience by the sceptre of affection. . . . But all
women are not as reasonable as ours of Philadelphia. The Boston ladies contend for the rights
of women. The New York girls aspire to mount
the rostrum, to do all the voting, and, we suppose,

all the fighting, too. . . . Our Philadelphia girls object to fighting and holding office. They prefer the baby-jumper to the study of Coke and Lyttleton, and the ball-room to the Palo Alto battle. They object to having a George Sand for President of the United States; a Corinna for Governor; a Fanny Wright for Mayor; or a Mrs. Partington for Postmaster. . . . Women have enough influence over human affairs without being politicians. . . . A woman is nobody. A wife is everything. A pretty girl is equal to ten thousand men, and a mother is, next to God, all powerful. . . . The ladies of Philadelphia, therefore, under the influence of the most 'sober second thoughts' are resolved to maintain their rights as Wives, Belles, Virgins, and Mothers, and not as Women."

From the "Editor's Table" of *Harper's New Monthly Magazine*, November, 1853: "Woman's Rights, or the movement that goes under that name, may seem to some too trifling in itself and too much connected with ludicrous associations to be made the subject of serious arguments. If nothing else, however, should give it consequence, it would demand our earnest attention from its intimate connection with all the radical and infidel movements of the day. A strange affinity seems to bind them all together. . . . But not to dwell on this remarkable connection— the claim of 'woman's rights' presents not only the common radical notion which underlies the whole class, but also a peculiar enormity of its

own; in some respects more boldly infidel, or
defiant both of nature and revelation, than that
which characterises any kindred measure. It is
avowedly opposed to the most time-honoured pro-
prieties of social life; it is opposed to nature;
it is opposed to revelation. . . . This unblushing
female Socialism defies alike apostles and prophets.
In this respect no kindred movement is so decidedly infidel, so rancorously and avowedly anti-
biblical.

"It is equally opposed to nature and the established order of society founded upon it. We do
not intend to go into any physiological argument.
There is one broad striking fact in the constitution
of the human species which ought to set the
question at rest for ever. This is the fact of
maternity. . . . From this there arise, in the first
place, physical impediments which, during the best
part of the female life, are absolutely insurmount-
able, except at a sacrifice of almost everything that
distinguishes the civilized human from the animal,
or beastly, and savage state. As a secondary, yet
inevitably resulting consequence, there come
domestic and social hindrances which still more
completely draw the line between the male
and female duties. . . . Every attempt to break
through them, therefore, must be pronounced as
unnatural as it is irreligious and profane. . . .
The most serious importance of this modern
'woman's rights' doctrine is derived from its
direct bearing upon the marriage institution. The

blindest must see that such a change as is proposed in the relations and life of the sexes cannot leave either marriage or the family in their present state. It must vitally affect, and in time wholly sever, that oneness which has ever been at the foundation of the marriage idea, from the primitive declaration in Genesis to the latest decision of the common law. This idea gone—and it is totally at war with the modern theory of 'woman's rights' —marriage is reduced to the nature of a contract simply. . . . That which has no higher sanction than the will of the contracting parties, must, of course, be at any time revocable by the same authority that first created it. That which makes no change in the personal relations, the personal rights, the personal duties, is not the holy marriage *union*, but the unholy *alliance* of concubinage."

In a speech of Senator George G. Vest, of Missouri, in the United States Senate, January 25, 1887, these: "I now propose to read from a pamphlet sent to me by a lady. . . . She says to her own sex: 'After all, men work for women; or, if they think they do not, it would leave them but sorry satisfaction to abandon them to such existence as they could arrange without us.'

"Oh, how true that is, how true!"

In 1890 a bill was introduced in the New York Senate to lower the "age of consent"—the age at which a girl may legally consent to sexual intercourse—from 16 to 14. It failed. In 1892 the brothel keepers tried again in the Assembly. The

bill was about to be carried by universal consent
when the chairman of the Judiciary Committee,
feeling the importance of the measure, called for
the individual yeas and nays, in order that the
constituents of the representatives might know
how their legislators voted. The bill thereupon
collapsed. In 1889 a motion was made in the
Kansas Senate to lower the age of consent from
18 to *12*. But the public heard of it; protests
flowed in; and under the pressure of these the law
was allowed to remain as it was.

Such are some typical examples of the warfare of
the opposition to all that pertains to advancing
the stătus of women. As I review the progress
of their rights, let the reader recollect that this
opposition was always present, violent, loud, and
often scurrilous.

In tracing the history of women's rights in the
United States my plan will be this: I shall first give
a general review of the various movements connected with the subject; and I shall then lay
before the reader a series of tables, wherein may
be seen at a glance the status of women to-day in
the various States.

In our country, as in England, single women
have at all times had practically the same legal
Single women. rights as men; but by no means the
same political, social, educational, or
professional privileges; as will appear more con-
clusively later on.

We may say that the history of the agitation for women's rights began with the visit of Frances Wright to the United States in 1820. Frances Wright was a Scotchwoman, born at Dundee in 1797, and early exhibited a keen intellect on all the subjects which concern political and social reform. For several years after 1820 she resided here and strove to make men and women think anew on old traditional beliefs—more particularly on theology, slavery, and the social degradation of women. The venomous denunciations of press and pulpit attested the success of her efforts. In 1832 Lydia Maria Child published her *History of Woman*, a résumé of the status of women; and this was followed by numerous works and articles, such as Margaret Fuller's *The Great Lawsuit, or Man vs. Woman: Woman vs. Man*, and Eliza Farnham's *Woman and her Era*. Various women lectured; such as Ernestine L. Rose—a Polish woman, banished for asserting her liberty. The question of women's rights received a powerful impetus at this period from the vast number of women who were engaged in the anti-slavery agitation. Any research into the validity of slavery perforce led the investigators to inquire into the justice of the enforced status of women; and the two causes were early united. Women like Angelina and Sarah Grimké and Lucretia Mott were pioneers in numerous anti-slavery conventions. But as soon as they dared to

History of agitation for women's rights.

address meetings in which men were present, a tempest was precipitated; and in 1840, at the annual meeting of the Anti-Slavery Association, the men refused to serve on any committee in which any woman had a part; although it had been largely the contributions of women which were sustaining the cause. Affairs reached a climax in London, in 1840, at the World's Anti-Slavery Convention.   Delegates from all anti-slavery organisations were invited to take part; and several American societies sent women to represent them.   These ladies were promptly denied any share in the proceedings by the English members, thanks mainly to the opposition of the clergy, who recollected with pious satisfaction that St. Paul permitted not a woman to teach.   Thereupon Lucretia Mott and Elizabeth Cady Stanton determined to hold a women's rights convention as soon as they returned to America; and thus a World's Anti-Slavery Convention begat an issue equally large.

Accordingly, the first Women's Rights Convention was held at Seneca Falls, New York, July 19–20, 1848.   It was organised by *divorced wives, childless women, and sour old maids*, the gallant newspapers declared; that is, by Mrs. Elizabeth Cady Stanton, Mrs. Lucretia Mott, Mrs. McClintock, and other fearless women, who not only lived the purest and most unselfish of domestic lives, but brought up many children besides.   Great crowds attended.   A *Declaration of Sentiments* was moved and adopted; and as this exhibits the temper of the convention and illustrates the then prevailing status of women very clearly, I shall quote it:

DECLARATION OF SENTIMENTS

"When, in the course of human events, it becomes necessary for one portion of the family of man to assume among the people of the earth a position different from that which they have hitherto occupied, but one to which the laws of nature and of nature's God entitle them, a decent respect to the opinions of mankind requires that they should declare the causes which impel them to such a course.

"We hold these truths to be self-evident: that all men and women are created equal; that they are endowed by their Creator with certain inalienable rights; that among these are life, liberty, and the pursuit of happiness; that to secure these rights governments are instituted, deriving their just powers from the consent of the governed. Whenever any form of government becomes destructive of those ends, it is the right of those who suffer from it to refuse allegiance to it, and to insist upon the institution of a new government, laying its foundation on such principles, and organising its powers in such form, as to them shall seem most likely to effect their safety and happiness. Prudence, indeed, will dictate that governments

long established should not be changed for light
or transient causes; and accordingly all experience
hath shown that mankind are more disposed to
suffer, while evils are sufferable, than to right
themselves by abolishing the forms to which they
were accustomed. But when a long train of
abuses and usurpations, pursuing invariably the
same object, evinces a design to reduce them
under absolute despotism, it is their duty to throw
off such government, and to provide new guards
for their future security. Such has been the
patient sufferance of the women under this government, and such is now the necessity which con-
strains them to demand the equal station to which
they are entitled.

"The history of mankind is a history of repeated
injuries and usurpations on the part of man
toward woman, having in direct object the establishment of an absolute tyranny over her. To prove
this, let facts be submitted to a candid world.

"He has never permitted her to exercise her
inalienable right to the elective franchise.

"He has compelled her to submit to laws, in
the formation of which she had no voice.

"He has withheld from her rights which are
given to the most ignorant and degraded men—
both natives and foreigners.

"Having deprived her of this first right of a
citizen, the elective franchise, thereby leaving her
without representation in the halls of legislation,
he has oppressed her on all sides.

"He has made her, if married, in the eye of the law, civilly dead.

"He has taken from her all right in property, even to the wages she earns.

"He has made her, morally, an irresponsible being, as she can commit many crimes with impunity, provided they be done in the presence of her husband. In the covenant of marriage, she is compelled to promise obedience to her husband, he becoming, to all intents and purposes, her master—the law giving him power to deprive her of her liberty, and to administer chastisement.

"He has so framed the laws of divorce, as to what shall be the proper causes, and, in case of separation, to whom the guardianship of the children shall be given, as to be wholly regardless of the happiness of women—the law in all cases going upon a false supposition of the supremacy of man, and giving all power into his hands.

"After depriving her of all rights as a married woman, if single, and the owner of property, he has taxed her to support a government which recognises her only when her property can be made profitable to it.

"He has monopolised nearly all the profitable employments, and from those she is permitted to follow she receives but a scanty remuneration. He closes against her all the avenues of wealth and distinction which he considers most honourable to himself. As a teacher of theology, medicine, or law, she is not known.

"He has denied her the facilities for obtaining a thorough education, all colleges being closed against her.

"He allows her in church, as well as state, but a subordinate position, claiming Apostolic authority for her exclusion from the ministry, and, with some exceptions, from any public participation in the affairs of the church.

"He has created a false public sentiment by giving to the world a different code of morals for men and women, by which moral delinquencies which exclude women from society are not only tolerated, but deemed of little account in man.

"He has usurped the prerogative of Jehovah himself, claiming it as his right to assign for her a sphere of action, when that belongs to her conscience and to her God.

"He has endeavoured, in every way that he could, to destroy her confidence in her own powers, to lessen her self-respect, and to make her willing to lead a dependent and abject life.

"Now, in view of this entire disfranchisement of one half the people of this country, their social and religious degradation; in view of the unjust laws above mentioned, and because women do feel themselves aggrieved, oppressed, and fraudulently deprived of their most sacred rights, we insist that they have immediate admission to all the rights and privileges which belong to them as citizens of the United States.

"In entering upon the great work before us,

we anticipate no small amount of misconception, misrepresentation, and ridicule; but we shall use every instrumentality within our power to effect our object. We shall employ agents, circulate tracts, petition the State and National legislatures, and endeavour to enlist the pulpit and press in our behalf. We hope this Convention will be followed by a series of Conventions embracing every part of the country."

Such was the defiance of the Women's Rights Convention in 1848; other conventions were held, as at Rochester, in 1853, and at Albany in 1854; the movement extended quickly to other States and touched the quick of public opinion. It bore its first good fruits in New York in 1848, when the Property Bill was passed. This law, amended in 1860, and entitled "An Act Concerning the Rights and Liabilities of Husband and Wife" (March 20, 1860), emancipated completely the wife, gave her full control of her own property, allowed her to engage in all civil contracts or business on her own responsibility, rendered her joint guardian of her children with her husband, and granted both husband and wife a one-third share of one another's property in case of the decease of either partner.

Thus New York became the pioneer. The movement spread, as I have mentioned, with amazing rapidity; but it was not so uniformly successful. Conventions were held, for example, in Ohio, at Salem, April 19–20, 1850; at Akron, May 28–29, 1851; at Massillon on May 27, 1852. Nevertheless, in 1857, the Legislature of Ohio passed a bill enacting that no married man should dispose of any personal property without having first obtained the consent of his wife; the wife was empowered, in case of a violation of this law, to commence a civil suit in her own name for the recovery of the property; and any married woman whose husband deserted her or neglected to provide for his family was to be entitled to his wages and to those of her minor children. A bill to extend suffrage to women was defeated, by a vote of 44 to 44; the petition praying for its enactment had received 10,000 signatures.

The course of events as it has been described in New York and Ohio, is practically the same in the case of the other States. The Civil War relegated these issues to a secondary place; but during that momentous conflict the heroism of Clara Barton on the battlefield and of thousands of women like her paved the way for a reassertion of the rights of woman in the light of her unquestioned exertions and unselfish labours for her country in its crisis. After the war, attention began to be concentrated more on the right to *vote*. By the Fourteenth Amendment the franchise was at once given to negroes; but the insertion of the word *male* effectually barred any national recognition of woman's right to vote. A vigorous effort was made by the suffrage leaders to have *male* stricken from the amendment; but the effort was futile. Legislators thought that the black man's vote ought to be secured first; as the *New York Tribune* (Dec. 12, 1866) puts it snugly: "We want to see the ballot put in the hands of the black without one day's delay added to the long postponement of his just claim. When that is done, we shall be ready to take up the next question" (i. e., woman's rights).

The first Women's Rights Convention after the Civil War had been held in New York City, May 10, 1866, and had presented an address to Congress. Such was the dauntless courage of the leaders, that Mrs. Stanton offered herself as a candidate for Congress at the November elections, in order to test the constitutional rights of a woman to run for office. She received twenty-four votes.

Six years later, on November 1, 1872, Miss Susan B. Anthony did a far more audacious thing. She went to the polls and asked to be registered. The two Republican members of the board were won over by her exposition of the Fourteenth Amendment and agreed to receive her name, against the advice of their Democratic colleague and a United States supervisor. Following Miss Anthony's example, some fifty other women of Rochester registered. Fourteen voted and were at once arrested under the enforcement act of Congress of May 31, 1870 (*section* 19). The case of Miss Anthony was argued ably by her attorney; but she was adjudged guilty. A *nolle prosequi* was entered for the women who voted with her.

Immediately after the decision in her case, the inspectors who had registered the women were put on trial because they "did knowingly and willfully register as a voter of said District one Susan B. Anthony, she, said Susan B. Anthony, then and there not being entitled to be registered as a voter of said District in that she, said Susan B. Anthony, was then and there a person of the female sex, contrary to the form of the statute of the United States of America in such case made and provided, and against the peace of the United States of America and their dignity." The defendants were ordered to pay each a fine of twenty-five dollars and the costs of the prosecution; but the sentence was revoked and an unconditional pardon given them by President Grant, in an order dated March 3, 1874. Miss Anthony was forced to pay her fine, in spite of an appeal to Congress.

Such were the stirring times when the agitation for women's rights was first brought to the fore as a national issue. Within a few years, various States, like New York and Kansas, put the question of equal suffrage for women before its voters; they in general rejected the measure. At present there are four States which give women complete suffrage and right to vote on all questions with the same privileges as men, viz., Wyoming (1869), Colorado (1893), Utah (1896), and Idaho (1896).

In 1838 Kentucky gave school suffrage to widows
with children of school age; in 1861 Kansas gave
it to all women. School suffrage was granted all
women in 1875 by Michigan and Minnesota, in
1876 by Colorado, in 1878 by New Hampshire and
Oregon, in 1879 by Massachusetts, in 1880 by
New York and Vermont, in 1883 by Nebraska,
in 1887 by North and South Dakota, Montana,
Arizona, and New Jersey. Kansas gave municipal
suffrage in 1887; and Montana gave tax-paying
women the right to vote upon all questions submitted to the tax-payers. In 1891 Illinois granted
school suffrage, as did Connecticut in 1893. Iowa
gave bond suffrage in 1894. In 1898 Minnesota
gave women the right to vote for library trustees,
Delaware gave school suffrage to tax-paying
women, and Louisiana gave tax-paying women
the right to vote upon all questions submitted to
the tax-payers. Wisconsin gave school suffrage
in 1900. In 1901 New York gave tax-paying
women in all towns and villages of the State the
right to vote on questions of local taxation; and
the Kansas Legislature voted down almost unani-
mously a proposal to repeal municipal suffrage.
In 1903 Kansas gave bond suffrage; and in 1907
the new State of Oklahoma continued school
suffrage. In 1908 Michigan gave all women who
pay taxes the right to vote upon questions of local
taxation and the granting of franchises.

The history of the "age of legal consent" has
an importance which through prudery and a wilful

ignorance of facts the public has never fully realised.   I shall have considerable to say of it
later.   It will suffice for the moment
Age of
legal   to remark that until the decade pre-
consent.   ceding 1898 the old Common Law
period of ten, sometimes twelve, years was the
basis of "age of consent" legislation in most States
and in the Territories under the jurisdiction of
the national government.   In 1885 the age in
Delaware was *seven*.

The Puritans, burning with an unquenchable
zeal for liberty, fled to America in order to build
a land of freedom and strike off the
The begin-
nings of high- shackles of despotism.   After they were
er education comfortably settled, they forthwith pro-
for women.
ceeded, with fine humour, to expel mistress Anne Hutchinson for venturing to speak
in public, to hang superfluous old women for
being witches, and to refuse women the right to an
education.   In 1684, when a question arose about
admitting girls to the Hopkins School of New
Haven, it was decided that "all girls be excluded
as improper and inconsistent with such a grammar
school as ye law enjoins and as in the Designs
of this settlement."   "But," remarks Professor
Thomas, "certain small girls whose manners seem
to have been neglected and who had the natural
curiosity of their sex, sat on the schoolhouse steps
and heard the boys recite, or learned to read and
construe sentences from their brothers at home,
and were occasionally admitted to school."

In the course of the next century the world moved a little; and in 1789, when the public school system was established in Boston, girls were admitted from April to October; but until 1825 they were allowed to attend primary schools only. In 1790 Gloucester voted that "two hours, or a proportional part of that time, be devoted to the instruction of females." In 1793 Plymouth accorded girls one hour of instruction daily.

The first female seminary in the United States was opened by the Moravians at Bethlehem, Pennsylvania, in 1749. It was unique. In 1803, of 48 academies or higher schools fitting for college in Massachusetts, only three were for girls, although a few others admitted both boys and girls.

The first instance of government aid for the systematic education of women occurred in New York, in 1819. This was due to the influence of a remarkable woman. Mrs. Emma Willard had begun teaching in Connecticut and by extraordinary diligence mastered not only the usual subjects of the curriculum, but in addition botany, chemistry, mineralogy, astronomy, and the higher mathematics. She had, moreover, striven always to introduce new subjects and new methods into her school, and with such success that Governor Clinton, of New York, invited her to that State and procured her a government subsidy. Her school was established first at Watervliet, but soon moved to Troy. This seminary was the first girls' school in which the higher mathematics formed a part of the course; and the first public examination of a girl in geometry, in 1829, raised a storm of ridicule and indignation—the clergy, as usual, prophesying the speedy dissolution of all family bonds and therefore, as they continued with remorseless logic, of the state itself. But Mrs. Willard continued her ways in spite of clerical disapproval and by-and-by projected a system of normal schools for the higher education of teachers, and even suggested women as superintendents of public schools. New York survived and does not even remember the names of the patriots who fought a lonely woman so valiantly.

The first female seminary to approach college rank was Mt. Holyoke, which was opened by Mary Lyon at South Hadley, Mass., in 1836. Vassar, the next, dates from 1865; and Radcliffe, the much-abused "Harvard Annex," was instituted in 1879. These were the first colleges exclusively for women. Oberlin College had from its foundation, in 1833, admitted men and women on equal terms; although it took pains to express its hearty disapproval of those women who, after graduation, had the temerity to advocate political rights for women—rights which that same Oberlin insisted should be given the negro at once. In 1858, when Sarah Burger and other women applied for admission to the University of Michigan, their request was refused.

It was hard enough for women to assert their rights to a higher education; to enter a profession

was almost impossible. Nevertheless, it was done.
The pioneer in medicine was Harriet K. Hunt who
practised in Boston from 1822 to 1872
without a diploma; but in 1853 the
Woman's Medical College of Pennsylvania conferred upon her the degree of Doctor of
Medicine. The first woman to receive a diploma
from a college after completing the regular course
was Elizabeth Blackwell, who attained that distinction at Geneva, New York, in 1848. The first adequate woman's medical institution was Miss
Blackwell's New York Infirmary, chartered in 1854.
In 1863, Dr. Zakrzewska, in co-operation with
Lucy Goddard and Ednah D. Cheney, established
the New England Hospital for Women and Children, which aimed to provide women the medical
aid of competent physicians of their own sex, to
assist educated women in the practical study of
medicine, and to train nurses for the care of the
sick.[1]

First women in medicine.

In law, it would seem that Mistress Brut
practised in Baltimore as early as 1647; but after
her the first woman lawyer in the United
States was Arabella A. Mansfield, of Mt.
Pleasant, Iowa. She was admitted to the bar in
1864. By 1879 women were allowed to plead
before the Supreme Court of the United States.[2]

In law.

[1] In 1900 there were 7399 female physicians and surgeons in
the United States, and 808 female dentists.

[2] In 1900 there were 1049 women lawyers in the United
States. The above statements are from Bliss, *Encyc.*, p. 1291.

Coming now to the consideration of the ministry, the first woman to attempt to assert a right to In the that profession was Anne Hutchinson, ministry. of Boston, in 1634. She was promptly banished. Among the Friends and the Shakers women like Lucretia Mott and Anne Lee preached; and among the primitive Methodists and similar bodies women were always permitted to exhort; but the first regularly ordained woman in the United States appears to have been Rev. Antoinette Brown Blackwell, of the Congregational Church, who was ordained in 1852. In 1864 Rev. Olympia Brown settled as pastor of the parish at Weymouth Landing, in Massachusetts; and the Legislature acknowledged marriages solemnised by women as legal. Phebe Hanaford, Mary H. Graves, and Lorenza Haynes were the first Massachusetts women to be ordained preachers of the Gospel; the latter was at one time chaplain of the Maine House of Representatives. The best known woman in the ministry at the present day is Rev. Anna Howard Shaw, a Methodist minister, president of the National American Woman's Suffrage Association.[1]

Women have from very early times been exceedingly active in newspaper work. Anna Frank- As newspaper lin printed the first newspaper in Rhode editors. Island, in 1732; she was made official printer to the colony. When the founder of the *Mercury*, of Philadelphia, died in 1742, his widow,

[1] In 1900 there were 3405 women clergy in the United States.

Mrs. Cornelia Bradford, carried it on for many years with great success, just as Mrs. Zenger continued the *New York Weekly Journal*—the second newspaper started in New York—for years after the death of her husband. Anna K. Greene established the *Maryland Gazette,* the first paper in that colony, in 1767. Penelope Russell printed *The Censor* in Boston, in 1771. In fact, there was hardly a colony in which women were not actively engaged in printing. After the Revolution they were still more active. Mrs. Anne Royal edited *The Huntress* for a quarter of a century. Margaret Fuller ran *The Dial,* in Boston, in 1840 and numbered Emerson and William Channing among her contributors. From 1840 to 1849 the mill girls of Lowell edited the *Lowell Offering.* These are but a few examples of what women have done in newspaper work. How very influential they are to-day every one knows who is familiar with the articles and editorial work appearing in newspapers and magazines; and that women are very zealous reporters many people can attest with considerable vigour.[1]

The enormous part which women now play in industry and in all economic production is a concomitant of the factory system, spe- **Women in** cialised industry, and all that makes **industry.** a highly elaborated and complex society. Be-

---

[1] In 1900 there were 2193 women journalists in the United States. This does not, of course, include women reporters and the like.

fore the introduction of machine industry, and in the simple society of the colonial days, women were no less a highly important factor in economic production; but not as wage earners. Their importance lay in the fact that spinning, weaving, brewing, cheese and butter making, and the like were matters attended to by each household to supply its own wants; and this was considered the peculiar sphere of the housewife. In 1840 Harriet Martineau found only seven employments open to women in the United States, viz., teaching, needlework, keeping boarders, working in cotton mills and in book binderies, type-setting, and household service.

I shall now present a series of fifty tables, by means of which the reader may see at a glance the status of women in all the States to-day. For convenience, I shall arrange the views alphabetically.

TABLES SHOWING THE PRESENT STATUS OF WOMEN IN THE UNITED STATES.

The right of "dower," as used in these tables, refers to the widow's right, under the Common Law, to the possession, for her life-time, of one third of the real estate of which her husband was possessed in fee-simple during the marriage.

"Curtesy" is the right of the husband after his wife's death to the life use of his wife's real estate, sometimes dependent on the birth of children, sometimes not; and usually the absolute right to her whole personal estate.

It must be remembered that the enforcement of certain laws, particularly in regard to child labour, is extremely lax in many States. It will be noted also that an unscrupulous employer could find loopholes in some of the statutes. The reader can observe these things for himself in his particular State.

Alabama

AGE OF LEGAL CONSENT: 14.

POPULATION: Male 916,764; female 911,933.

HUSBAND AND WIFE: Wife controls own earnings and has full control of own property; but she cannot mortgage her real and personal property or alienate it without husband's consent. Married women may execute will without concurrence of husband and may bar latter's right of curtesy. Husband may appoint guardian for children by will; but wife has custody of them until they are fourteen. If a wife commits a crime in partnership with her husband she cannot be punished (except for murder and treason). Husband is not required by law to support the family.

DIVORCE: Absolute divorce is granted for incurable impotence, adultery, desertion for two years, imprisonment for two years or more, crimes against nature, habitual drunkenness after marriage; in favour of husband if wife was pregnant at time of marriage without his knowledge or agency, in favour of wife for physical violence on part of husband endangering life or health, or when there is reasonable apprehension of such violence.

Limited divorce is granted for cruelty in either of the parties or any other cause which would justify absolute divorce, if the party desires only a divorce from bed and board.

LABOUR LAWS: Women not allowed to work in mines. Children under 12 not permitted to work in any factory. All employers of women must provide seats and must allow women to rest when not actively engaged.

SUFFRAGE, POLITICAL CONDITION, INDUSTRIAL AND PROFESSIONAL STATUS: There is no suffrage. Women not eligible for any elective office; they may be notaries public. There are 18 women in the ministry, 12 journalists, 1 dentist, 3 lawyers, 16 doctors, 3 professors, 2 bankers, 5 saloon keepers, 4 commercial travellers, 11 carpenters, etc.

Arizona

AGE OF LEGAL CONSENT: 17.

POPULATION: Male 71,795; female 51,136.

HUSBAND AND WIFE: Husband controls wife's earnings. Wife has control of property which she had before marriage. Wife may contract debts for necessaries for herself and children upon credit of husband. She may sue and be sued and make contracts in her own name as regards her separate property, but must sue jointly with husband for personal injuries, and damages recovered are community property and in his control. Father is legal guardian of minor children; at his death mother becomes guardian as long as she remains unmarried.

DIVORCE: Absolute divorce for excesses, cruelty, or outrage, adultery, impotence, conviction for a felony, desertion for one year, neglect of husband to provide for one year, habitual intemperance; in favour of husband if wife was pregnant at time of marriage without his knowledge or agency.

There is no limited divorce; but when the husband wilfully abandons his wife, she can maintain an action against him for permanent maintenance and support.

LABOUR LAWS: No woman or minor may work or give any exhibition in a saloon.

SUFFRAGE, POLITICAL CONDITION, INDUSTRIAL AND PROFESSIONAL STATUS: Women 21 years old or more who are mothers or guardians of a child of school age are eligible to the office of school trustee and may vote for such officers. There are 12 women in the ministry, 1 dentist, 2 journalists, 4 lawyers, 4 doctors, 628 saloon keepers, 2 bankers, etc.

Arkansas

AGE OF LEGAL CONSENT: 16.
POPULATION: Male 675,312; female 636,252.

HUSBAND AND WIFE: Wife controls own earnings. Dower exists, but not curtesy. Wife may sell or transfer her separate real estate without husband's consent. Father is legal guardian of children, but cannot apprentice them or create testamentary guardianship for them without wife's consent. At husband's death wife may be guardian of persons of children, but not of their property, unless derived from her.

DIVORCE: Absolute or limited divorce for impotence, wilful desertion for a year, when husband or wife had a former wife or husband living at the time of the marriage sought to be set aside, conviction for felony or other infamous crime, habitual drunkenness for one year, intolerable indignities, and adultery subsequent to marriage.

LABOUR LAWS: Labour contracts of married women, approved by their husbands, are legal and binding. No woman may work in a mine.

SUFFRAGE, POLITICAL CONDITION, INDUSTRIAL AND PROFESSIONAL STATUS: No suffrage. 13 women are ministers, 6 journalists, 9 lawyers, 39 doctors, 3 professors, 3 saloon keepers, 9 commercial travellers, etc.

California

AGE OF LEGAL CONSENT: 16.

POPULATION: Male 820,531; female 664,522.

HUSBAND AND WIFE: Wife controls own earnings. Wife may dispose of separate property without husband's consent. In torts of a personal nature she must sue jointly with her husband. Husband is guardian of minor children; wife becomes so at his death. Husband must provide for family. If husband has no property or is disabled, wife must support him and the family out of her property or earnings.

DIVORCE: Absolute divorce for adultery, extreme cruelty, wilful desertion for one year, wilful neglect for one year, habitual intemperance for one year, conviction for felony.

There are no statutory provisions for limited divorce. But when the wife has any cause for action as provided in the code, she may, without applying for a divorce, maintain an action against her husband for permanent support and maintenance of herself or of herself and children.

LABOUR LAWS: Sex shall be no disqualification for entering any business, vocation, or profession. Children under 16 may not be let out for acrobatic performances or any exhibition endangering life or morals. Any one who sends a minor under the age of 18 to a saloon, gambling house, or brothel, is guilty of a misdemeanour. One day of rest each week must be given all employees.

SUFFRAGE, POLITICAL CONDITION, INDUSTRIAL AND PROFESSIONAL STATUS: No suffrage. May be elected school trustees. May be notaries public. There are 201 women in the ministry, 52 dentists, 116 journalists, 60 lawyers, 522 doctors, 8 professors, 129 saloon keepers, 9 bankers, 23 commercial travellers, etc.

Colorado

AGE OF LEGAL CONSENT: 18.

POPULATION: Male 295,332; female 244,368.

HUSBAND AND WIFE: Wife controls own earnings. No assignment of wages by a married man is valid without the consent of his wife. Neither dower nor curtesy obtains. Husband and wife have same rights in making wills. Wife can sue and be sued as if unmarried. She is joint guardian of children with husband and has equal powers. Husband must support family.

DIVORCE: Absolute divorce for impotence, when husband or wife had a wife or husband living at time of marriage, adultery subsequent to marriage, wilful desertion for one year, cruelty (including the infliction of mental suffering as well as physical violence), neglect to provide for one year, habitual drunkenness for one year, conviction for felony.

There is no limited divorce.

LABOUR LAWS: Eight hours the usual day's work. Children under 12 may not work in mines; none under 14 may exhibit in saloons, variety theatres, or any place endangering morals. No female help may be sent to any place of bad repute. Children under 14 may not be employed in mills or factories. No woman may work underground in a mine. All employers of women must provide seats.

SUFFRAGE, POLITICAL CONDITION, INDUSTRIAL

AND PROFESSIONAL STATUS: Full suffrage. Women are eligible to all offices; 10 have served
in the Legislature. There are 39 women in the
ministry, 23 dentists, 28 journalists, 17 lawyers,
172 doctors, 4 professors, 17 saloon keepers, 12
bankers, 8 commercial travellers, etc.

Connecticut

AGE OF LEGAL CONSENT: 16.
POPULATION: Male 454,294; female 454,126.
HUSBAND AND WIFE: Wife controls own earnings. No dower or curtesy. Survivor gets one
third of property. Wife controls own property.
Wife and husband joint guardians of children with
equal powers. Husband must support family.

DIVORCE: Absolute divorce for adultery,
fraudulent contract, wilful desertion for three
years with total neglect of duty, seven years'
absence when absent party is not heard from during that period, habitual intemperance, intolerable cruelty, sentence to imprisonment for life,
any infamous crime involving a violation of conjugal duty and punishable by imprisonment.

There is no limited divorce.

LABOUR LAWS: No child under 12 may give
exhibition endangering limbs or morals. Employers of females may not send them to any place
of bad repute. Eight hours is a day's work.
Women employees must have seats to rest. No
woman shall be forced to labour more than ten
hours a day.

SUFFRAGE, POLITICAL CONDITION, INDUSTRIAL
AND PROFESSIONAL STATUS: Women have school
suffrage and may be elected school trustees.
There are 45 women in the ministry, 6 dentists,
122 doctors, 1 professor, 28 saloon keepers, 4 bankers, 13 commercial travellers, 14 carpenters, etc.

Delaware

AGE OF LEGAL CONSENT: 18.

POPULATION: Male 94,158; female 90,577.

HUSBAND AND WIFE: Wife controls own earnings. If there is a child or lawful issue of a child
living, widow has a life interest in one third of the
real estate and one third absolutely of the personal
property. If there is no child nor the descendant
of a child living, widow has a life interest in one
half of the real estate and one half absolutely of
the personal estate. If there are neither descendants nor kin of husband, she gets the entire real
estate for her life, and all the personal estate
absolutely. Father is legal guardian of children
and he alone may appoint a guardian at his death.
Husband must support family.

DIVORCE: Absolute divorce for adultery, desertion for three years, habitual drunkenness, impotence, extreme cruelty, conviction for felony,
procurement of marriage by fraud for want of
age, wilful neglect to provide for three years.

Limited divorce may be decreed, in the discretion of the court, for the last two causes
mentioned.

LABOUR LAWS: All female employees must be provided with seats. Sunday labour forbidden. No minor under 15 may be let out for any gymnastic or other exhibition endangering body or morals. Separate lunch, wash-rooms, etc., for all women employees; the rooms must be kept reasonably heated. Using indecent or profane language towards a female employee is a misdemeanour. The governor must appoint a *female* factory inspector who shall see that these laws are enforced. Children under 14 may not work in mills and factories; and no child under 16 shall be forced to labour more than nine hours daily.

SUFFRAGE, POLITICAL CONDITION, INDUSTRIAL AND PROFESSIONAL STATUS: Women in Milford, Townsend, Wyoming, and Newark who pay a property tax may vote for Town Commissioners. All such women in the State may vote for school trustees. There are 4 women in the ministry, 3 dentists, 1 journalist, 1 lawyer, 7 doctors, 8 saloon keepers, 1 commercial traveller, 2 carpenters, etc.

District of Columbia

AGE OF LEGAL CONSENT: 16.

POPULATION: Male 132,004; female 146,714.

HUSBAND AND WIFE: Wife controls own earnings and property, may be sued and sue, carry on business, etc., as if unmarried. Husband and wife are equal guardians of children. Husband must furnish reasonable support if he have property. Both dower and curtesy obtain.

DIVORCE: Absolute divorce for bigamy, insanity at time of marriage, impotence, adultery, habitual drunkenness for three years, cruel treatment endangering life or health.

Limited divorce for drunkenness, cruelty, and desertion.

In case of absolute divorce, only the innocent party may remarry; but the divorced parties may marry each other again.

LABOUR LAWS: No child under 14 may be let out for any public exhibition endangering body or morals. Seats must be provided for women employees. Employment agencies must not send applicants to places of bad repute. Children under 14 may not be employed in any factory, hotel, etc.; but judge of juvenile court may give dispensation to child between 12 and 14. No girl under 16 may be bootblack or sell papers or any other wares publicly.

SUFFRAGE, POLITICAL CONDITION, INDUSTRIAL AND PROFESSIONAL STATUS: No suffrage. Women may be notaries public and members of Board of Education. 17 women in the ministry, 7 dentists, 38 journalists, 23 lawyers, 56 doctors, 18 saloon keepers, 1 banker, 7 commercial travellers, 2 carpenters, etc.

Florida

AGE OF LEGAL CONSENT: 16 (but 10 practically, as penalty above 10 is insignificant).

POPULATION: Male 275,246; female 253,296.

HUSBAND AND WIFE: Wife controls own earnings and owns separate estate; but cannot transfer her real or personal property without husband's consent. Dower prevails, but not curtesy. Wife may make a will as if unmarried. Husband is legal guardian of children. Husband must support family.

DIVORCE: Absolute divorce for impotence, where the parties are within the degrees prohibited by the law, adultery, bigamy, extreme cruelty, habitual indulgence in violent and ungovernable temper, habitual intemperance, desertion for one year, if husband or wife has obtained a divorce elsewhere and if the applicant has been a citizen of Florida for two years.

There is no limited divorce. But the wife may claim alimony, without applying for a divorce, for any of these causes except bigamy.

LABOUR LAWS: Ten hours legal day's work. Employers of women must provide seats. No child under 14 may be let out for any public exhibition endangering body or morals. Sunday labour forbidden. No child under 12 may be employed in any factory, or any place where intoxicating liquor is sold; and no child under 12 may labour more than nine hours a day.

SUFFRAGE, POLITICAL CONDITION, INDUSTRIAL AND PROFESSIONAL STATUS: No suffrage. Women may be notaries public. 19 women in the ministry, 1 dentist, 9 journalists, 4 lawyers, 21 doctors, 1 banker, 3 commercial travellers, 6 carpenters, etc.

Georgia

AGE OF LEGAL CONSENT: 10.

POPULATION: Male 1,103,201; female 1,113,130.

HUSBAND AND WIFE: Wife controls own earnings and own property. Dower prevails, but not curtesy. Husband is legal guardian of children and at his death may appoint a guardian to the exclusion of his wife. Husband must support family.

DIVORCE: Absolute divorce for intermarriage within the prohibited degrees of consanguinity and affinity, mental incapacity at time of marriage, impotence at time of marriage, force, menace, duress, or fraud in obtaining marriage, pregnancy of wife at time of marriage unknown to husband, adultery, wilful desertion for three years, conviction for an offence involving imprisonment for two years or longer.

Absolute or limited divorce for cruelty or habitual intoxication. Limited divorce for any ground held sufficient in English courts prior to May 4, 1784.

LABOUR LAWS: No boss or other superior in any factory shall inflict corporal punishment on minor labourers. Seats must be provided for female employees. Sunday labour forbidden. No minors may be employed in barrooms. To let

out children for gymnastic exhibition or any indecent exhibition is a misdemeanour. Children
under 12 may not work in factories. No child
under 14 may work between 7 P.M. and 6 A.M.

SUFFRAGE, POLITICAL CONDITION, INDUSTRIAL
AND PROFESSIONAL STATUS: No suffrage. 33
women in the ministry, 2 dentists, 37 journalists,
6 lawyers, 43 doctors, 4 professors, 2 saloon
keepers, 4 bankers, 9 commercial travellers, 10
carpenters, etc.

Idaho

AGE OF LEGAL CONSENT: 18.

POPULATION: Male 93,367; female 68,405.

HUSBAND AND WIFE: Husband controls wife's
earnings. Wife can secure control of own property only by going into court and showing that
her husband is mismanaging it. Husband is legal
guardian of the children.

DIVORCE: Absolute divorce for adultery, extreme cruelty, wilful desertion for one year, wilful neglect for one year, habitual intemperance
for one year, conviction of felony, permanent
insanity.

There is no limited divorce.

LABOUR LAWS: No Sunday labour. Children
under 14 may not work in mine, factory, hotel,
or be messenger; no child under 16 shall work
more than nine hours per day; nor be let out for
any exhibition or vocation which endangers health

or morals; nor ever be sent to any immoral resort or serve or handle intoxicating liquors.

SUFFRAGE, POLITICAL CONDITION, INDUSTRIAL AND PROFESSIONAL STATUS: Full suffrage. Women are eligible to all offices. 7 women are in the ministry, 4 journalists, 2 lawyers, 15 doctors, 1 saloon keeper, 1 commercial traveller, 1 carpenter, etc.

Illinois

AGE OF LEGAL CONSENT: 16.

POPULATION: Male 2,472,782; female 2,348,768.

HUSBAND AND WIFE: Wife controls own earn-ings. Dower prevails. Wife has full disposal of property, can sue, etc., as if unmarried. Wife and husband are equal guardians of children. Wife is entitled to support suited to her condition in life; husband is entitled to same support out of her individual property. They are jointly liable for family expenses.

DIVORCE: Absolute divorce for impotence, bigamy, adultery, wilful desertion for two years, habitual drunkenness for two years, attempt to murder, extreme and repeated cruelty, conviction for felony or other infamous crime.

No limited divorce; but married women living separate through no fault of their own have an action in equity for reasonable maintenance, if they so desire.

LABOUR LAWS: No Sunday labour. No minor

shall be allowed to sell indecent literature, etc., nor be let out as acrobat or mendicant or for any immoral occupation. Eight hours a legal day's work. No person shall be debarred from any occupation or profession on account of sex; but females shall not be required to work on streets or roads or serve on juries. No child under 14 to be employed in any place where intoxicating liquors are sold or in factory or bowling alley; and shall not labour more than eight hours. No child under 16 shall engage in occupations dangerous to life or morals; and no female under 16 shall engage in any employment which requires her to stand constantly. Seats must be provided for all female employees. No woman shall work more than ten hours a day in stores and factories.

SUFFRAGE, POLITICAL CONDITION, INDUSTRIAL AND PROFESSIONAL STATUS: Women have school suffrage and are eligible to all school offices and can be notaries public. There are 292 women in the ministry, 117 dentists, 240 journalists, 113 lawyers, 820 doctors, 31 professors, 196 saloon keepers, 8 bankers, 101 commercial travellers, 24 carpenters, etc.

Indiana

AGE OF LEGAL CONSENT: 16.

POPULATION: Males 1,285,404; females 1,231,058.

HUSBAND AND WIFE: Wife controls own earnings. No dower or curtesy. Wife may sue in her own name for injuries, etc. Neither husband nor wife can alienate their separate real estate without each other's consent. A wife can act as executor or administrator of an estate only with her husband's consent. No married woman can become a surety for any person. Husband is guardian of children.

DIVORCE: Absolute for adultery, impotency, desertion for two years, cruel and inhuman treatment, habitual drunkenness, neglect of husband to provide for two years, conviction of an infamous crime.

Limited divorce for adultery, desertion or neglect for six months, habitual cruelty or constant strife, gross and wanton neglect of conjugal duty for six months.

LABOUR LAWS: No child under 12 may work in a mine. Children under 15 may not be let out for acrobatic or any immoral exhibition or to work in any place where liquor is sold. Seats must be provided for female employees. Eight hours a legal day's work. No female under 18 may work more than ten hours a day in any factory, laundry, renovating works, bakery, or printing office; no woman shall be employed in any factory between 10 P.M and 6 A.M. Suitable dressing rooms must be provided and not less than sixty minutes given for the noonday meal. Sweat-shops under strict supervision of a State inspector. No woman may work in a mine. No Sunday labour.

SUFFRAGE, POLITICAL CONDITION, INDUSTRIAL AND PROFESSIONAL STATUS: No suffrage. Women may be notaries public. 130 women in the ministry, 34 dentists, 79 journalists, 40 lawyers, 195 doctors, 6 professors, 27 saloon keepers, 2 bankers, 44 commercial travellers, 7 carpenters, etc.

Indian Territory

AGE OF LEGAL CONSENT: 16.

POPULATION: Male 208,952; female 183,108.

HUSBAND AND WIFE: Husband controls wife's earnings. Dower is in force and curtesy. Woman controls separate estate absolutely in practice; for though at common law any money or property given her husband for investment becomes his, by statute it does not. Husband and wife are equal guardians of children.

DIVORCE: Absolute or limited for impotence, wilful desertion for one year, bigamy, conviction for felony or other infamous crime, habitual drunkenness for one year, cruel treatment endangering life, intolerable indignities, adultery, incurable insanity subsequent to marriage.

LABOUR LAWS: No Sunday labour.

SUFFRAGE, POLITICAL CONDITION, INDUSTRIAL AND PROFESSIONAL STATUS: No suffrage. 6 women in ministry, 1 dentist, 4 journalists, 13 doctors, 4 professors, 1 banker, etc.

Iowa

AGE OF LEGAL CONSENT: 15.

POPULATION: Male 1,156,849; female 1,075,004.

HUSBAND AND WIFE: Wife controls own earnings. Any assignment of wages must have written consent of both husband and wife. No dower or curtesy; surviving husband or wife is entitled to one third in fee simple of both real and personal estate of other at his or her death. Wife controls own property, can sue, etc., as if single. Husband and wife are equal guardians of children. Support and education of family is chargeable equally on husband's and wife's property.

DIVORCE: Absolute for adultery, wilful desertion for two years, conviction of felony after marriage, habitual drunkenness, inhuman treatment endangering life, pregnancy of wife at time of marriage by another man, unless the husband have an illegitimate child living unknown to wife.

No limited divorce.

Annulment for prohibited degrees, impotence, bigamy, insanity or idiocy at time of marriage.

LABOUR LAWS: No female may be employed in any place where intoxicating liquors are sold. Seats must be provided for female employees. Children under 16 not to assist in operating dangerous machinery. No Sunday labour. No person under 14 may work in a factory, mine, laundry, slaughter-house, store where more than eight persons are employed; no child under 16 shall be employed in any vocation endangering life or morals, nor shall work more than ten hours a day.

SUFFRAGE, POLITICAL CONDITION, INDUSTRIAL AND PROFESSIONAL STATUS: Women have bond suffrage and can vote on increase of taxes. They may serve as school trustees and superintendents. 117 women in ministry, 52 dentists, 74 journalists, 53 lawyers, 260 doctors, 27 professors, 8 saloon keepers, 1₁ bankers, 34 commercial travellers, 7 carpenters, etc.

Kansas

AGE OF LEGAL CONSENT: 18.

POPULATION: Male 768,716; female 701,779.

HUSBAND AND WIFE: Wife controls own earnings. Husband and wife are equal guardians of children. Wife controls her separate property, can sue, etc., as if unmarried. Neither husband nor wife can convey or encumber real estate without consent of other; nor dispose by will of more than one half of the separate property without other's consent. If there are no children, the surviving husband or wife takes all the property, real and personal; if there are children, one half. Husband must support family.

DIVORCE: Absolute for bigamy, desertion for one year, adultery, impotency, when wife at time of marriage was pregnant by another than her husband, extreme cruelty, fraudulent contract, habitual drunkenness, gross neglect of duty, conviction and imprisonment for felony subsequent to marriage.

No limited divorce; but wife may obtain alimony without divorce for any causes above mentioned.

LABOUR LAWS: People employing children under 14 in acrobatic or mendicant occupations are guilty of a misdemeanour. No Sunday labour. Seats must be provided for female employees. No child under 14 may work in coal mine, nor in any factory or packing house. No child under 16 may work at any occupation endangering body or morals.

SUFFRAGE, POLITICAL CONDITION, INDUSTRIAL AND PROFESSIONAL STATUS: Women have municipal, school, and bond suffrage. 63 women in ministry, 21 dentists, 39 journalists, 43 lawyers, 190 doctors, 21 professors, 9 saloon keepers, 7 bankers, 20 commercial travellers, 19 carpenters, etc.

Kentucky

AGE OF LEGAL CONSENT: 12.

POPULATION: Male 1,090,227; female 1,056,947.

HUSBAND AND WIFE: Husband controls wife's earnings. Curtesy and dower are equalised. After the death of either husband or wife, the survivor is given a life interest in one third of the realty of the deceased and an absolute estate in one half of the personalty. Wife controls her personal property, but cannot dispose of real estate without husband's consent; the husband can convey real estate without his wife's signature, but it is subject to her dower. Husband is legal guardian of children. He must furnish support according to his condition, but if he has only his wages there is no law to punish him for non-support.

DIVORCE: Absolute to both husband and wife for impotence or inability to copulate and for living apart for five consecutive years without any cohabitation. Also to the party not in fault for desertion for one year, adultery, condemnation for felony, concealment of any loathsome disease at time of marriage or contracting it afterwards, force, duress, or fraud in obtaining marriage, uniting with any creed or religious society requiring a renunciation of the marriage covenant or forbidding husband and wife to cohabit. To the wife, when not in like fault, for confirmed drunkenness of husband leading to neglect to provide, habitual behaviour by husband for six months indicating aversion to wife and causing her unhappiness, physical injury or attempt at it. To the husband for wife's pregnancy at time of marriage unknown to him, adultery of wife, or such conduct as proves her to be unchaste without proof of adultery, and habitual drunkenness of wife.

Limited divorce for any of these causes or any other cause as the court may deem sufficient.

LABOUR LAWS: Forbidden to let or employ any children under 16 in any acrobatic or mendicant or immoral occupations. No Sunday labour. No child under 14 shall work in factory, mill, or mine unless said child shall have no other means of support. No child under 16 shall work more than ten hours per day. Seats and suitable dressing-rooms must be provided for female employees.

SUFFRAGE, POLITICAL CONDITION, INDUSTR'AL AND PROFESSIONAL STATUS: In the country districts any widow having a child of school age and any widow or spinster having a ward of school age may vote for school trustees and school taxes. In Louisville, five third-class, and twenty or more fourth-class cities no woman has any vote. Women may be notaries public. 39 women in ministry, 4 dentists, 21 journalists, 16 lawyers, 98 doctors, 5 professors, 35 saloon keepers, 3 bankers, 20 commercial travellers, 9 carpenters, etc.

Louisiana

AGE OF LEGAL CONSENT: 16.

POPULATION: Male 694,733; female 686,892.

HUSBAND AND WIFE: Husband controls wife's earnings. Wife cannot appear in court without her husband's consent, and needs this consent in all matters connected with her separate estate. She may make her will without the authority of her husband. No woman can be a witness to a testament. No married woman can be executor without husband's consent. The dowry is given to the husband, for him to enjoy as long as the marriage shall last. Husband is legal guardian of children.

DIVORCE: Absolute or limited for adultery, condemnation to an infamous punishment, habitual and intolerable intemperance, insupportable excess or outrages, public defamation on the part of one of the married persons toward the other, desertion, attempted murder, proof of guilt of husband or wife who has fled from justice when charged with an infamous offence.

LABOUR LAWS: No female to be employed in any place where liquor is sold. No Sunday labour. No child under 15 to engage in any acrobatic or theatrical public exhibition. Seats must be provided for female employees, who are also to have at least thirty minutes for lunch. No girl under 14 may be employed in any mill or factory; and no woman shall be worked more than ten hours a day. Seats, suitable dressing-rooms, and stairs must be provided. An inspector, male or female, is appointed.

SUFFRAGE, POLITICAL CONDITION, INDUSTRIAL AND PROFESSIONAL STATUS: Tax-paying women can vote on all questions of taxation. 14 women in ministry, 4 dentists, 21 journalists, 8 lawyers, 25 doctors, 16 professors, 31 saloon keepers, 2 bankers, 18 commercial travellers, 9 carpenters, etc.

Maine

AGE OF LEGAL CONSENT: 16.

POPULATION: Male 350,995; female 343,471.

HUSBAND AND WIFE: Wife controls own earnings and has full control of separate property. Wife and husband are equal guardians of children. If there is no will, the interest of the husband or wife in the real estate of the other is the same— one third absolutely, if there is issue living, one half if there is no issue, the whole if there is neither issue nor kindred.

DIVORCE: Absolute for adultery, impotence, extreme cruelty, desertion for three years, gross and confirmed habits of intoxication whether from liquors or drugs, cruel and abusive treatment, wilful neglect to provide.

No limited divorce.

LABOUR LAWS: Ten hours a day the legal limit for female employees. No child under 14 may work in a factory. No Sunday labour. No child under 16 may be employed in any acrobatic, mendicant, immoral, or dangerous occupation.

SUFFRAGE, POLITICAL CONDITION, INDUSTRIAL AND PROFESSIONAL STATUS: No suffrage. Women can be justices of the peace, town clerks, and registers of probate. They cannot be notaries public. 39 women in ministry, 4 dentists, 33 journalists, 4 lawyers, 67 doctors, 1 professor, 3 bankers, 5 carpenters, etc.

Maryland

AGE OF LEGAL CONSENT: 16.

POPULATION: Male 589,275; female 598,769.

HUSBAND AND WIFE: Wife controls own earnings. No assignment of wages to be made without consent of both husband and wife. Wife controls separate property absolutely. Inheritance of property is the same for widow and widower. Husband is legal guardian of children and must support family.

DIVORCE: Absolute for impotence, any cause which by the laws of the State renders a marriage null and void *ab initio*, adultery, desertion for three years, illicit sexual intercourse *of the woman before* marriage unknown to husband (*but the wife cannot obtain a divorce from her husband if he has been guilty of such an offence*). Limited divorce for cruelty, excessively vicious conduct, or desertion. In all cases where an absolute divorce is granted for adultery or abandonment, the court may decree that the guilty party shall not contract marriage with any other person during the lifetime of the other party. Annulment is given for bigamy or marriage within the prohibited degrees of consanguinity and affinity.

LABOUR LAWS: Seats must be provided for female employees. No Sunday labour. No child under 14 may be employed in any mendicant or acrobatic occupation. No child under 8 may be employed in peddling. Women may not be wait-

resses in any place where liquor is sold. Children
under 12 may not be employed in any business
except in the counties, from June 1 to Oct. 15.
Ten hours a legal day's work.

SUFFRAGE, POLITICAL CONDITION, INDUSTRIAL
AND PROFESSIONAL STATUS: No suffrage. Women serve as notaries public. 35 women in
ministry, 6 dentists, 23 journalists, 6 lawyers, 87
doctors, 4 professors, 2 bankers, 13 commercial
travellers, 10 carpenters, etc.

Massachusetts

AGE OF LEGAL CONSENT: 16.

POPULATION: Male 1,367,474; female 1,437,872.

HUSBAND AND WIFE: Wife controls own earnings and has control of her separate property subject only to the husband's interests. She can
be executor, make contracts, etc., as if unmarried.
The husband is legal guardian of minor children;
he may dispose of them and may appoint a
guardian at his death. Husband must support
family. In distributing the estate, no distinction is made between real and personal property.
The surviving husband or wife takes one third,
if deceased leaves children or their descendants;
5000 dollars and one half of the remaining estate
if the deceased leaves no issue; and the whole, if
deceased leaves no kin. This is taken absolutely
and not for life. Curtesy and dower exist; but
the old-time curtesy is cut down to a life-interest

in one third, the same as dower; and in order to be entitled to dower or curtesy, the surviving husband or wife must elect to take it in preference to the above provisions.

DIVORCE: Absolute for adultery, impotency, utter desertion for three years, gross and confirmed habits of intoxication, cruel and abusive treatment, wilful neglect to provide, sentence to imprisonment for five years.

No limited divorce.

LABOUR LAWS: No Sunday labour. Ten hours a legal day's work. No woman to labour between 10 P.M. and 6 A.M. in any manufacturing establishment, nor between 6 P.M. and 6 A.M. in any textile works. No child under 14 and no illiterate under 16 and over 14 may be employed in any factory or mercantile establishment. No child under 14 may be employed between 7 P.M. and 6 A.M., or during the time when the public schools are in session. Seats must be provided for females. No woman or young person shall be required to work more than six hours without thirty minutes for lunch. No child under 15 may engage in any gymnastic or theatrical exhibition.

SUFFRAGE, POLITICAL CONDITION, INDUSTRIAL AND PROFESSIONAL STATUS: Women have school suffrage. They may be justices of the peace. 188 women in ministry, 38 dentists, 180 journalists, 47 lawyers, 729 doctors, 38 professors, 8 saloon keepers, 3 bankers, 73 commercial travellers, 31 carpenters, etc.

Michigan

AGE OF LEGAL CONSENT: 16.

POPULATION: Male 1,248,905; female 1,172,077.

HUSBAND AND WIFE: Husband controls wife's earnings.   Dower prevails, but not curtesy. When the wife has separate real estate, she controls it as if single.   The husband cannot give full title to his real estate unless the wife joins so as to cut off her dower.   Father is guardian of the children.   Husband must support.

DIVORCE: Absolute for adultery, impotence, imprisonment for three years, desertion for two years, habitual drunkenness, if husband or wife has obtained a divorce in another State.

Limited or absolute divorce at the discretion of the court for extreme cruelty, desertion for two years, neglect to provide.

LABOUR LAWS: No female may be employed in any place where liquor is sold.   Seats must be provided for female employees.   Ten hours a legal day's work.   No Sunday labour.   No child under 16 may take part in any acrobatic or mendicant or dangerous or immoral occupation, nor shall any minor be given obscene literature to sell.   No female under 21 may be employed in any occupation endangering life, health, or morals. At least forty-five minutes must be allowed for lunch.

SUFFRAGE, POLITICAL CONDITION, INDUSTRIAL AND PROFESSIONAL STATUS: All women who pay taxes may vote upon questions of local taxation and the granting of franchises. Parents and guardians have also school suffrage. Women serve as notaries public. 105 women in ministry, 17 dentists, 81 journalists, 27 lawyers, 270 doctors, 26 professors, 23 saloon keepers, 13 bankers, 53 commercial travellers, 32 carpenters, etc.

Minnesota

AGE OF LEGAL CONSENT: 16.

POPULATION: Male 932,490; female 818,904.

HUSBAND AND WIFE: Wife controls own earnings, but cannot convey or encumber her separate real estate without husband's consent. No dower or curtesy. If either husband or wife die intestate, the survivor, if there is issue living, is entitled to the homestead for life and one third of the rest of the estate in fee simple. If there are no descendants, the entire estate goes absolutely to the survivor. Husband is guardian of children and must support family.

DIVORCE: Absolute for adultery, impotency, cruel and inhuman treatment, sentence to imprisonment after marriage, wilful desertion for one year, habitual drunkenness for one year.

Limited divorce—to wife only—for cruel and inhuman treatment, on part of husband, or such conduct as may make it unsafe and improper for her to cohabit with him, desertion and neglect to provide.

LABOUR LAWS: Children between 8 and 18 must be sent to school during whole period schools are in session, except in cases of unusual poverty. Ten hours a legal day's work. Seats must be provided for female employees. No Sunday labour. No child under 18 may engage in any occupation between 6 P.M. and 7 A.M.; nor in any mendicant, acrobatic, immoral, or dangerous business. No child under 14 may work in factory or mine. A *female* factory inspector must be appointed.

SUFFRAGE, POLITICAL CONDITION, INDUSTRIAL AND PROFESSIONAL STATUS: Women have school suffrage and may vote for library trustees. 80 women in ministry, 18 dentists, 75 journalists, 21 lawyers, 199 doctors, 16 professors, 17 saloon keepers, 10 bankers, 46 commercial travellers, 8 carpenters, etc.

Mississippi

AGE OF LEGAL CONSENT: 10.

POPULATION: Male 781,451; female 769,819.

HUSBAND AND WIFE: Husband controls wife's earnings. He manages her separate property, but must give an account of it annually. No dower or curtesy. If husband or wife dies intestate, the entire estate goes to the survivor; if there is issue, surviving husband or wife has a child's share of the estate. Each has equal rights in making a will. Father is legal guardian of children, but cannot deprive mother of custody of their persons. Husband must support.

DIVORCE: Absolute for marriage within prohibited degrees, natural impotence, adultery, sentence to the penitentiary, wilful desertion for two years, habitual drunkenness or excessive use of drugs, habitually cruel treatment, pregnancy of wife at time of marriage unknown to husband, bigamy, insanity, or idiocy when party applying did not know of it.

No limited divorce. The court may decree that the guilty party must not marry again.

LABOUR LAWS: No Sunday labour. There are no other laws.

SUFFRAGE, POLITICAL CONDITION, INDUSTRIAL AND PROFESSIONAL STATUS: A woman as a freeholder or lease-holder may vote at a county election to decide as to the adoption or non-adoption of a law permitting stock to run at large. If a widow and the head of a family, she may vote on leasing certain portions of land in the township which are set apart for school purposes. Widows in country districts may also vote for school trustees. Women cannot be notaries public. 13 women in ministry, 2 dentists, 19 journalists, 4 lawyers, 16 doctors, 3 professors, 1 saloon keeper, 3 bankers, 9 commercial travellers, 13 carpenters, etc.

Missouri

AGE OF LEGAL CONSENT: 18.
POPULATION: Male 1,595,710; female 1,510,955.
HUSBAND AND WIFE: Wife controls own

earnings.   Her separate property is liable for
debts contracted by the husband for necessaries
for the family.   Wife can sue and be sued, make
contracts, etc., in her own name.   She may hold
real property under three different tenures: an
equitable separate estate created by certain technical words in the conveyance, and this she can dispose of without husband's consent; a legal separate
estate, which she cannot convey without his
joinder; and a common law estate in fee, of which
the husband is entitled to the rents and profits.
Dower and curtesy prevail.   Husband is guardian
of children and must support.

DIVORCE: Absolute for impotence, bigamy,
adultery, desertion for one year, conviction for
felony or infamous crime, habitual drunkenness
for one year, cruel treatment endangering life
or intolerable indignities, vagrancy of husband,
pregnancy of wife at time of marriage unknown
to husband.

No limited divorce.

LABOUR LAWS: Seats must be provided for female employees.   No woman may be employed
in any place where liquor is served except wife,
daughter, mother, or sister of owner.   No child
under 14 to engage in any acrobatic, mendicant,
dangerous, or immoral occupation.   No Sunday
labour.   No female may work underground in a
mine.   Children between 8 and 14 must go to
school.   No child under 14 may work in any
theatre, concert hall, factory; but this applies

only to cities with 10,000 or more inhabitants. No female may labour more than 54 hours a week.

SUFFRAGE, POLITICAL CONDITION, INDUSTRIAL AND PROFESSIONAL STATUS: No suffrage. Women may be notaries public. 138 women in ministry, 32 dentists, 87 journalists, 61 lawyers, 303 doctors, 17 professors, 44 saloon keepers, 30 bankers, 37 commercial travellers, 15 carpenters, etc.

Montana

AGE OF LEGAL CONSENT: 16.

POPULATION: Male 149,842; female 93,487.

HUSBAND AND WIFE: Wife controls own earnings. There is dower, but not curtesy. Wife controls separate property. Husband is guardian of children and must furnish support; but wife must help, if necessary. Her personal property is subject to debts incurred for family expenses.

DIVORCE: Absolute for adultery, extreme cruelty, wilful desertion, wilful neglect, habitual intemperance, conviction of felony.

No limited divorce; but wife may have an action for permanent maintenance, at discretion of court, even though absolute divorce is denied.

LABOUR LAWS: Children under 16 may not be employed in mines. Children between 8 and 14 must go to school. No child under 16 may take part in any acrobatic, mendicant, or wandering occupation. No Sunday labour. No child under

16 may work in mill, factory, railroad, in any place where machinery is operated, or in any messenger company.

SUFFRAGE, POLITICAL CONDITION, INDUSTRIAL AND PROFESSIONAL STATUS: Women may vote for school trustees. Those owning property may vote on all questions submitted to tax-payers. They cannot be notaries public. 22 women in ministry, 3 dentists, 6 journalists, 3 lawyers, 16 doctors, 7 saloon keepers, 2 commercial travellers, 2 carpenters, etc.

Nebraska

AGE OF LEGAL CONSENT: 18.

POPULATION: Male 564,592; female 501,708.

HUSBAND AND WIFE: Wife controls own earnings and separate property. Both dower and curtesy prevail; but wife can mortgage or sell her real estate without husband's consent and without regard for his right of curtesy. He can do the same with his separate property, but subject to her dower. Husband and wife are equal guardians of the children. Husband must provide; but wife's separate property can be levied on for necessaries furnished the family, if husband has no property. Wife is not "next of kin" and cannot sue, for example, for damages to a minor child, even though she is divorced and has custody of children.

DIVORCE: Absolute for adultery, impotence,

imprisonment for three years, desertion for two years, habitual drunkenness, imprisonment for life, extreme cruelty, neglect to provide.

Limited divorce also for last three causes. Annulment for bigamy, when one party is white and other has one fourth or more negro blood, insanity or idiocy at time of marriage, consanguinity, obtaining marriage by fraud or force, when there has been no subsequent cohabitation.

LABOUR LAWS: Children must go to school between 7 and 15. Ten hours a legal day's labour. Sunday labour forbidden. Females to be employed between 6 A.M. and 10 P.M. Seats must be provided. No child under 14 may be employed in any place where liquor is sold, factory, hotel, laundry, messenger work. No child under 14 may be employed at all during school term.

SUFFRAGE, POLITICAL CONDITION, INDUSTRIAL AND PROFESSIONAL STATUS: Women who are mothers of children of school age or who are assessed on real or personal property have school suffrage; but they cannot vote for State or county superintendents or county supervisors. Women act as notaries public. 95 women in ministry, 16 dentists, 35 journalists, 23 lawyers, 134 doctors, 11 professors, 10 saloon keepers, 15 commercial travellers, 12 carpenters, etc.

Nevada

AGE OF LEGAL CONSENT: 14.

POPULATION: Male 25,603; female 16,732.

HUSBAND AND WIFE: Wife controls own earnings. She may control her separate property,
if a list of it is filed with the county recorder, but
unless it is kept constantly inventoried and recorded, it becomes community property. The
community property, both real and personal, is
under absolute control of husband and at wife's
death it all belongs to him. On death of the husband, wife is entitled to half of it. A wife's
earnings are hers if her husband has allowed her
to appropriate them to her own use, when they
are regarded as a gift from him to her. Husband is legal guardian of children. Husband
must provide; but there is no penalty if he does
not.

DIVORCE: Absolute for impotence, adultery
since marriage remaining unforgiven, wilful desertion for one year, conviction for felony or
infamous crime, habitual drunkenness which in-
capacitates party from contributing his or her
share to support of family, extreme cruelty, wilful neglect to provide for one year.

No limited divorce.

LABOUR LAWS: There are none dealing with
women and children.

SUFFRAGE, POLITICAL CONDITION, INDUSTRIAL
AND PROFESSIONAL STATUS: No suffrage. Women cannot serve as notaries public. 2 women in
ministry, 4 dentists, 1 journalist, 1 lawyer, 6
doctors, 5 saloon keepers.

New Hampshire

AGE OF LEGAL CONSENT: 16.

POPULATION: Male 205,379; female 206,209.

HUSBAND AND WIFE: Wife controls own earnings. Dower and curtesy prevail. Wife can sue and be sued and make contracts without husband's consent. Husband is legal guardian of children, and must provide.

DIVORCE: Absolute for impotence, adultery, extreme cruelty, imprisonment for one year, treatment seriously injuring health or endangering reason, absence for three years without being heard from, habitual drunkenness for three years, joining any religious sect which believes relation of husband and wife unlawful, desertion for three years with neglect to provide.

No limited divorce.

LABOUR LAWS: No child under 12 may be employed in any factory, nor any child under 14 while schools are in session. Nine hours and forty minutes the legal limit for female labour per day. No child under 14 shall engage in any acrobatic exhibition or in the selling of obscene literature. No Sunday labour. Seats must be provided for female employees. No female may sell or serve liquor.

SUFFRAGE, POLITICAL CONDITION, INDUSTRIAL AND PROFESSIONAL STATUS: Women have school suffrage. They may be notaries public. 25 women in ministry, 3 dentists, 12 journalists, 2 lawyers, 61 doctors, 3 professors, 9 saloon keepers, 6 commercial travellers, 5 carpenters, etc.

New Jersey

AGE OF LEGAL CONSENT: 16.

POPULATION: Male 941,760; female 941,909.

HUSBAND AND WIFE: Wife controls own earnings. Dower and curtesy prevail. She has full disposal of her personal property by will; but must get husband's consent to convey or encumber her separate estate. Husband is guardian of children. Husband must furnish support; but wife must contribute, if he is unable.

DIVORCE: Absolute for bigamy, marriage within prohibited degrees, adultery, wilful desertion for two years, impotence.

Limited divorce for extreme cruelty.

In case of desertion and neglect to provide, wife has an action for support.

LABOUR LAWS: Seats must be provided for female employees. Hours for labour must be from 7 A.M. to 12 M. and from 1 P.M to 6 P.M., except in fruit canning and glass factories. Sunday labour forbidden. No child under 18 may engage in any acrobatic, immoral, or mendicant occupation. No child under 15 may engage in any vocation unless he or she shall have attended school within twelve months immediately preceding. No child under 14 may work in a factory. No female

employee shall be sent to any place of bad
repute.

SUFFRAGE, POLITICAL CONDITION, INDUSTRIAL
AND PROFESSIONAL STATUS: Women in villages
and country districts have school suffrage. They
may be notaries public. 87 women in ministry,
19 dentists, 45 journalists, 23 lawyers, 176 doctors,
4 professors, 208 saloon keepers, 4 bankers, 11
commercial travellers, 12 carpenters, etc.

New Mexico

AGE OF LEGAL CONSENT: 14.

POPULATION: Male 104,228; female 91,082.

HUSBAND AND WIFE: Wife controls own earnings. Curtesy prevails. Neither husband nor
wife can convey real property without consent
of other. Husband is legal guardian of children,
but is not required by law to support the family.

DIVORCE: Absolute for adultery, cruel treatment, desertion, impotency, neglect to provide,
habitual drunkenness, conviction for felony and
imprisonment subsequent to marriage, pregnancy
of wife at time of marriage unknown to husband.

No limited divorce. But when husband and
wife have permanently separated, wife has an action for support.

LABOUR LAWS: No Sunday labour. There are
no other laws relating to women and children.

SUFFRAGE, POLITICAL CONDITION, INDUSTRIAL
AND PROFESSIONAL STATUS: No suffrage. Wo-

men may be notaries public.   10 women in ministry, 2 dentists, 5 doctors, 3 professors, 2 saloon keepers, 1 commercial traveller, 3 carpenters, etc.

New York

AGE OF LEGAL CONSENT: 18.   (Trials may be held privately, and it is almost impossible to secure a conviction.)

POPULATION: Male 3,614,780; female 3,654,114.

HUSBAND AND WIFE: Wife controls own earnings.   Dower and curtesy prevail.   Wife holds separate property free from control of husband. Both husband and wife can make wills without knowledge or consent of other.   Wife can mortgage or convey her whole estate without husband's consent; he can do this with his personal property; but not with his real estate.   Husband and wife are equal guardians of the children.   Husband must provide.

DIVORCE: Absolute for adultery only.

Limited for cruelty, conduct rendering cohabitation unsafe or improper, desertion, neglect to provide.

Court refuses to allow party guilty of adultery to marry again, but may modify this after five years if conduct of defendant has been uniformly good.   Adultery is now a crime in New York.

LABOUR LAWS: No child under 16 may take part in any acrobatic, mendicant, theatrical, wandering, dangerous, or immoral occupation.   Children

must attend school between 8 and 16. No child
under 14 may be employed in any occupation
during school term. Eight hours a day's work.
Seats must be provided for female employees.
No child under 14 may work in a factory. Female
labour is confined between 6 A.M. and 9 P.M., and
must not exceed 10 hours. No girl under 16
shall sell papers or periodicals in any public place.
Female employment agencies may not send applicant to any place of bad repute.

SUFFRAGE, POLITICAL CONDITION, INDUSTRIAL
AND PROFESSIONAL STATUS: Tax-paying women
in towns and villages may vote on questions of
local taxation. Parents and widows with children
have school suffrage in towns and villages. Women may be notaries public. 511 women in
ministry, 108 dentists, 365 journalists, 124 lawyers,
103 commercial travellers, 925 doctors, 49 professors, 348 saloon keepers, 81 bankers, 84 carpenters, etc.

North Carolina

AGE OF LEGAL CONSENT: 14.

POPULATION: Male 938,677; female 955,133.

HUSBAND AND WIFE: Wife controls own earnings. Dower and curtesy prevail. Wife controls separate property. Wife is not bound by a
contract unless husband joins in writing. In
actions against her he must be served with
the suit. Wife cannot be sole trader without

husband's written consent. Husband is legal guardian of children, and must provide.

DIVORCE: Absolute for adultery, impotence, pregnancy of wife at time of marriage unknown to husband.

Limited for desertion, turning partner maliciously out of doors, cruel treatment endangering life, intolerable indignities, habitual drunkenness.

Wife has an action for separate maintenance if husband neglects to provide or is a drunkard or spendthrift.

LABOUR LAWS: No Sunday labour. No child under 12 may be employed in factory, except oyster canning concerns which pay for opening oysters by the bushel. No person under 18 shall be required to labour more than 66 hours per week. No child under 12 shall work in a mine. No boy or girl under 14 shall work in a factory between 8 P.M. and 5 A.M.

SUFFRAGE, POLITICAL CONDITION, INDUSTRIAL AND PROFESSIONAL STATUS: No suffrage. Women cannot be notaries public. 25 women in ministry, 6 journalists, 22 doctors, 2 professors, 2 saloon keepers, 3 bankers, 4 commercial travellers, 6 carpenters, etc.

North Dakota

AGE OF LEGAL CONSENT: 18.
POPULATION: Male 177,493; female 141,653.
HUSBAND AND WIFE: Wife controls own earn-

ings and separate property absolutely. Dower and curtesy do not prevail; if husband or wife dies intestate, survivor takes one half of the estate, if there is only one child living or the lawful issue of one child; if there are more, survivor gets one third. If husband is unable to support family, wife must maintain him and the children. Husband is guardian of children.

DIVORCE: Absolute for adultery, extreme cruelty, wilful desertion for one year, wilful neglect for one year, habitual intemperance for one year, conviction of felony.

No limited divorce.

LABOUR LAWS: Children under 12 may not work in mines, factories, or workshops. Children must go to school between 8 and 14, unless they have already been taught adequately and poverty compels them to work. No Sunday labour. No woman under 18 shall labour more then ten hours per day.

SUFFRAGE, POLITICAL CONDITION, INDUSTRIAL AND PROFESSIONAL STATUS: Women have school suffrage and are eligible to all school offices. They may be notaries public. 15 women in ministry, 5 dentists, 2 journalists, 6 lawyers, 15 doctors, 1 professor, 1 commercial traveller, 4 carpenters, etc.

Ohio

AGE OF LEGAL CONSENT: 16.

POPULATION: Male 2,102,655; female 2,054,890.

HUSBAND AND WIFE: Husband controls wife's earnings, but wife controls separate property. Either husband or wife on the death of the other is entitled to one third of the real estate for life. Husband is legal guardian of children, and must provide; but if he is unable, wife must assist.

DIVORCE: Absolute for bigamy, desertion for three years, adultery, impotence, extreme cruelty, fraudulent contract, any gross neglect of duty, habitual drunkenness for three years, imprisonment in penitentiary, procurement of divorce in another State. No limited divorce; but wife has an action for alimony without divorce for adultery, any gross neglect of duty, desertion, separation on account of ill treatment by husband, habitual drunkenness, sentence and imprisonment in penitentiary.

LABOUR LAWS: No child under 14 may work in a mine. Children must go to school between 8 and 14. Seats and suitable toilet rooms must be provided for female employees. No child under 14 may be employed in any establishment or take part in any acrobatic, mendicant, dangerous, or immoral vocation. Hours for girls under 18 confined between 6 A.M. and 7 P.M., nor may they work more than ten hours per day. No Sunday labour. No labour agency shall send any female to an immoral resort.

SUFFRAGE, POLITICAL CONDITION, INDUSTRIAL AND PROFESSIONAL STATUS: Women may vote for members of boards of education, but not for

State commissioner nor on bonds and appropriations. They cannot be notaries. 206 women in ministry, 40 dentists, 151 journalists, 66 lawyers, 451 doctors, 26 professors, 337 saloon keepers, 15 bankers, 62 commercial travellers, 31 carpenters, etc.

Oklahoma

AGE OF LEGAL CONSENT: 16.

POPULATION: Male 214,359; female 182,972.

HUSBAND AND WIFE: Wife controls own earnings and separate property absolutely. If husband or wife dies intestate, leaving one child or lawful issue of child, survivor receives one third of the estate; otherwise one half. If there are no kin, survivor takes all. Husband is guardian of children, and is expected to provide; but law assigns no penalty if he does not.

DIVORCE: Absolute for bigamy, desertion for one year, impotence, pregnancy of wife at time of marriage by other than husband, extreme cruelty, fraudulent contract, habitual drunkenness, gross neglect of duty, conviction and imprisonment for felony after marriage.

Wife may have an action for separate maintenance for any of these causes without applying for divorce.

LABOUR LAWS: No children under 15 may be employed in any occupation injurious to body or morals. No Sunday labour. Ten hours per day legal labour for children under 14.

SUFFRAGE, POLITICAL CONDITION, INDUSTRIAL AND PROFESSIONAL STATUS: Women may vote for school trustees. They may be notaries public. 29 women in ministry, 1 dentist, 5 journalists, 5 lawyers, 26 doctors, 1 professor, 4 commercial travellers, 3 carpenters, etc.

Oregon

AGE OF LEGAL CONSENT: 16.

POPULATION: Male 232,985; female 183,972.

HUSBAND AND WIFE: Wife controls own earnings. By registering as a sole trader, she can carry on business in her own name. Civil disabilities are same for husband and wife except as to voting and holding office. If husband or wife dies intestate, and there are no descendants living, survivor takes whole estate. If there is issue living, the widow receives one half of husband's real estate and one half of his personal property. The widower takes a life interest in all the wife's real estate, whether there are children or not, and all her personal property absolutely if there are no descendants living; otherwise one half. Husband and wife are equal guardians of children. Husband must provide.

DIVORCE: Absolute for impotency, adultery, conviction for felony, habitual drunkenness for one year, wilful desertion for one year, cruel treatment or indignities making life burdensome.

No limited divorce. Annulment if either party is one fourth negro or Mongolian blood.

LABOUR LAWS: No Sunday labour. No child under 14 shall work in factory, mill, mine, telegraph, telephone, or public messenger service; and no child under 14 shall be employed at all during school session. Attendance at school compulsory between 8 and 14. Hours of work for children under 16 to be confined between 7 A.M. and 6 P.M. Seats must be provided for female employees. Ten hours a day the legal limit for female labour.

SUFFRAGE, POLITICAL CONDITION, INDUSTRIAL AND PROFESSIONAL STATUS: Women having property in school districts have school suffrage and may be elected school trustees. They may be notaries. 40 women in ministry, 15 dentists, 17 journalists, 8 lawyers, 82 doctors, 7 professors, 5 saloon keepers, 10 bankers, 18 commercial travellers, 7 carpenters, etc.

Pennsylvania

AGE OF LEGAL CONSENT: 16.

POPULATION: Male 3,204,541; female 3,097,574.

HUSBAND AND WIFE: Wife controls own earnings. Dower and curtesy prevail. Wife cannot mortgage separate estate without husband's consent; cannot sue or be sued or contract without his consent; and in order to carry on business in her own name must secure special permission from the court. Husband is legal guardian of children, and must provide.

DIVORCE: Absolute for impotence, bigamy,

adultery, desertion for two years, cruelty or intolerable indignities, marriage within prohibited degrees of consanguinity or affinity, fraud, conviction for felony for more than two years, lunacy for ten years.

Limited divorce for desertion, turning wife out of doors, cruelty, adultery.

LABOUR LAWS: Seats must be provided for female employees. Employment of females in mines forbidden. Children under 18 may not engage in any mendicant occupations; those under 15 may not exhibit in any place where liquor is sold nor take part in any acrobatic or immoral vocation. Sunday labour forbidden. No female may work in bakery or macaroni or other establishment more than twelve hours per day. Children must go to school between 8 and 16. No child under 16 may work in any anthracite coal mine. No child under 14 shall be employed in any establishment. One hour must be allowed for lunch. No employment bureau shall send any female to an immoral resort.

SUFFRAGE, POLITICAL CONDITION, INDUSTRIAL AND PROFESSIONAL STATUS: No suffrage. 290 women in ministry, 73 dentists, 125 journalists, 73 lawyers, 601 doctors, 38 professors, 183 saloon keepers, 17 bankers, 44 commercial travellers, 40 carpenters, etc.

Rhode Island

AGE OF LEGAL CONSENT: 16.

POPULATION: Male 210,516; female 218,040.

HUSBAND AND WIFE: Wife controls own earnings and separate estate, subject to husband's right to curtesy. Curtesy and dower both prevail. Husband is legal guardian of children and must provide.

DIVORCE: Absolute or limited for marriages originally void by law, conviction for crime involving loss of civil status, when either party may be presumed to be naturally dead from absence, etc., impotence, adultery, desertion for any time at discretion of court, continued drunkenness, neglect to provide, any gross misbehaviour.

LABOUR LAWS: No child under 13 may be employed except during vacation. No child under 15 may be employed unless he or she has school certificate. No child under 14 to work in factory. Hours of labour for children under 16 confined between 6 A.M. and 8 P.M. Seats must be provided for all female employees. No child under 16 shall be employed in any acrobatic, mendicant, dangerous, or immoral occupation. Hours for female labour confined to ten. Sunday labour forbidden.

SUFFRAGE, POLITICAL CONDITION, INDUSTRIAL AND PROFESSIONAL STATUS: No suffrage. 24 women in ministry, 5 dentists, 7 journalists, 3 lawyers, 56 doctors, 2 saloon keepers, 5 commercial travellers, 6 carpenters, etc.

South Carolina

AGE OF LEGAL CONSENT: 14.
POPULATION: Male 664,895; female 675,421.

HUSBAND AND WIFE: Wife controls own earnings and separate estate absolutely. Dower prevails, but not curtesy. Husband is legal guardian of children, and is required to provide, but law as it stands offers many loopholes.

DIVORCE: There are no divorce laws in South Carolina.

LABOUR LAWS: Seats must be provided for female employees. Sunday labour forbidden. No child under 12 to work in factory, mill, or textile establishment, except in cases of extreme poverty duly attested; all such labour to be confined between 6 A.M. and 8 P.M.

SUFFRAGE, POLITICAL CONDITION, INDUSTRIAL AND PROFESSIONAL STATUS: No suffrage. Women cannot be notaries. 17 women in ministry, 1 dentist, 6 journalists, 3 lawyers, 17 doctors, 13 professors, 3 saloon keepers, 2 commercial travellers, 13 carpenters, etc.

South Dakota

AGE OF LEGAL CONSENT: 16.

POPULATION: Male 216,164; female 185,406.

HUSBAND AND WIFE: Wife controls own earnings and controls separate estate. Joint real estate can be conveyed only by signature of both husband and wife, but husband can dispose of joint personal property without wife's consent. In order to control her separate property, wife must keep it recorded in the office of the county register. No dower and no curtesy. Survivor gets one half of estate, if there is one child or issue of child; otherwise one third; unless there are neither children nor kin, when survivor takes all. On the death of an unmarried child, father inherits all its property. If he is dead and there are no other children, mother succeeds; but if there are brothers and sisters, she inherits a child's share. Husband is guardian and must support; but if he is infirm, wife must do so.

DIVORCE: Absolute for adultery, extreme cruelty, wilful desertion or neglect or habitual intemperance for one year, conviction of felony.

No limited divorce.

Party guilty of adultery cannot marry any other, except the innocent party, until death of latter.

LABOUR LAWS: Sunday labour forbidden. No woman under 18 may labour more than ten hours a day. No child under 15 may work in mine, hotel, laundry, factory, elevator, bowling alley, or any place where liquor is sold. No child under 15 shall be employed at all while schools are in session.

SUFFRAGE, POLITICAL CONDITION, INDUSTRIAL AND PROFESSIONAL STATUS: Women can vote for school trustees. They may be notaries. 29 women in ministry, 3 dentists, 4 journalists, 12 lawyers, 24 doctors, 7 professors, 3 saloon keepers, 3 commercial travellers, etc.

Tennessee

AGE OF LEGAL CONSENT: 18.

POPULATION: Male 1,021,224; female 999,392.

HUSBAND AND WIFE: Husband controls wife's earnings, and wife can do nothing with her separate estate without his consent. Dower and curtesy prevail. Husband has right to all rents and profits of wife's estate. No law requires husband to provide. Husband is guardian of children.

DIVORCE: Absolute for impotence, bigamy, adultery, desertion for two years, conviction for felony, attempted murder, pregnancy of woman at time of marriage without knowledge of husband, habitual drunkenness.

Limited for wife only for cruel treatment by husband or intolerable indignities, and desertion or refusal to provide.

Party guilty of adultery cannot marry person with whom adultery has been committed during life of former partner.

LABOUR LAWS: No Sunday labour. No child under 14 may be employed in factory, workshop, or mine. Seats must be provided for female employees. Hours for labour of women confined to 60 per week.

SUFFRAGE, POLITICAL CONDITION, INDUSTRIAL AND PROFESSIONAL STATUS: No suffrage. 30 women in ministry, 1 dentist, 19 journalists, 14 lawyers, 48 doctors, 9 professors, 6 saloon keepers, 4 bankers, 16 commercial travellers, 6 carpenters, etc.

Texas

AGE OF LEGAL CONSENT: 15.

POPULATION: Male 1,578,900; female 1,469,810.

HUSBAND AND WIFE: Husband controls wife's earnings and wife can do nothing with her separate property without his consent. No dower or curtesy. Husband and wife succeed equally to each other's estate. Husband is guardian of children and may be required to provide out of his wife's estate.

DIVORCE: Absolute for excesses or outrages; in favour of husband when wife is taken in adultery or has deserted him for three years; in favour of wife, if husband has deserted her for three years or has abandoned her and lives in adultery with another woman. In favour of either husband or wife on conviction for felony.

No limited divorce.

LABOUR LAWS: No Sunday labour. No child under 12 may be employed in any establishment using machinery. No females shall be employed in any place where liquor is sold except immediate members of owner's family.

SUFFRAGE, POLITICAL CONDITION, INDUSTRIAL AND PROFESSIONAL STATUS: No suffrage. Women can be notaries. 50 women in ministry, 12 dentists, 51 journalists, 17 lawyers, 100 doctors, 3 professors, 26 saloon keepers, 18 bankers, 29 commercial travellers, 12 carpenters, etc.

Utah

AGE OF LEGAL CONSENT: 18.

POPULATION: Male 141,687; female 135,062.

HUSBAND AND WIFE: Wife controls own earnings.   No dower or curtesy.   Husband and wife
succeed equally to each other's estate at death.
Woman controls separate estate absolutely.
Husband is legal guardian of children.   There is
no penalty for non-support.

DIVORCE: Absolute for impotence, adultery, desertion for one year, neglect to provide, habitual
drunkenness, conviction of felony, cruel treatment
causing bodily injury or mental distress, permanent insanity.

No limited divorce; but wife has an action for
separate maintenance in case of desertion or
neglect to provide on part of husband.

LABOUR LAWS: No females may work in mines.
No Sunday labour.

SUFFRAGE, POLITICAL CONDITION, INDUSTRIAL
AND PROFESSIONAL STATUS: Full suffrage; therefore all offices are open to women.   20 women
in ministry, 5 dentists, 7 journalists, 1 lawyer,
34 doctors, 2 saloon keepers, 1 banker, 3 commercial travellers, 1 carpenter, etc.

Vermont

AGE OF LEGAL CONSENT: 16.

POPULATION: Males 175,138; females 168,503.

HUSBAND AND WIFE: Wife controls own earnings and controls separate property.   No dower
or curtesy.   Husband and wife have same powers

of mutual inheritance, except that widower does not take his wife's personal property. Husband is guardian of children and must support.

DIVORCE: Absolute or limited for adultery, sentence to hard labour, intolerable severity, desertion for three years, neglect to provide, absence for seven years without being heard from.

LABOUR LAWS: No child under 16 to be employed after 8 P.M. No child under 12 may work in mill, factory, railroad, quarry, or messenger service. No female shall be employed in barrooms. No Sunday labour.

SUFFRAGE, POLITICAL CONDITION, INDUSTRIAL AND PROFESSIONAL STATUS: Women have school suffrage. They may be notaries. 17 women in ministry, 3 dentists, 15 journalists, 21 doctors, 1 professor, 2 saloon keepers, 11 commercial travellers, 3 carpenters, etc.

Virginia

AGE OF LEGAL CONSENT: 14.

POPULATION: Male 925,897; female 928,287.

HUSBAND AND WIFE: Wife controls own earnings and separate property absolutely. Dower and curtesy prevail. Husband is guardian of children and must support.

DIVORCE: Absolute for adultery, impotence, sentence to penitentiary, conviction of an infamous offence prior to marriage without knowledge of other party, desertion for three years, pregnancy of wife at time of marriage or previous prostitution without knowledge of husband.

Limited for cruelty, reasonable apprehension of bodily hurt, desertion.

LABOUR LAWS: Seats must be provided for female employees. Hours of female labour confined to ten. No child under 12 may work in factory or mine; no child under 14 shall work between 6 P.M. and 7 A.M. No child under 14 shall be hired for any mendicant, acrobatic, dangerous, or immoral occupation. No Sunday labour.

SUFFRAGE, POLITICAL CONDITION, INDUSTRIAL AND PROFESSIONAL STATUS: No suffrage. 37 women in ministry, 1 dentist, 12 journalists, 7 lawyers, 32 doctors, 20 professors, 19 saloon keepers, 13 commercial travellers, 9 carpenters, etc.

Washington

AGE OF LEGAL CONSENT: 18.

POPULATION: Male 304,178; female 213,925.

HUSBAND AND WIFE: Wife controls own earnings and controls separate estate; but control of community property is vested absolutely in the husband; this includes everything acquired after marriage by the joint or separate efforts of either. Husband and wife have equal rights of inheritance to one another's estate; but are not equal guardians of the children, as husband can exclude wife by will. Support of the family is chargeable upon the property of both husband or wife, or either of them. No dower or curtesy.

DIVORCE: Absolute for any cause deemed by court sufficient, when court is satisfied that parties can no longer live together, fraudulent contract, adultery, impotence, desertion for one year, cruel treatment, habitual drunkenness, neglect to provide, imprisonment.

No limited divorce.

LABOUR LAWS: No female may be employed in a mine. Every profession and occupation open to women, but they may not hold public office. No Sunday labour. Females shall not be employed in any place where liquor is sold. Seats must be provided for female employees. Hours limited to ten. No child under 14 shall labour in factory, mill, or workshop except at discretion of juvenile judge. Children must go to school between 8 and 15.

SUFFRAGE, POLITICAL CONDITION, INDUSTRIAL AND PROFESSIONAL STATUS: Women have school and bond suffrage, but cannot vote for State or county superintendents. 38 women in ministry, 7 dentists, 13 journalists, 13 lawyers, 62 doctors, 3 professors, 8 saloon keepers, 1 banker, 8 commercial travellers, etc.

West Virginia

AGE OF LEGAL CONSENT: 14.

POPULATION: Male 499,242; female 459,558.

HUSBAND AND WIFE: Wife controls own earnings, but cannot sell or encumber her separate property without husband's consent. Husband is legal guardian and must provide. Dower and curtesy prevail.

DIVORCE: Absolute for adultery, impotence, imprisonment in penitentiary, conviction of an infamous offence before marriage, desertion for three years, pregnancy of wife at time of marriage or prostitution before without knowledge of husband, in favour of wife when husband was notoriously a licentious person before marriage without her knowledge.

Limited for cruelty, reasonable apprehension of bodily hurt, desertion, habitual drunkenness.

LABOUR LAWS: No Sunday labour. No child under 12 may work in factory or mill and no child under 14 shall be employed during school session. No child under 15 may be employed in any mendicant, acrobatic, immoral, or dangerous occupation, nor in any place where liquor is sold. Seats must be provided for female employees. No female may work in mine.

SUFFRAGE, POLITICAL CONDITION, INDUSTRIAL AND PROFESSIONAL STATUS: No suffrage. Women cannot be notaries. 26 women in ministry, 4 dentists, 4 journalists, 4 lawyers, 18 doctors, 4 professors, 9 saloon keepers, 2 bankers, 3 commercial travellers, 2 carpenters, etc.

Wisconsin

AGE OF LEGAL CONSENT: 18.

POPULATION: Male 1,067,562; female 1,001,480.

HUSBAND AND WIFE: Wife controls own earnings. Assignment of wages of husband must have wife's written consent. Wife controls separate property absolutely. Dower and curtesy prevail. Husband is guardian of children and must provide.

DIVORCE: Absolute for impotence, adultery, sentence to imprisonment for three years prior to marriage. Limited or absolute for desertion for one year, cruelty, habitual drunkenness, neglect to provide, conduct of husband rendering it improper or unsafe for wife to live with him.

LABOUR LAWS: Female labour confined to eight hours per day. No child under 14 may work in factory, workshop, bowling alley, or mine. Children between 14 and 16 must get permission from juvenile judge. No child under 16 shall be employed on dangerous machinery. None under 14 shall take part in theatrical or circus exhibition as musician unless accompanied on tours by parent or guardian. Authorities shall in all cases determine whether occupation is dangerous or immoral for children under 14. No Sunday labour.

SUFFRAGE, POLITICAL CONDITION, INDUSTRIAL AND PROFESSIONAL STATUS: Women have school suffrage. They may be notaries. 65 women in ministry, 24 dentists, 32 journalists, 23 lawyers, 154 doctors, 12 professors, 143 saloon keepers, 2 bankers, 27 commercial travellers, 9 carpenters, etc.

Wyoming

AGE OF LEGAL CONSENT: 21.

POPULATION: Male 58,184; female 34,347.

HUSBAND AND WIFE: Wife controls own earnings and separate property absolutely. Neither dower nor curtesy prevail. Husband and wife have same rights of mutual inheritance. Husband is legal guardian of children, but there is no penalty if he does not provide.

DIVORCE: Absolute for adultery, impotence, conviction for felony, desertion for one year, habitual drunkenness, extreme cruelty, neglect to provide for one year, intolerable indignities, vagrancy of husband, conviction of felony prior to marriage unknown to other party, pregnancy of wife at time of marriage unknown to husband.

No limited divorce.

LABOUR LAWS: No female shall work in mine. Acrobatic, mendicant, dangerous, or immoral occupations forbidden to children under 14. No Sunday labour. Seats must be provided for female employees.

SUFFRAGE, POLITICAL CONDITION, INDUSTRIAL AND PROFESSIONAL STATUS: Full suffrage. Women are eligible for all offices. 2 women in ministry, 2 journalists, 12 doctors, 1 professor, no saloon keepers, lawyers, or dentists, 2 carpenters, etc.

In studying these tables, it should be remembered that new laws are being made constantly;

and that the census of 1910 will give figures which as soon as they appear must supersede those of 1900.

SOURCES

I. The Statutes of the Several States, from earliest times to the present day. Published by Authority.

II. All newspapers and periodicals.

III. The Census Reports, especially the various separate reports such as that on "Marriage and Divorce"; and the Reports of the Commissioner of Labour.

IV. The History of Woman Suffrage: edited by Elizabeth Cady Stanton, Susan B. Anthony, Matilda Joslyn Gage, and Ida Husted Harper, 4 vols. [First two published by Fowler and Wells, New York, 1881 and 1882; last two by Susan B. Anthony, Rochester, 1887 and 1902.]

V. The Encyclopedia of Social Reforms: edited by William D. P. Bliss, with the Co-operation of many Specialists. Funk and Wagnalls, New York and London, 1898.

CHAPTER IX

GENERAL CONSIDERATIONS

IT is twenty-three centuries since Plato gave to the world his magnificent treatise on the State. The dream of the Greek philosopher of equal rights for all intelligent citizens, among whom he includes women, has in large part been realised; but much is yet wanting to bring society to the standard of the Ideal Republic. In not a few States of the world the conditions affecting property rights are inequitable; in all but very few States woman is still barred from the field of politics and from the legitimate rights of citizenship; and the day seems far distant when the States possessing a representative government will be prepared to accept the woman citizen as eligible for administrative positions.

It will, therefore, be my purpose in this chapter first to consider five of the most serious objections to the granting of equal suffrage, that is to say, to the concession to women of full citizens' rights under the law. It will be found that these objections are based on a presumed inferiority of women to men in various respects. I shall give consideration next in order to the question of the

inferiority or superiority of one sex over the other.
In view, furthermore, of the new ferment in
thought in modern society, it will be useful to
analyse certain habits of mind and to indicate the
necessity for a readjustment of old beliefs in
the light of recent evolution. I shall conclude
my history with a suggestion for definite reforms
which, I believe, must be brought about, whether
equal suffrage is granted or not, before women can
attain their maximum of efficiency.

The opposition to the granting of equal suffrage is, as I have said, based mainly upon five
classes of contentions:

    I.   The theological.
    II. The physiological.
    III. The social or political.
    IV. The intellectual.
    V. The moral.

A consideration and an analysis of these five
classes of objections will constitute a summary of
the relations of woman to the community, and
may also serve as a guide or suggestion to the
possibility of a legitimate development, in the
near future, of her rights as a citizen.

I. The theological argument is based upon
the distinctly evil conception of woman, presented
in *Genesis*, as the cause of misery in this world
and upon the subordinate position assigned to her
by Paul and Peter. Christ himself has left us
no teachings on the subject. The Hebrew and
Oriental creed of woman's sphere permeated the

West as Christianity expanded and forced to
extinction the Roman principle of equality. Only
within fifty years, has the female sex regained the
rights enjoyed by women under the law of the
Empire seventeen centuries ago. The Apostolic
theory of complete subordination gained strength
with each succeeding age. I have already cited
instances of ecclesiastical vehemence. As a final
example I may recall that when, early in the
nineteenth century, chloroform was first used
to help women in childbirth, a number of Protestant divines denounced the practice as a sin
against the Creator, who had expressly commanded that woman should bring forth in sorrow
and tribulation. Yet times have so far changed
within two decades that the theological argument
is practically obsolete among Protestants, although it is still influential in the Roman Catholic
Church, which holds fast to the doctrine laid
down by the Apostles. We may say, however,
that of all the objections, the theological has, in
practice, the least weight among the bulk of the
population. The word *obey* in the clerical formula
love, honour, and obey provokes a smile.

II. The physiological argument is more powerful. Its supporters assert that the constitution
of woman is too delicate, too finely wrought to
compete with man in his chosen fields. The
physiological argument makes its appearance most
persistently in the statement that woman should
have no vote because she could not defend her

property or her country in time of war. In reply to this some partisans of equal suffrage have thought it necessary to prove that women are physically equal in all respects to men. But the issues between nations which in the centuries past it had been believed could be adjusted only by war, by being fought out (not, of course, to any logical conclusion, but to a result which showed simply that one party was stronger than the other), are now, in the great majority of cases, determined by the more reasonable, the more civilised, method of arbitration.

As a matter of fact, the cause of woman's rights will suffer no harm by a frank admission that women are not, in general, the peers of men in brute force. The very nature of the female sex, subjected, as it is, to functional strains from which the male is free, is sufficient to invalidate such a claim. A refutation of the physiological objection to equal suffrage is, however, not hard to find. Even in war, as it is practised to-day, physical force is of little significance compared with strategy which is a product of the intellect. In a naval battle for instance, ships no longer engage at close range, where it is possible for the crew of one to board the opposing ship and engage in hand to hand conflict with the enemy; machinery turns the guns and even loads them; the whole fight is simply a contest between trained gunners, who must depend for success on cool mathematical computation.

Nevertheless, it is true that under stress or the need of making a livelihood women in many instances do show physical endurance equal to that of men. Women who are expert ballet dancers and those who are skilled acrobats can hardly be termed physiological weaklings. In Berlin, you may see women staggering along with huge loads on their backs; in Munich, women are street-cleaners and hod-carriers; on the island of Capri, the trunk of the tourist is lifted by two men onto the shoulder of a woman, who carries it up the steep road to the village. In this country many women are forced to do hard bodily labour ten hours a day in sweat-shops. In all countries and in all ages there have been examples of women who, disguised as men, have fought side by side with the male and with equal efficiency. The case of Joan of Arc will at once occur to the reader; and those who are curious about this subject may, by consulting the records of our Civil War, find exciting material in the story of "Belle Boyd," "Frank Miller," and "Major Cushman." [1]

Doubtless women are stronger physically than they were a half-century ago, when it was considered unladylike to exercise. If you will read the novels of that time, you will find that the heroine faints on the slightest provocation or weeps copiously, like Amelia in *Vanity Fair*,

[1] See an excellent article on "The American Woman" by Miss Ida M. Tarbell, in the *American Magazine* for April, 1910.

whenever the situation demands a grain of will-power or of common-sense. But to-day women seldom faint or weep in literature; they play tennis or row. When, in 1844, Pauline Wright Davis lectured on physiology before women in America and displayed the manikin, some of her auditors dropped their veils, some ran from the room, and some actually became unconscious, because their sense of delicacy was put to so sharp a test.

It should be borne in mind, in connection with the contention that the privileges of a citizen ought to be accorded only to those persons who are physically capable of helping to defend the community by force, that no such principle is applied in fixing the existing qualifications for male citizenship. A large number of the voters of every community are, on the ground either of advanced years or of invalidism, physically disqualified for service as soldiers, sailors, or policemen. This group of citizens includes a very large proportion of the thinking power of the community. No intelligently directed state would, however, be prepared to deprive itself of the counsels, of the active political co-operation, and of the service from time to time in the responsibility of office, of men of the type of Gladstone (at the age of seventy-five), of John Stuart Mill (always a physical weakling), of Washington (serving as President after he was sixty), on the ground that these citizens were no longer capable of carrying muskets in the ranks.

Any classification of citizens, any privileges extended to voters, ought, of course, to be arrived at on a consistent and impartial principle.

Further, under the conditions obtaining in this twentieth century, governments, whether of nations, of states, or of cities, are carried on not by force but by opinion. In the earlier history of mankind, each family was called upon to maintain its existence by physical force. The families the members of which (female as well as male) were not strong enough to fight for their existence were crushed out. Far into the later centuries, issues between individuals were adjusted by the decision of arms. Up to within a very recent date, it may be admitted that issues between nations could be settled only by war. It is, however, at this time the accepted principle of representative government in all communities that matters of policy are determined by the expression of opinion, that is by means of the votes given by the majority of its citizens. It is by intelligence and not by brute force that the world is now being ruled, and with the growth of intelligence and a better understanding of the principles of government, it is in order not only on the grounds of justice but for the best interests of the state to widen the foundations of representative government, so as to make available for voting and for official responsibilities all the intelligence that is comprised within the community. This is in my judgment the most conclusive reply to the objection that the physical weakness of woman unfits her for citizenship.

III. According to the social or political argument, if woman is given equal rights with man, the basis of family life, and hence the foundation of the state itself, is undermined, as a house divided against itself cannot stand. It is said that (1) there must be some one authority in a household and that this should be the man; (2) woman will neglect the home if she is left free to enter politics or a profession; (3) politics will degrade her; (4) when independent and self-asserting she will lose her influence over man; and (5) most women do not want to vote or to enter politics.

It is astonishing with what vehemence men will base arguments on pure theory and speculation, while they wilfully close their eyes to any facts which may contradict their assumptions. It is inconceivable to a certain type of mind that a husband and wife can differ on political questions and may yet maintain an even harmony, while their love abates not one whit. In the four States where women vote—Wyoming, Colorado, Utah, and Idaho—there is no more divorce than in other States; and any one who has travelled in these communities can attest that no domestic unhappiness results from the suffrage. Nor does it in New Zealand.

It is said that there must be some one supreme authority; but this depends on the view taken of marriage. Under the old Common Law, the personality of the wife was merged completely in that of her husband; marriage was an absolute despotism. Under the Canon Law, woman is man's obedient and unquestioning subject; marriage is a benevolent despotism. To-day people are more inclined to look upon matrimony as a partnership of equal duties, rights, and privileges.

Sophocles argued in one of his tragedies that children belong entirely to the father, that the mother can assert no valid claim for anything. Lawyers have found this logic excellent; and the records are full of instances of children being taken from a hard-working mother in order to be handed over to a drunken father who wants their wages for his support. It is no longer so in most states. Civilisation has advanced so far, that the pains of bringing forth and raising children are acknowledged to give the mother a right almost equal to that of the father to determine all that concerns the child. There is some reason, therefore, for believing that she should have a voice also in passing upon laws which may make or undo for ever the welfare of the boys and girls for whom she struggles during the years that they are growing to manhood and womanhood. Men are for the greater part so engrossed in business that on certain questions they are far less competent to be "authorities" than women. Against stupid pedagogy, against red-tape, against the policy that morality must never interfere with business principles, against civic dirtiness, against brothel and saloon, women are more active than men, because they see more clearly how vitally the interests of their children are affected by these evil conditions. Wherever women vote, these questions are to the fore.

Closely connected with the "one authority" argument is the old contention, so often resorted to and relied upon, that women, if they are permitted to vote, will neglect the home, and that, if the professions are opened to them, they will find these too absorbingly attractive. Much weight should, however, be given to the great power of the domestic instinct implanted in the nature of woman. In the States where women vote and are eligible for political offices, there are fewer unmarried women in proportion to the population than in States where they have no such rights. The great leaders of the woman suffrage movement from Mrs. Stanton to Mrs. Snowden have in their home circle led lives as beautiful and have raised families as large and as well equipped morally and intellectually as those who are content to sit by the fire and spin.

Thus far I have argued from the orthodox view, that matrimony ought to be the goal of every woman's ambition. But if a woman wishes to remain single and devote herself exclusively to the realisation of some ideal, it is hard to see why she should not. Men who take this course are eulogised for their noble self-sacrifice in immolating themselves for the advancement of the cause of civilisation; women who do precisely the same thing are sometimes unthinkingly spoken of in terms of contempt or with that complacent pity which is far worse. It is difficult for us to realise adequately what talented women like Rosa Bonheur had to undergo because of this curious attitude of humanity.

"The home is woman's sphere." This shibboleth is the logical result of the attitude mentioned. Doubtless, the home is woman's sphere; but the home includes all that pertains to it— city, politics and taxes, laws relating to the protection of minors, municipal rottenness which may corrupt children, schools and playgrounds and museums which may educate them. Few doctrines have been productive of more pain than the "woman's sphere" argument. It is this which has, for a thousand years, made the unmarried woman, the *Old Maid*, the butt of the contemptible jibes of Christian society, whereof you will find no parallel in pagan antiquity. Dramatic writers have held her up to ridicule on the stage on account of the peculiarities of character which are naturally acquired when a person is isolated from participation in the activities of life. It is the doctrine which has made women glad to marry drunkards and rakes, to bring forth children tainted with the sins of their fathers, and to suffer hell on earth rather than incur the ridicule of the Christian gentleman who may, without incurring the protest of society, remain unmarried and sow an unlimited quantity of wild oats. It is this doctrine which was indirectly responsible for the hanging and burning of eccentric old women on the charge that they were witches. As men found a divine sanction for keeping women in subjection, so in those days of superstition did they blaspheme their Creator by digging out of the Old Testament, as a justification for their brutality, the text, "Thou shalt not suffer a witch to live."

"Politics will degrade women"—this naïve confession that politics are rotten is a fairly strong argument that some good influence is needed to make them cleaner. Generally speaking, it is difficult to imagine how politics could be made any worse. If a woman cannot go to the polls or hold office without being insulted by rowdies, her vote will be potent to elect officials who should be able to secure for the community a standard of reasonable civilisation. There is no case in which more sentimentality is wasted. Lovely woman is urged not to allow her beauty, her gentleness, her tender submissiveness to become the butt of the lounger at the street corner; and in most instances lovely woman, like the celebrated Maître Corbeau, is cajoled effectively. Meanwhile the brothel and the sweat-shop continue on their prosperous way. By a curious inconsistency, man will permit woman to help him out of a political dilemma and will then suavely remark that suffrage will degrade her.

During the Civil War, Anna Dickinson by her remarkable lecture entitled, "The National Crisis" saved New Hampshire and Connecticut for the Republicans; Anna Carroll not only gave such a crushing rejoinder to Breckinridge's secession speech that the government printed and distributed it, but she also, as is now generally believed, planned the campaign which led to the fall of Forts Henry and Donelson and opened the Mississippi to Vicksburg. How many men realise these facts?

The theory that politics degrade women will not find much support in such States as Colorado and Wyoming. Here, where equal suffrage obtains, women have been treated with uniform courtesy at the polls; they have even been elected to legislatures with no diminution of their womaniiness; and the House of Wyoming long ago made a special resolution of its approval of equal rights and attested the beneficial results that have followed the extension of the suffrage to women.[1] Judge Lindsey of Colorado has said that his election, and consequent power to work out his great reforms in juvenile delinquency, was due to the backing of women at a time when men, for

[1] In 1893. "Be it resolved by the Second Legislature of the State of Wyoming:

"That the possession and exercise of suffrage by the women of Wyoming for the past quarter of a century has wrought no harm and has done great good in many ways; that it has largely aided in banishing crime, pauperism, and vice from this State, and that without any violent and oppressive legislation," etc.

"business reasons," were averse to extend their aid. "No one would dare to propose its repeal [i.e., the repeal of equal suffrage], and if left to the men of the State any proposition to revoke the rights bestowed on women would be overwhelmingly defeated." Experience in Colorado and elsewhere has shown that any important moral issue will bring out the women voters in great force; but after election they are content to resume their domestic duties; and they have shown no great desire for political office. [1]

[1] Women in Colorado have been of greatest service in establishing the following laws:

1—Establishing a State Home for dependent children, three of the five members of the board to be women.

2—Requiring that at least three of the six members of the county visitors shall be women.

3—Making mothers joint guardians of their children with the fathers.

4—Raising the age of protection for girls to 18 years.

5—Establishing a State Industrial School for girls. There had long been one for boys, but the women could not get one for girls until they had the vote.

6—Removing the emblems from the Australian ballots. This is a little, indirect step toward educational qualifications for voting.

7—Establishing the indeterminate sentence for prisoners.

8—Requiring one physician on the board of the Insane Asylum to be a woman.

9—Establishing truant schools.

10—Making better provision for the care of the feeble-minded.

11—For tree preservation.

12—For the inspection of private eleemosynary institutions by the State Board of Charities.

13—Various steps toward prevention of cruelty to animals.

14—Providing that foreign life and accident insurance companies, when sued, must pay the costs.

Before I leave the discussion as to whether politics degrade women, it will not be out of place to consider the question whether certain women may not, if they have a vote, degrade politics. Of such women there are two classes— the immoral and the merely ignorant. As to the former, much fear has been expressed that they would be the very agents for unscrupulous politicians to use at the polls. Exact data on this

---

15—Establishing a juvenile court.

16—Making education compulsory for all children between the ages of 8 and 16, except those who are ill or those who are 14 and have completed the eighth grade, or those whose parents need their help and support.

17—Making the mother and father joint heirs of a deceased child.

18—Providing for union high schools.

19—Establishing a State travelling library commission.

20—Providing that any person employing a child under 14 in any mine, mill, or factory be punished by imprisonment in addition to a fine.

21—Requiring the joint signature of the husband and wife to a mortgage of a homestead.

22—Forbidding the insuring of the lives of children under 10.

23—Forbidding children of 16 or under to work more than six hours a day in any mill, factory, or other occupation that may be unhealthful.

24—Making it a criminal offence to contribute to the delinquency of children—the parental responsibility act.

25—Making it a misdemeanour to fail to support aged or infirm parents.

26—Providing that no woman shall work more than eight hours a day at work requiring her to be on her feet.

27—Restricting the time for shooting doves.

28—Abolishing the binding out of girls committed to the Industrial School until the age of 21.

29—A pure food law in harmony with the national law.

matter are not available. I shall content myself
with quoting a statement by Mrs. Ida Husted
Harper [1] :

"That 'immoral' class," said Mrs. Harper, "is
a bogey that has never materialised in States
where women have the suffrage. Those women
don't vote. Indeed, Denver's experience has
been interesting in that respect. When equal
suffrage was first granted, women of that class
were compelled by the police to register. It was
a question of doing as the police said, of course,
or being arrested. The women did not want to
vote. They don't go under their real names; they
have no fixed residence, and so on. Anyway,
the last thing they wanted was to be registered
voters.

"But the corrupt political element needed their
vote, and were after it, through the police. These
women actually appealed to a large woman's
political club to use its influence to keep the police
from forcing them to register. A committee was
appointed; it was found that the story was true;
coercion was stopped, and the women's vote
turned out the chief of police who attempted it.
There is now no coercion, and this class simply
pays no attention to politics at all."

The doubling of the number of ignorant voters
by giving all women alike the ballot would be a
more serious affair. A remedy for that, however,
lies in making an educational test a necessary

[1] In the *Boston Herald* for June 4, 1910.

qualification for all voters. In this connection the remarks of Mr. G. H. Putnam are suggestive[1]: "If I were a citizen of Massachusetts or of any State which, like Massachusetts, possesses such educational qualification, I should be an active worker for the cause of equal suffrage. As a citizen of New York who has during the last fifty years done his share of work in the attempt to improve municipal conditions, I am forced to the conclusion that it will be wiser to endure for a further period the inconsistency, the stupidity, and the injustice of the disfranchisement of thousands of intelligent women voters rather than to accept the burden of an increase in the mass of unintelligent voters. The first step toward 'equal suffrage' will, in my judgment, be a fight for an educational qualification for all voters."

Those who maintain that when women are independent and self-asserting, they will lose their influence over men, assume that we view things to-day as they did a century ago and that the thoughts of men are not widened with the progress of the suns. The woman who can share the aspirations, the thoughts, the complete life of a man, who can understand his work thoroughly and support him with the sympathy born of perfect comprehension, will exert a far vaster influence over him than the milk-and-water ideal who was advised "to smile when her husband smiled, to frown when he frowned, and to be

[1] Quoted in the *New York Times* of Jan. 9, 1910.

discreetly silent when the conversation turned on subjects of importance." It is a good thing for women to be self-asserting and independent. There is and always has been a class of men who, like Mr. Murdstone, are amenable to justice and reason only when they know that their proposed victim can at any time break the chains with which they would bind her.

This brings us to the last of the social or political arguments, viz., "Most women do not want to vote."[1] Precisely the same argument has been used by slave owners from time immemorial —the slaves do not wish to be free. As Professor Thomas writes[2]: "Certainly the negroes of Virginia did not greatly desire freedom before the idea was developed by agitation from the outside, and many of them resented this outside interference. 'In general, in the whole western Sahara desert, slaves are as much astonished to be told that their relation to their owners is wrong and that they ought to break it, as boys amongst us would be to be told that their relation to their fathers was wrong and ought to be broken.' And it is reported from eastern Borneo that a white man could hire no natives for wages. 'They thought it degrading to work for wages, but if he would buy them, they would work for him.'" It is akin to the old

[1] See, for example, Lyman Abbott in the *Outlook* for Feb. 19, 1910.
[2] *American Magazine*, July, 1909.

contention of despots that when their subjects
are fit for freedom, they will make them free;
but nobody has ever seen such a time.

Reform of evil conditions does not come from
below; leaders with visions of the future must
point the way.   I once heard of a very respectable
lady of Boston who exclaimed indignantly against
certain proposed changes in child labour laws in
North Carolina, where she owned shares in a cotton mill.   She maintained that the children who
worked at the looms ten hours a day expressed
no discontent; it kept them off the streets; and
the operators, in the kindness of their hearts, had
actually had the looms made especially to ac-
commodate conveniently the diminutive size of
the little workers.   Some people might, with
great profit to themselves, read Plato's superb
allegory of the men in the cave.

The fact that various women's associations have
been instituted in opposition to the extension of
woman suffrage—as in Boston and New York—
is no argument for depriving all women of the
franchise.   If the women who compose these
societies do not care to vote, they do not need to;
but they have no right to deprive of their rights
those who do so desire.   It is said that good
women will not go to the polls; yet there are
in every large city hundreds of respectable males
who disdain to vote.   A woman is more likely to
have a sense of duty to vote than a man.   It is
the old cry, "Don't disturb the old order of things.

If you make us think for ourselves, we shall *be* so unhappy." So Galileo was brought to trial, so Anne Hutchinson was banished; and so persecuted they the prophets before them.

IV. Another argument that is made much of is the intellectual inferiority of woman. For ages women were allowed no higher education than reading, writing, and simple arithmetic, often not even these; yet Elizabeth Barrett Browning, George Sand, George Eliot, Harriet Martineau, Jane Austen, and some scores of others did work which showed them to be the peers of any minds of their day. And if no woman can justly claim to have attained an eminence such as that of Shakespeare in letters or of Darwin in science, we may question whether Shakespeare would have been Shakespeare or Darwin Darwin if the society which surrounded them had insisted that it was a sin for them to use their minds and that they should not presume to meddle with knowledge. When a girl for the first time in America took a public examination in geometry, in 1829, men wagged their heads gravely and prophesied the speedy dissolution of family and state.

To the list of women whose service for their fellows would have been lost if the old-time barriers had been maintained, may be added the name of the late Dr. Mary Putnam Jacobi. Mary Putnam secured her preliminary medical education in the early '60's, and found herself keenly troubled and dissatisfied at the inadequacy of the facilities extended to women for the study of medicine. She insisted that if women practitioners were to be, as she expressed it, "turned loose" upon the community with license to practise, they should, not only as a matter of justice to themselves but of protection for the women and children whose lives they would have in their hands, be properly qualified.

At the time in question, the medical profession took the ground that women might enjoy the benefit of a little medical education but they were denied the facilities for any thorough training or for any research work. Mary Putnam secured her graduate degree from the great medical school of the University of Paris, being the first woman who had been admitted to the school since the fourteenth century. Returning after six years of thorough training, she did much during the remaining years of her life to secure and to maintain for women physicians the highest possible standard of training and of practice. It was natural that with this experience of the requirement of equal facilities for women in her own work, she should always have been a believer in the extension of equal facilities for any citizen's work for which, after experience, women might be found qualified. She was, therefore, an ardent advocate of equal suffrage.

One needs but recall the admirable intellectual work of women to-day to wonder at the imbecility of those who assert that women are intellectually

the inferiors of men. Madame Curie in science,
Miss Tarbell in political and economic history,
Miss Jane Addams in sociological writings and
practice, the Rev. Anna Howard Shaw in the
ministry, Mrs. Hetty Green in business, are a
few examples of women whose mental ability
ought to bring a blush to the Old Guard. Mrs.
Harriman and Mrs. Sage, who manage properties
of many millions, are denied the privilege of
voting in regard to the expenditure of their taxes;
but every ignorant immigrant can cast a vote,
thanks to the doctrine that the political acumen
of a man, however degraded, is superior to that
of a woman, however great her genius—an admirable obedience to the saw in *Ecclesiasticus*
that the badness of men is better than the goodness of women. Let me quote again from Professor Thomas: "The men have said that women
are not intelligent enough to vote, but the women
have replied that more of honesty than of intelligence is needed in politics at present, and that
women certainly do not represent the most ignorant portion of the population. They claim that
voting is a relatively simple matter anyway, that
political freedom 'is nothing but the control of
those who do make politics their business by those
who do not,' and that they have enough intelligence 'to decide whether they are properly governed, and whom they will be governed by.'
They point out also that already, without the
ballot, they are instructing men how to vote and

teaching them how to run a city; that women have
to journey to the legislature at every session to
instruct members and committees at legislative
hearings, and that it is absurd that women who
are capable of instructing men how to vote should
not be allowed to vote themselves.   To the suggestion that they would vote like their husbands
and that so there would be no change in the political situation, women admit that they would
sometimes vote like their husbands, because their
husbands sometimes vote right; but ex-Chief-
Justice Fisher of Wyoming says: 'When the
Republicans nominate a bad man and the Democrats a good one, the Republican women do not
hesitate a moment to "scratch" the bad and sub-
stitute the good.   It is just so with the Democrats;
hence we almost always have a mixture of office-
holders.   I have seen the effects of female suffrage,
and, instead of being a means of encouragement
to fraud and corruption, it tends greatly to purify
elections and to promote better government.'
Now, 'scratching' is the most difficult feature of
the art of voting, and if women have mastered
this, they are doing very well.   Furthermore, the
English suffragettes have completely outgeneralled
the professional politicians.   They   discovered
that no cause can get recognition in politics unless
it is brought to the attention, and that John Bull
in particular will not begin to pay attention 'until
you stand on your head to talk to him.'   They
regretted to do this, but in doing it they secured

the attention and interest of all England. They
then followed a relentless policy of opposing the
election of any candidate of the party in power.
The Liberal men had been playing with the Liberal
women, promising support and then laughing the
matter off. But they are now reduced to an
appeal to the maternal instinct of the women.
They say it is unloving of them to oppose their
own kind. Politics is a poor game, but this is
politics."

V. The last objection I would call the *moral*.
It embraces such arguments as, that woman is too
impulsive, too easily swayed by her emotions to
hold responsible positions, that the world is very
evil and slippery, and that she must therefore
constantly have man to protect her—a pious duty,
which he avows solemnly it has ever been his
special delight to perform. The preceding pages
are a commentary on the manner in which man
has discharged this duty. In Delaware, for instance, the age of legal consent was until 1889
seven years. The institution of Chivalry, to take
another example, is usually praised for the high
estimation and protection it secured for women;
yet any one who has read its literature knows
that, in practice, it did nothing of the sort. The
noble lord who was so gallant to his lady love
—who, by the way, was frequently the wife of another man—had very little scruple about se-
ducing a maid of low degree. The same gallantry
is conspicuous in the *Letters* of Lord Chesterfield,

beneath whose unctuous courtesy the beast of sensuality is always leering.

In the past the main function of woman outside of the rearing of children has been to satisfy the carnal appetite of man, to prepare his food, to minister to his physical comfort; she was barred from participation in the intellectual. In order to hold her to these bonds a Divine Sanction was sought. The Mohammedan found it in the Koran; the Christian, in the Bible—just as slavery was justified repeatedly from the story of Ham, just as the Stuarts and the Bourbons believed firmly that they were the special favourites of God.

Strangely enough, men who are so sensitive about the moral welfare of women will visit a dance hall where women are degraded nightly, and will allow their daughters to marry "reformed" rakes. Men will not permit any mention of sexual matters in their homes, and will let their children get their information on the street; and all for the very simple reason that they are afraid the truth will hurt, will make people think. Men have been remarkably sensitive about having women speak in public for their rights; but they watch with zest a woman screaming nonsense on the stage.

It is quite possible that many women are swayed too easily by their emotions. We must recollect, however, that for some thousands of years woman has been carefully drilled to believe that she is an emotional creature. If a dozen people conspire to tell a man that he is looking badly, it is not unlikely that he will feel ill. Certainly Florence Nightingale and Clara Barton exhibited no lack of firmness on the shambles of battlefields; and there are few men living who cannot recall instances of women who have, in the face of disaster and evil fortune, shown a steady perseverance and will-power in earning a living for themselves and their children that men have not surpassed.

Having in the preceding pages considered the five capital objections to the concession of equal suffrage, I shall now, in accordance with my plan, say something of the much-mooted question of the superiority or inferiority of one sex to the other. It might be concluded from the foregoing account that I see little difference in the aptitudes and powers of the sexes physically, morally, or intellectually. That does not necessarily follow. It is possible to conceive of each sex as the complement of the other; and between complements there can be no question either of superiority or of inferiority. The great historian of European Morals has analysed the constitutional differences of the sexes as he conceived them; and I may quote his remarks as pertinent to my theme. Lecky writes as follows [1]:

"Physically, men have the indisputable super-

[1] *History of European Morals*, vol. ii, pp. 379 and following. New York, D. Appleton & Co., 1869.

iority in strength, and women in beauty. Intellectually, a certain inferiority of the female sex can hardly be denied when we remember how almost exclusively the foremost places in every department of science, literature, and art have been occupied by men, how infinitesimally small is the number of women who have shown in any form the very highest order of genius, how many of the greatest men have achieved their greatness in defiance of the most adverse circumstances, and how completely women have failed in obtaining the first position, even in music or painting, for the cultivation of which their circumstances would appear most propitious.   It is as impossible to find a female Raphael, or a female Handel, as a female Shakespeare or Newton.   Women are intellectually more desultory and volatile than men; they are more occupied with particular instances than with general principles; they judge rather by intuitive perceptions than by deliberate reasoning or past experience.   They are, however, usually superior to men in nimbleness and rapidity of thought, and in the gift of tact or the power of seizing speedily and faithfully the finer inflections of feeling, and they have therefore often attained very great eminence as conversationalists, as letter-writers, as actresses, and as novelists.

"Morally, the general superiority of women over men is, I think, unquestionable.   If we take the somewhat coarse and inadequate criterion of police statistics, we find that, while the male and

female populations are nearly the same in number,
the crimes committed by men are usually rather
more than five times as numerous as those committed by women; and although it may be justly
observed that men, as the stronger sex, and the
sex upon whom the burden of supporting the
family is thrown, have more temptations than
women, it must be remembered, on the other hand,
that extreme poverty which verges upon starv-
ation is most common among women, whose
means of livelihood are most restricted, and whose
earnings are smallest and most precarious. Self-
sacrifice is the most conspicuous element of a
virtuous and religious character, and it is certainly
far less common among men than among women,
whose whole lives are usually spent in yielding to
the will and consulting the pleasures of another.
There are two great departments of virtue: the
impulsive, or that which springs spontaneously
from the emotions, and the deliberative, or that
which is performed in obedience to the sense of
duty; and in both of these I imagine women are
superior to men. Their sensibility is greater,
they are more chaste both in thought and act, more
tender to the erring, more compassionate to the
suffering, more affectionate to all about them. . . .
In active courage women are inferior to men. In
the courage of endurance they are commonly
their superiors. . . . In the ethic of intellect
they are decidedly inferior. To repeat an expression I have already employed, women very rarely

love truth, though they love passionately what they call 'the truth' or opinions they have received from others, and hate vehemently those who differ from them. They are little capable of impartiality or doubt; their thinking is chiefly a mode of feeling; though very generous in their acts, they are rarely generous in their opinions. . . . They are less capable than men of perceiving qualifying circumstances, of admitting the existence of elements of good in systems to which they are opposed, of distinguishing the personal character of an opponent from the opinions he maintains. Men lean most to justice, and women to mercy. Men are most addicted to intemperance and brutality, women to frivolity and jealousy. Men excel in energy, self-reliance, perseverance, and magnanimity, women in humility, gentleness, modesty, and endurance. . . . Their religious or devotional realisations are incontestably more vivid. . . . But though more intense, the sympathies of women are commonly less wide than those of men. Their imaginations individualise more, their affections are, in consequence, concentrated rather on leaders than on causes. . . . In politics, their enthusiasm is more naturally loyalty than patriotism. In history, they are even more inclined than men to dwell exclusively upon biographical incidents or characteristics as distinguished from the march of general causes.''

Experience, by which alone mankind has ever

learned or can learn, will show how far the characteristics enumerated by Lecky are innate and
how far they have been acquired in the course of
ages by certain habits of belief and education.

The securing of citizens' rights for woman will
of necessity depend on the attitude of society.
There may be numerous laws for her relief on the
statute books; but if society frowns on her appearance in court, it will be only in exceptional
cases that she will appeal to the courts. To one
who is familiar with the records of daily life a
hundred years ago there is little doubt that conjugal infidelity on the part of the husband was
more flagrant then than it is to-day; but there
were infinitely fewer divorces. The reason for
this is simply that public sentiment on the subject has changed. A century ago, a divorced
woman could do nothing; the wife was exhorted
to bear her husband's faults with meekness;
and the expansion of industry had not yet opened
to her that opportunity of making her own living
which she now possesses in a hundred ways.
Women were entirely dependent on men; and the
men knew it. To-day they are not so sure.

The old conception of woman's position was
subjection, based on mental and physical inferiority and supported by Biblical arguments. The
newer conception is that of a complement, in
which neither inferiority nor superiority finds
place. The old conception was based, like every

institution of the times, on fear. Men were warned against heresy by being reminded of the tortures of hell fire; against crime by appealing to their dread of the gallows. Between the death of Anne and the reign of George III one hundred and eighty-eight capital offences were added to the penal code; and crime at once increased to an amazing degree. In a system that is founded on fear, when once that fear is removed—as it inevitably will be with the growth of enlightenment—there remains no basis of action, no incentive to good. It has been tried for centuries and has yielded only Star Chambers and Spanish Inquisitions. It is time that we try a new method. An appeal to the sense of *fair play*, an appeal to the sense of duty and of natural affection may yield immeasurably superior results. It has been my experience and personal observation that the standard of honour in our non-sectarian schools, where the *fair play* spirit is most insisted on, is vastly greater than it was in the old sectarian institutions where boys were told morning, noon, and night that they would go to hell if they did not behave.

The new spirit is not going to be accepted at once by society. There must first be some wailing and much gnashing of teeth; and the monster, custom, which all sense doth eat, will still for a time be antagonistic as it has been in the past. "In no society has life ever been completely controlled by the reason," remarks Professor Thomas, "but mainly by the instincts and the habits and the customs growing out of these. Speaking in a general way, it may be said that all conduct both of men and animals tends to be right rather than wrong. They do not know why they behave in such and such ways, but their ancestors behaved in those ways and survival is the guaranty that the behaviour was good. We must admit that within the scope of their lives the animals behave with almost unerring propriety. Their behaviour is simple and unvarying, but they make fewer mistakes than ourselves. The difficulty in their condition is, that having little power of changing their behaviour they have little chance of improvement. Now, in human societies, and already among gregarious animals, one of the main conditions of survival was common sentiment and behaviour. So long as defence of life and preying on outsiders were main concerns of society, unanimity and conformity had the same value which still attaches to military discipline in warfare and to team work in our sports. Morality therefore became identified with uniformity. It was actually better to work upon some system, however bad, than to work on none at all, and early society had no place for the dissenter. Changes did take place, for man had the power of communicating his experiences through speech and the same power of imitation which we show in the adoption of fashions, but these changes took place with almost imperceptible slowness, or if they did not, those who proposed them were considered sinners and punished with death or obloquy.

"And it has never made any difference how bad the existing order of things might be. Those who attempted to reform it were always viewed with suspicion. Consequently our practices usually run some decades or centuries behind our theories and history is even full of cases where the theory was thoroughly dead from the standpoint of reason before it began to do its work in society. A determined attitude of resistance to change may therefore be classed almost with the instincts, for it is not a response to the reason alone, but is very powerfully bound up with the emotions which have their seat in the spinal cord.

"It is true that this adhesion to custom is more absolute and astonishing in the lower races and in the less educated classes, but it would be difficult to point out a single case in history where a new doctrine has not been met with bitter resistance. We justly regard learning and freedom of thought and investigation as precious, and we popularly think of Luther and the Reformation as standing at the beginning of the movement toward these, but Luther himself had no faith in 'the light of reason' and he hated as heartily as any papal dogmatist the 'new learning' of Erasmus and Hutten. . . . We are even forced to realise that the law of habit continues to do its perfect work in a strangely resentful or apathetic manner even when there is no moral issue at stake. . . . Up to the year 1816, the best device for the application of electricity to telegraphy had involved a separate wire for each letter of the alphabet, but in that year Francis Ronalds constructed a successful line making use of a single wire.   Realising the importance of his invention, he attempted to get the British government to take it up, but was informed that 'telegraphs of any kind are now wholly unnecessary, and no other than the one in use will be adopted.' "

The reader will doubtless be able to add from his own experience and observation examples which will support Professor Thomas's admirable account of the power of custom.   Among many barbarous tribes certain foods, like eggs, are *taboo;* no one knows why they should not be eaten; but tradition says their use produces bad results, and one who presumes to taste them is put to death.   To-day, we believe ourselves rather highly civilised; but the least observation of society must compel us to acknowledge that *taboo* is still a vital power in a multitude of matters.

There is a still more forcible opposition to a re-casting of the status of women by those men who have beheld no complete regeneration of society through the extension of the franchise in four of our States.   Curiously oblivious of the fact that partial regeneration through the instrumentality of women is something attained, they take this as a working argument for the uselessness of extending the suffrage. They point to other evils that have followed and tell you that if this is the result of the emancipation of women, they will have none of it. For example, there can be no doubt that one may see from time to time the pseudo-intellectual woman. She affects an interest in literature, attends lectures on Browning and Emerson, shows an academic interest in slum work, and presents, on the whole, a selfishness or an egotism which repels. There never has been a revolution in society, however beneficial eventually, which did not bring at least some evil in its train. I cannot do better in this connection than to quote Lord Macaulay's splendid words (from the essay on Milton): "If it were possible that a people, brought up under an intolerant and arbitrary system, could subvert that system without acts of cruelty and folly, half the objections to despotic power would be removed. We should, in that case, be compelled to acknowledge that it at least produces no pernicious effects on the intellectual and moral character of a people. We deplore the outrages which accompany revolutions. But the more violent the outrages, the more assured we feel that a *revolution was necessary*. The violence of these outrages will always be proportioned to the ferocity and ignorance of the people; and the ferocity and ignorance of the people will be proportioned

to the oppression and degradation under which
they have been accustomed to live. Thus it was
in our civil war. The rulers in the church and
state reaped only what they had sown. They
had prohibited free discussion—they had done
their best to keep the people unacquainted with
their duties and their rights. The retribution was
just and natural. If they suffered from popular
ignorance, it was because they had themselves
taken away the key to knowledge. If they were
assailed with blind fury, it was because they had
exacted an equally blind submission.

"It is the character of such revolutions that we
always see the worst of them at first. Till men
have been for some time free, they know not how
to use their freedom. The natives of wine-coun-
tries are always sober. In climates where wine
is a rarity, intemperance abounds. A newly-
liberated people may be compared to a northern
army encamped on the Rhine or the Xeres. It is
said that when soldiers in such a situation first
find themselves able to indulge without restraint
in such a rare and expensive luxury, nothing
is to be seen but intoxication. Soon, however,
plenty teaches discretion; and after wine has been
for a few months their daily fare, they become
more temperate than they had ever been in their
own country. In the same manner, the final and
permanent fruits of liberty are wisdom, moderation, and mercy. Its immediate effects are often
atrocious crimes, conflicting errors, skepticism on

points the most clear, dogmatism on points the most mysterious.   It is just at this crisis that its enemies love to exhibit it.   They pull down the scaffolding from the half-finished edifice; they point to the flying dust, the falling bricks, the comfortless rooms, the frightful irregularity of the whole appearance; and then ask in scorn where the promised splendour and comfort are to be found?   If such miserable sophisms were to prevail, there never would be a good house or a good government in the world. . . . There is only one cure for the evils which newly acquired freedom produces—and that cure is *freedom*. When a prisoner leaves his cell, he cannot bear the light of day—he is unable to discriminate colours or to recognise faces.   But the remedy is not to remand him into his dungeon, but to accustom him to the rays of the sun.   The blaze of truth and liberty may at first dazzle and bewilder nations which have become half-blind in the house of bondage.   But let them gaze on, and they will soon be able to bear it. In a few years men learn to reason.   The extreme violence of opinion subsides.   Hostile theories correct each other.   The scattered elements of truth cease to conflict, and begin to coalesce. And at length a system of justice and order is educed out of the chaos.

"Many politicians of our time are in the habit of laying it down as a self-evident proposition, that no people ought to be free till they are

fit to use their freedom. The maxim is worthy
of the fool in the old story, who resolved not to
go into the water till he had learnt to swim. If men
are to wait for liberty till they become wise and
good in slavery, they may indeed wait for ever."

The speedy dissolution of family and state was
prophesied by men when first a girl took a public
examination in geometry; whenever women have
been given complete control of their own property; when they have been received into the professions and industries; and now in like manner
people dread the condition of things that they
imagine might follow if women are given the right
to vote and to hold office. We may well believe,
with Lecky, that there are "certain eternal moral
landmarks which never can be removed." But
no matter what our views may be of the destinies,
characteristics, functions, or limitations of the
sex, certain reforms are indispensable before woman and, through her, family life can reach their
highest development. Of these reforms I shall
speak briefly and with them close my history.

   I. The double standard of morality for the
sexes must gradually be abolished.[1] Of all the

---

[1] Note, for example, that in Maryland a man can get a divorce
if his wife has had sexual intercourse before marriage; *but a wife
cannot get a divorce from her husband if he has been guilty of the
same thing.* In Texas, adultery on the part of the wife entitles
the husband to a divorce; but the wife can obtain divorce from
her husband only if he has *abandoned* her and *lived* in adultery
with another woman.

sad commentaries on Christian nations none is so pathetic or so tragical as the fact that for nineteen centuries men have been tacitly and openly allowed, at least before marriage, unrestrained liberty to indulge in sexual vice and intemperance, while one false step on the part of the woman has condemned her to social obloquy and, frequently, to a life on the street. This strange system, a blasphemy against the Christ who suffered death in order to purify the earth, has had its defenders not merely among the uneducated who do not think, but even among the most acute intellects. The philosopher Hume justifies it by commenting on the vastly greater consequences attendant on vice in women than in men; divines like Jeremy Taylor have encouraged it by urging women meekly to bear the sins of their husbands. This subject is one of the great *taboos* in modern society. Let me exhort the reader to go to any physician and get from him the statistics of gonorrhea and syphilis which he has met in his practice; let him learn of the children born blind and of wives rendered invalid for life because their husbands once sowed a crop of wild oats with the sanction of society; let him read the Report of the Committee of Fifteen in New York (G. P. Putnam's Sons, 1902) on *The Social Evil*, the records of the Watch and Ward Society in Boston, or the recent report of the special jury in

New York which investigated the "White Slave Traffic." [1]

The plain facts are not pleasant. A system which has been in vogue from the beginning of history cannot be changed in a decade; but the desired state of things will be more speedily achieved and immediate good will be accomplished by three reforms which may be begun at once—have begun, in fact. In the first place, the "age of legal consent" should be uniformly twenty-one. In most States to-day it is fourteen or sixteen. [2] To the ordinary mind it is a self-evident proposition that a girl of those ages, the slippery period of puberty, can but seldom realise what she is doing when she submits herself to the lust of scoundrels. But the minds of legislators pass understanding; and when, a few years ago, a woman in the Legislature of Colorado proposed to have the age of consent raised from sixteen to twenty-one, such a storm of protest came from her male colleagues that the measure had to be abandoned. In the second place the public should be made better acquainted with the facts of prostitution. When people once realise thoroughly what sickness and social ulcers result from the

[1] On Jan. 12, 1910, a bill was introduced in the House of Representatives to check the "White Slave Traffic" by providing a penalty of ten years' imprisonment and a fine of five thousand dollars for any one who engages in it.

[2] In some it is even lower; *ten* in Georgia and Mississippi for example.

presence in the city of New York of 100,000 debauched women (and the estimate is conservative)—when they begin to reflect that their children must grow up in such surroundings, then perhaps they will question the expediency of the double standard of morality and will insist that what is wrong for a woman is wrong for a man. It is a fact, to be borne carefully in mind, that the vast majority of prostitutes begin their career below the age of *eighteen* and usually at the instigation of adult *men*, who take advantage of their ignorance or of their poverty.   If the miserable Thaw trial did nothing else, it at least once more called public attention to conditions which every intelligent man knows have existed for years.   Something can also be done by statute. New York has made adultery a crime; and the State of Washington requires a physical examination of the parties before marriage.   In the third place, physicians should take more pains to educate men to the knowledge that a continent life is not a detriment to health—the contrary belief being more widely spread than is usually suspected.

II.   In the training of women, care should be taken to impress upon them that they are not toys or spoiled children, but fellow-citizens, devoted to the common task of advancing the ideals of the nation to their goal.

The woman's cause is man's; they rise or sink
Together, dwarf'd or godlike, bond or free:

If she be small, slight-natured, miserable,
How shall men grow?

TENNYSON, *The Princess.*

A Being breathing thoughtful breath,
A Traveller between life and death;
The reason firm, the temperate will,
Endurance, foresight, strength, and skill;
A perfect Woman, nobly planned,
To warn, to comfort, and command;
And yet a Spirit still, and bright
With something of an angel light.

WORDSWORTH.

Towards a higher conception of their duties, women are steadily advancing. It often happens that the history of words will give a hint of the progress of civilisation. Such a story is told by the use of *lady* and *woman.* Not many decades ago the use of the word *woman* in referring to respectable members of the sex was interpreted as a lack of courtesy. To-day, women prefer to be called *women.*

III. Women should be given the full right to enter any profession or business which they may desire. As John Stuart Mill says:

"The proper sphere for any human being is the highest sphere that being is capable of attaining; and this cannot be ascertained without complete liberty of choice."

"We are, as always, in a period of transition," remarks Mr. Björkman, [1] "the old forms are

[1] In *Collier's Weekly*, Feb. 5, 1910.

falling away from us on every side. Concerning
the new ones we are still uncertain and divided.
Whether woman shall vote or not, is not the main
issue. She will do so sooner or later if it suits
her. No, the imperative question confronting us
is this: What are we to do that her life once
more may be full and useful as it used to
be? That question cannot be answered by anybody but herself. Furthermore, it can only be
answered on the basis of actual experience. And
urged onward by her never-failing power of in-
tuition, woman has for once taken to experiment-
ing. She has, if you please, become temporarily
catabolic. But it means merely that she is seek-
ing for new means to fulfil her nature, not for
ways of violating it. And the best thing—nay,
the only thing—man can do to help her is to stand
aside and keep his faith, both in her and in life.
Whether it be the franchise, or the running of
railroads, or public offices, that her eager hands
and still more eager soul should happen to reach
out for, he must give her free way. All she
wants is to find herself, and for this purpose
she must try everything that once was foreign
to her being: the trial over, she will instinctively
and unfailingly pick out the right new things
to do, and will do them."

The opening up of professions and industries to
woman has been of incalculable benefit to her.
Of old the unmarried woman could do little except sit by the fire and spin or make clothing for

the South Sea Islanders.   Her limited activities
caused a corresponding influence on her character.
People who have nothing to do will naturally
find an outlet for their superfluous energy in
gossip and all the petty things of life; if isolated
from a share in what the world is doing, they will
no less naturally develop eccentricities of character
and will grow old prematurely.   To-day, by being
allowed a part in civic and national movements,
women can "get out of themselves"—a powerful
therapeutic agent.   Mrs. Ella Young, a woman of
sixty, was last year made Superintendent of the
great Public School System of Chicago.   Fräulein
Anna Heinrichsdorff is the first woman in Germany to get an engineer's diploma, very recently
bestowed upon her; an "excellent" mark was given
Fräulein Heinrichsdorff in every part of her examination by the Berlin Polytechnic Institute.
Miss Jean Gordon, the only factory inspector
in Louisiana, is at present waging a strong fight
against the attempt to exempt "first-class"
theatres from the child-labour law.   Mrs. Nellie
Upham, of Colorado, is President and General
Manager of the Gold Divide Mining, Milling,
and Tunnel Company of Colorado and directs
300 workmen.   These are a few examples out of
some thousands of what woman is doing.[1]   And

[1] Note what the officers of the Chicago Juvenile Protective Association, many of whom are women, accomplished in 1909-1910.
These women are fighting the agencies which make for juvenile
crime mostly and each officer has a specified " beat " to patrol.
Last year their work amounted to the following:

yet there are men who do not believe she should do anything but wash dishes and scrub.

Much more serious is the glaring discrepancy in the wages paid to men and to women. For doing precisely the same work as a man and often doing it better, woman receives a much lower

Complaints of selling liquors to minors investigated...... 295
Complaints of selling tobacco to minors investigated.... 52
Complaints of selling obscene postcards investigated..... 49
Complaints of poolrooms investigated.................. 203
Complaints of dance halls investigated................ 92
Five and ten cent theatres visited.....................1,013
Penny arcades visited............................... 67
Saloons visited...................................... 735
Relief visits.. 174
Cases referred to relief organisations................... 374
Legal aid cases referred.............................. 105
Referred to Visiting Nurses' Association............... 7
Housing cases referred.............................. 51
Applications for work referred........................ 264
Placed in hospitals.................................. 103
Sent to dispensaries................................. 192
Children placed in homes............................ 240
Slot machines removed.............................. 223
Work found for men................................ 57
Work found for women.............................. 81
Work found for boys................................ 84
Work found for girls................................ 90
Visits to ice-cream parlors........................... 356
Visits to candy stores............................... 805

VISITS TO COURTS

Juvenile.. 451
Municipal..1,809
Criminal.. 211
County... 86
Grand Jury... 26
Conferences with state or city officials..................1,244

wage. The reasons are several and specious. We are told that men have families to support, that women do not have such expensive tastes as men, that they are incapable of doing as much as men, that by granting them equal wages one of the inducements to marry is removed. These arguments are generally used with the greatest gravity by bachelors. If men have families to support, women by the hundreds support brothers and sisters and weak parents. That they are incapable of doing as much sounds unconvincing

PROSECUTIONS

Cases of abandonment	99
Assault and battery	8
Contributing to delinquency and dependency of children	232
Crimes against children	12
Disorderly conduct	141
Immoral dancing	4
Intoxicating liquors	33
Juvenile Court cases	78
Larceny	4
Tobacco	10
Sale of cocaine	4
Other cases	110
Total prosecutions	738

RESULTS

Convictions	311
Settled out of court	100
Nolle pros. or nonsuit	52
Dismissed	93
Acquittals	50
Pending	92
Total complaints received	5,047

to one who has seen the work of sweat-shops.   The argument that men have more expensive tastes to satisfy is too feeble to deserve attention. Finally, when men argue that women should be forced to marry by giving them smaller wages, they are simply reverting to the time-honoured idea that the goal of every woman's ambition should be fixed as matrimony.   If the low wages of women produced no further consequence, one might dismiss the matter as not of essential importance; but inadequate pay has been found too frequently to be a direct cause of prostituition. No girl can well keep body and soul together on four dollars a week; and some business managers have been known to inform their women employees with frankness that a "gentleman friend" is a necessary adjunct to a limited income.

The women who suffer most from low wages are probably the teachers in our primary schools. They start usually on a salary of about three hundred and fifty dollars a year.   For this each teacher performs all the minute labour and bears all the nervous strain of instructing sixty pupils six and a half hours a day and of correcting dozens of papers far into the night.   And when crime increases or the pupils are not universally successful in business, the school teacher has the added pleasure of getting blamed for it, being told that she ought to have trained them better. These facts lend some colour to Mark Twain's sage reflection that God at first made idiots—

that was for practice; then he made school boards.

One of the most interesting examples of recent evolution in the industrial status of women is the decision of the Supreme Court of Illinois in the so-called Ritchie Case. The last Legislature of Illinois passed a law limiting to ten hours the working day of women in factories and stores. Now, as far back as 1893, the Legislature had passed a similar law limiting woman's labour to *eight* hours; but the Supreme Court in 1895 declared it unconstitutional on the ground that it was an arbitrary and unreasonable interference with the right of women to contract for the sale of their labour. When, therefore, this year a ten-hour bill was tried, W. C. Ritchie, who had secured the nullification of the act of 1893, again protested. The decision of the Court, rendered April 21, 1910, is an excellent proof of the great advance made within two decades in the position of women. Reversing completely its judgment of 1895, the Court left far behind it mere technicalities of law and found a sanction for its change of front in the experience of humanity and of common sense. These are its conclusions:

"It is known to all men, and of what we know as men we cannot profess to be ignorant as judges:

"That woman's physical structure and the performance of maternal functions place her at a great disadvantage in the battle of life.

"That while a man can work for more than ten

hours a day without injury to himself, a woman, especially when the burdens of motherhood are upon her, cannot.

"That while a man can work standing upon his feet for more than ten hours a day, day after day, without injury to himself, a woman cannot.

"That to require a woman to stand upon her feet for more than ten hours in any one day and to perform severe manual labour while thus standing has the effect of impairing her health.

"And as weakly and sickly women cannot be the mothers of vigorous children, it is of the greatest importance to the public that the State take such measures as may be necessary to protect its women from the consequences produced by long-continued manual labour in those occupations which tend to break them down physically.

"It would seem obvious, therefore, that legislation which limits the number of hours which women shall be permitted to work to ten hours in a single day in such employments as are carried on in mechanical establishments, factories, and laundries would tend to preserve the health of women and assure the production of vigorous offspring by them and would conduce directly to the health, morals, and general welfare of the public, and that such legislation would fall clearly within the police powers of the State."

IV. All phenomena that concern family life should be carefully studied and their bearing on the state ascertained as exactly as possible. There is no subject, for example, from which such wild conclusions are drawn as the matter of divorce. The average moralist, but more particularly the clergy, seeing the fairly astonishing increase in divorce during the last decade, jump to the conclusion that family life is decadent and immorality flagrantly on the increase. They point to the indubitable fact that a century ago divorces were insignificant in number; and they infer that morality was then on a much higher level than it is now. Such alarmists neglect certain elementary facts. The flippant manner in which marriage is treated by the Restoration dramatists and by novelists of the 18th century, the callous sexual morality revealed in diaries and in the conversations of men like Johnson alone are sufficient to suggest the need of a readjustment of one's view regarding the standard of morality in the past. A century ago it was the duty of a gentleman to drink to excess; and it was presumed that a guest had not enjoyed his dinner unless he was at least comfortably the worse for liquor. This view of drunkenness is admirably depicted in Dickens's *Pickwick Papers*, where intoxication is treated throughout as something merely humorous.

There were just as many unhappy marriages formerly in proportion to the population as there are to-day; but the wife was held effectually from application for a divorce not only by rigid laws but by the sentiment of society, which ostracised a divorced woman, and furthermore by her lack of means and of opportunity for earning an independent livelihood. To-day women are not inclined to tolerate a husband who is brutal or debauched. Alarmists make a mistake when they place too much emphasis on the seeming triviality of the reasons, justifying their course, which wives advance when applying for a separation. For example, the phrase "incompatibility of temperament" is in a great number of cases merely a euphemism for something much worse. The clergy will counsel a woman to bear with what they call Christian resignation a husband addicted to drink or scarred by the diseases that are a consequence of sin. Abstractly considered, this may conceivably be good advice. But viewed in a common-sense way it is the duty of a woman to reflect on the consequences of conceiving children from such a man; and the researches of physicians will furnish her with incontrovertible facts regarding the impaired health of the offspring of such a union. A law which would permit of no divorce under such conditions, instead of benefiting the state, would injure it in its most vital asset—healthy children, the coming citizens. Doubtless the divorce laws in many States are too lax. But sweeping generalities based on theory will not remedy matters. Divorce may simply be a symptom, not a disease; a revolt against unjust conditions; and the way to do away with divorce or reduce the frequency of it is to remedy the evil social conditions which, in a great many instances, are responsible.

The fact is, the institution of marriage is going through a crisis. The old view that marriage is a complete merging of the wife in the husband and that the latter is absolute monarch of his home is being questioned. When a man with this idea and a woman with a far different one marry, there is likely to be a clash. Marriage as a real partnership based on equality of goods and of interests finds an increasing number of advocates. There is great reason to believe that the issue will be only for the good and that from doubt and revolt a more enduring ideal will arise, based on a sure foundation of perfect understanding.

CHAPTER X

FURTHER CONSIDERATIONS

IN the four years intervening since this book was first written, the progress of equal rights for women has been so rapid that the summary on pages 175–235 is now largely obsolete; but it is useful for comparison. In the United States at present (August, 1914), Wyoming, Colorado, Utah, Idaho, Washington, California, Oregon, Kansas, Arizona, and Alaska have granted full suffrage to women. In the following States the voters will pass upon the question in the autumn of 1914: Montana, Nevada, North Dakota, South Dakota, Missouri, Nebraska, and Ohio, the last three by initiative petition. In New Jersey, Pennsylvania, Iowa, New York, and Massachusetts a constitutional amendment for equal suffrage has passed one legislature and must pass another before being submitted to the people. The advance has been world-wide. Thus, in 1910 the Gaekwar of Baroda in India allowed the women of his dominions a vote in municipal elections, and Bosnia bestowed the parliamentary suffrage on women who owned a certain amount of real estate; Norway in 1913 and Iceland in 1914 were won to full suffrage. The following table presents a convenient historical summary of the progress in political rights:

On July 2, 1776, two days before the Declaration of Independence was signed, New Jersey, in her first State constitution, enfranchised the women by changing the words of her provincial charter from "Male freeholders worth £50" to "*all inhabitants worth £50*," and for 31 years the women of that State voted.

GAINS IN EQUAL SUFFRAGE

Eighty years ago women could not vote anywhere, except to a very limited extent in Sweden and in a few other places in the Old World.

TIME	PLACE	KIND OF SUFFRAGE
1838	Kentucky	School suffrage to widows with children of school age.
1850	Ontario	School suffrage, women married and single.
1861	Kansas	School suffrage.
1867	New South Wales	Municipal suffrage.
1869	England	Municipal suffrage, single women and widows.
	Victoria	Municipal suffrage, married and single women.
	Wyoming	Full suffrage.
1871	West Australia	Municipal suffrage.
1875	Michigan	School suffrage.
	Minnesota	Do.
1876	Colorado	Do.
1877	New Zealand	Do.
1878	New Hampshire	Do.
	Oregon	Do.
1879	Massachusetts	Do.
1880	New York	Do.
	Vermont	Do.
	South Australia	Municipal suffrage.
1881	Scotland	Municipal suffrage to the single women and widows.
	Isle of Man	Parliamentary suffrage.
1883	Nebraska	School suffrage.
1884	Ontario	Municipal suffrage.
	Tasmania	Do.
1886	New Zealand	Do.
	New Brunswick	Do.
1887	Kansas	Do.
	Nova Scotia	Do.
	Manitoba	Do.
	North Dakota	School suffrage.
	South Dakota	Do.

TIME	PLACE	KIND OF SUFFRAGE
1887	Montana................	School suffrage
	Arizona................	Do.
	New Jersey.............	Do.
	Montana................	Tax-paying suffrage.
1888	England................	County suffrage.
	British Columbia.........	Municipal Suffrage.
	Northwest Territory......	Do.
1889	Scotland...............	County suffrage.
	Province of Quebec.......	Municipal suffrage, single women and widows.
1891	Illinois.................	School suffrage.
1893	Connecticut.............	Do.
	Colorado................	Full suffrage.
	New Zealand............	Do.
1894	Ohio....................	School suffrage.
	Iowa...................	Bond suffrage.
	England................	Parish and district suffrage, married and single women.
1895	South Australia..........	Full State suffrage.
1896	Utah...................	Full suffrage.
	Idaho..................	Do.
1898	Ireland................	All offices except members of Parliament.
	Minnesota..............	Library trustees.
	Delaware...............	School suffrage to tax-paying women.
	France.................	Women engaged in commerce can vote for judges of the tribunal of commerce.
	Louisiana..............	Tax-paying suffrage.
1900	Wisconsin..............	School suffrage.
	West Australia..........	Full State suffrage.
1901	New York..............	Tax-paying suffrage; local taxation in all towns and villages of the State.
	Norway................	Municipal suffrage.
1902	Australia...............	Full suffrage.
	New South Wales........	Full State suffrage.
1903	Kansas.................	Bond suffrage.
	Tasmania...............	Full State suffrage.
1905	Queensland.............	Do.
1906	Finland................	Full suffrage; eligible to all offices.
1907	Norway................	Full parliamentary suffrage to the 300,000 women who already had municipal suffrage.
	Sweden................	Eligible to municipal offices.
	Denmark...............	Can vote for members of boards of public charities and serve on such boards.
	England................	Eligible as mayors, aldermen, and county and town councilors.
	Oklahoma..............	New State continued school suffrage for women.
1908	Michigan...............	Taxpayers to vote on questions of local taxation and granting of franchises.
	Denmark...............	Women who are taxpayers or wives of taxpayers vote for all officers except members of Parliament.
	Victoria................	Full State suffrage.
1909	Belgium................	Can vote for members of the conseils des prudhommes, and also eligible.
	Province of Voralberg (Austrian Tyrol)......	Single women and widows paying taxes were given a vote.
	Ginter Park, Va.........	Tax-paying women, a vote on all municipal questions.
1910	Washington............	Full suffrage.
	New Mexico............	School suffrage.

TIME	PLACE	KIND OF SUFFRAGE
1910	Norway...............	Municipal suffrage made universal. Three-fifths of the women had it before.
	Bosnia...............	Parliamentary vote to women owning a certain amount of real estate.
	Diet of the Crown Prince of Krain (Austria)........	Suffrage to the women of its capital city Laibach.
	India (Gaekwar of Baroda)	Women of his dominions vote in municipal elections.
	Wurttemberg, Kingdom of	Women engaged in agriculture vote for members of the chamber of agriculture; also eligible.
	New York...............	Women in all towns, villages, and third-class cities vote on bonding propositions.
1911	California...............	Full suffrage.
	Honduras...............	Municipal suffrage in capital city, Belize.
	Iceland................	Parliamentary suffrage for women over 25 years.
1912	Oregon.................	Full suffrage.
	Arizona................	Do.
	Kansas................	Do.
1913	Alaska................	Do.
	Norway................	Do.
	Illinois................	Suffrage for statutory officials (including presidential electors and municipal officers).
1914	Iceland................	Full suffrage.

In the United States the struggle for the franchise has entered national politics, a sure sign of its widening scope. The demand for equal suffrage was embodied in the platform of the Progressive Party in August, 1912. This marks an advance over Col. Roosevelt's earlier view, expressed in the *Outlook* of February 3, 1912, when he said: "I believe in woman's suffrage wherever the women want it. Where they do not want it, the suffrage should not be forced upon them." When the new administration assumed office in March, 1913, the friends of suffrage worked to secure a constitutional amendment which should make votes for women universal in the United States.

The inauguration ceremonies were marred by an attack of hoodlums on the suffrage contingent of the parade. Mr. Hobson in the House denounced the outrage and mentioned the case of a young lady, the daughter of one of his friends, who was insulted by a ruffian who climbed upon the float where she was. Mr. Mann, the Republican minority leader, remarked in reply that her daughter ought to have been at home. Commenting on this dialogue, *Collier's Weekly* of April 5, 1913, recalled the boast inscribed by Rameses III of Egypt on his monuments, twelve hundred years before Christ: "To unprotected women there is freedom to wander through the whole country wheresoever they list without apprehending danger." If one works this out chronologically, said the editor, Mr. Mann belongs somewhere back in the Stone Age. In the Senate an active committee on woman suffrage was formed under the chairmanship of Mr. Thomas, of Colorado. The vote on the proposed new amendment was taken in the Senate on March 19, 1914, and it was rejected,[1] 35 to 34, two-thirds being necessary

[1] Twenty-six senators did not vote. The question of negro suffrage complicated the matter with Southern senators. Mr. Williams of Mississippi wished to limit the franchise to "white citizens"; but his amendment was voted down. The list of senators voting for and against the woman suffrage amendment appears on page 5472 of the Congressional Record, March 19, 1914. The debate is contained in pages 5454–5472. Senator Tillman of South Carolina inserted a vicious attack on northern women by the late Albert Bledsoe, who advised them to "cut

before the measure could be submitted to the States for ratification.   In the House Mr. Under-wood, Democratic minority leader, took the stand that suffrage was purely a State issue.   Mr. Heflin of Alabama was particularly vigorous in denunciation of votes for women.   He said[1]:

"I do not believe that there is a red-blooded man in the world who in his heart really believes in woman suffrage.   I think that every man who favours it ought to be made to wear a dress.   Talk about taxation without representation!   Do you say that the young man who is of age does not represent his mother?   Do you say that the young man who pledges at the altar to love, cherish, and protect his wife, does not represent her and his children when he votes?   When the Christ of God came into this world to die for the sins of human-ity, did he not die for all, males and females? What sort of foolish stuff are you trying to inject into this tariff debate? . . . There are trusts and monopolies of every kind, and these little feminine fellows are crawling around here talking about woman suffrage.   I have seen them here in this Capitol.   The suffragette and a little henpecked fellow crawling along beside her; that is her hus-band.   She is a suffragette, and he is a mortal suffering yet."

---

their hair short, and their petticoats, too, and enter à la bloomer the ring of political prizefighters." Bledsoe's article will be found in the Record, July 28, 1913, 3115–3119.

[1] Record, May 6, 1913, 1221–1222.

Mr. Falconer of Washington rose in reply. He remarked: [1]

"I want to observe that the mental operation of the average woman in the State of Washington, as compared to the ossified brain operation of the gentleman from Alabama, would make him look like a mangy kitten in a tiger fight. The average woman in the State of Washington knows more about social economics and political economy in one minute than the gentleman from Alabama has demonstrated to the members of this House that he knows in five minutes."

On February 2, 1914, a delegation of women called upon President Wilson to ascertain his views. The President refused to commit himself. He was not at liberty, he said, to urge upon Congress policies which had not the endorsement of his party's platform; and as the representative of his party he was under obligations not to promulgate or intimate his individual convictions. On February 3, 1914, the Democrats of the House in caucus, pursuant to a resolution of Mr. Heflin, refused to create a woman suffrage committee. So the constitutional amendment was quite lost. In the following July Mr. Bryan suddenly issued a strong appeal for equal suffrage in the *Commoner*. Among his arguments were these:

"As man and woman are co-tenants of the earth and must work out their destiny together, the presumption is on the side of equality of treatment

[1] Record, May 6, 1913, 1222.

in all that pertains to their joint life and its opportunities. The burden of proof is on those who
claim for one an advantage over the other in determining the conditions under which both shall
live. This claim has not been established in the
matter of suffrage. On the contrary, the objections raised to woman suffrage appear to me to be
invalid, while the arguments advanced in support of
the proposition are, in my judgment, convincing."

"Without minimising other arguments advanced in support of the extending of suffrage to
woman, I place the emphasis upon the mother's
right to a voice in molding the environment which
shall surround her children—an environment
which operates powerfully in determining whether
her offspring will crown her latter years with joy
or 'bring down her gray hairs in sorrow to the
grave.' . . .

"For a time I was imprest by the suggestion
that the question should be left to the women to
decide—a majority to determine whether the
franchise should be extended to woman; but I find
myself less and less disposed to indorse this test.
. . . Why should any mother be denied the use
of the franchise to safeguard the welfare of her
child merely because another mother may not
view her duty in the same light?"

The change in the status of women has been
significant not only in the political field, but also
in every other direction. A brief survey of the
legislation of various States in the past year, 1913,

reveals the manifold measures already adopted for
the further protection of women and indicates
the trend of laws in the near future. Acts were
passed in Arkansas, Kansas, Missouri, New Mexico,
and Ohio to punish the seduction of girls and women for commercialised vice, the laws being known
as "White Slave Acts"; laws for the abatement
of disorderly houses were passed in California,
Minnesota, Oregon, Pennsylvania, and Washington; Oregon decreed that male applicants for a
marriage license must produce a physician's certificate showing freedom from certain diseases;
and it authorised the sterilisation of habitual
criminals and degenerates. The necessity of
inculcating chastity in the newer generation,
whether through the teaching of sex hygiene in
the schools or in some other form, was widely
discussed throughout the country. Mothers' pensions were granted by fourteen States; minimum
wage boards were established by three; and three
passed laws for the punishment of family desertion, in such wise that the family of the offender
should receive a certain daily sum from the State
while he worked off his sentence. Tennessee removed the disability of married women arising
from coverture. Ten States further limited the
hours of labour for women in certain industries,
the tendency being to fix the limit at fifty-four
or fifty-eight hours a week with a maximum of
nine or ten in any one day. The hours of labour
of children and the age at which they are allowed

to work were largely restricted. A National
Children's Bureau, under the charge of Miss Julia
Lathrope, has been created at Washington; and
Mrs. J. Borden Harriman was appointed to the
Industrial Relations Commission. The minute-
ness and thoroughness of modern legislation for
the protection of women may be realised by noting
that in 1913 alone New York passed laws that no
girl under sixteen shall in any city of the first,
second, or third class sell newspapers or magazines
or shine shoes in any street or public place; that
separate wash rooms and dressing rooms must be
provided in factories where more than ten women
are employed; that whenever an employer requires a physical examination, the employee, if a
female, can demand a physician of her own sex;
that the manufacture or repair for a factory of
any article of food, dolls' clothing, and children's
apparel in a tenement house be prohibited except
by special permit of the Labor Commission; that
the State Industrial Board be authorised to make
special rules and regulations for dangerous employments; and that the employment of women
in canning establishments be strictly limited
according to prescribed hours.

The unmistakable trend of legislation in the
United States is towards complete equality of the
sexes in all moral, social, industrial, professional,
and political activities.

In England the House of Commons rejected
parliamentary suffrage for women. Incensed at

the repeated chicanery of politicians who alter-
nately made and evaded their promises, a group
of suffragettes known as the "militants" resorted
to open violence. When arrested for damaging
property, they went on a "hunger strike," refus-
ing all nourishment. This greatly embarrassed
the government, which in 1913 devised the so-
called "Cat and Mouse Act," whereby those who
are in desperate straits through their refusal to eat
are released temporarily and conditionally, but
can be rearrested summarily for failure to comply
with the terms of their parole. The weakness in
the attitude of the militant suffragettes is their
senseless destruction of all kinds of property and
the constant danger to which they subject innocent
people by their outrages. If they would confine
themselves to making life unpleasant for those who
have so often broken their pledges, they could
stand on surer ground. The English are commonly regarded as an orderly people, especially
by themselves. Nevertheless, it is true that hardly
any great reform has been achieved in England
without violence. The men of England did not
secure the abolition of the "rotten-borough"
system and extensive manhood suffrage until, in
1831, they smashed the windows of the Duke of
Wellington's house, burned the castle of the Duke
of Newcastle, and destroyed the Bishop's palace
at Bristol. In 1839 at Newport twenty chartists
were shot in an attempt to seize the town; they
were attempting to secure reforms like the aboli-

tion of property qualifications for members of
Parliament. The English obtained the permanent
tenure of their "immemorial rights" only by
beheading one king and banishing another. In
our own country, the Boston Tea Party was a
typical "militant outrage," generally regarded
as a fine piece of patriotism. If the tradition of
England is such that violence must be a preliminary to all final persuasion, perhaps censure of
the militants can find some mitigation in that fact.

Some things move very slowly in England. In
1909 a commission was appointed to consider reform in divorce. Under the English law a husband can secure a divorce for infidelity, but a
woman must, in addition to adultery, prove aggravated cruelty. This is humorously called
"British fair play." In November, 1912, the
majority of the commission recommended that
this inequality be removed and that the sexes be
placed on an equal footing; and that in addition
to infidelity, now the only cause for divorce allowed, complete separation be also granted for
desertion for three years, incurable insanity, and
incurable habitual drunkenness. The majority,
nine commissioners, found that the present stringent restrictions and costliness of divorce are
productive of immorality and illicit relations,
particularly among the poorer classes. The majority report was opposed by the three minority
members, the Archbishop of York, Sir William
Anson, and Sir Lewis Dibdin, representing the

Established Church of England and the Roman Catholic Church. Thus far, Parliament has not yet acted and the old law is still in force.

On the Continent, with the exception of a few places like Finland, the movement for equal suffrage, while earnestly pressed by a few, is not yet concentrated. Women have won their rights to higher education and are admitted to the universities. They can usually enter business and most of the professions. Inequities of civil rights are gradually being swept away. For example, in Germany a married woman has complete control of her property, but only if she specifically provided for it in the marriage contract; many German women are ignorant that they possess such a right. The Germans may be divided into two classes: the caste which rules, largely Prussian, militaristic, and bureaucratic; and that which, although desirous of more republican institutions and potentially capable of liberal views, is constrained to obey the first or ruling class. This upper class is not friendly to the modern women's-rights movement. Perhaps it has read too much Schopenhauer. This amiable philosopher, whose own mother could not endure living with him, has this to say of women[1]:

"A woman who is perfectly truthful and does not dissemble, is perhaps an impossibility. In a

[1] Essays of Schopenhauer. Translated by Mrs. Rudolf Dircks. Pages 64–79.

court of justice women are more often found guilty
of perjury than men. . . . Women are directly
adapted to act as the nurses and educators of our
early childhood, for the simple reason that they
themselves are childish, foolish, and shortsighted.
. . . Women are and remain, taken altogether,
the most thorough and incurable Philistines; and
because of the extremely absurd arrangement
which allows them to share the position and title
of their husbands they are a constant stimulus to
his ignoble ambitions. . . . Where are there any
real monogamists? We all live, at any rate for a
time, and the majority of us always, in polygamy.
. . . It is men who make the money, and not
women; therefore women are neither justified in
having unconditional possession of it nor capable
of administering it. . . . That woman is by nature
intended to obey, is shown by the fact that every
woman who is placed in the unnatural position
of absolute independence at once attaches herself
to some kind of man, by whom she is controlled
and governed; that is because she requires a
master. If she is young, the man is a lover; if she
is old, a priest."

Essentially the opinion of Schopenhauer is that
of the Prussian ruling class to-day. It is indisputable that in Germany, as elsewhere on the
Continent, chastity in men outside of marriage is
not expected, nor is the wife allowed to inquire
into her husband's past. The bureaucratic German expects his wife to attend to his domestic

comforts; he does not consult her in politics. The natural result when the masculine element has not counterchecks is bullying and coarseness. To find the coarseness, the reader can consult the stories in papers like the *Berliner Tageblatt* and much of the current drama; to observe the bullying, he will have to see it for himself, if he doubts it. This is not an indictment of the whole German people; it is an indictment of the militaristic-bureaucratic ruling class, which, persuaded of its divine inspiration and intolerant of criticism,[1] has plunged the country into a devastating war. It is not unlikely that the end of the conflict will mark also the overthrow of the Hohenzollern dynasty. The spirit of the Germans of 1848, who labored unsuccessfully to make their country a republic, may awake again and realise its dreams.

In concluding this chapter, I wish to enlarge somewhat upon the philosophy of suffrage as exhibited in the preceding chapter. The "woman's sphere" argument is still being worked overtime by anti-suffrage societies, whose members rather inconsistently leave their "sphere," the

[1] Any criticism of the Kaiser leads to arrest. The most vigorous checks to Bourbon rule come from the Socialists, who in 1912 polled 4,250,300 votes. But as the Kaiser, as King of Prussia, controls a majority of votes in the Bundesrath, or Federal Council, can dissolve the Reichstag, or House of Representatives, at any time with the consent of the Bundesrath, has sole power to appoint the chancellor, and is lord supreme of the army and navy, anything like real popular government is far off.

home, to harangue in public and buttonhole legislators to vote against the franchise for women.
"A woman's place," says the sage Hennessy, "is
in th' home, darning her husband's childher. I
mean——" "I know what ye mean," says Mr.
Dooley. "'Tis a favrite argument iv mine whin I
can't think iv annything to say." A century ago,
the home was the woman's sphere. To-day the
man has deliberately dragged her out of it to
work for him in factory and store because he can
secure her labor more cheaply than that of men
and is, besides, safer in abusing her when she has
no direct voice in legislation. Are the manufac-
turers willing to send their 1,300,000 female employees back to their "sphere"? If they are not,
but desire their labor, they ought in fairness to
allow them the privileges of workmen—that is, of
citizens, participating actively in the political,
social, and economic development of the country.

As women enter more largely into every profession and business, certain results will inevitably
follow. We shall see first of all what pursuits are
particularly adapted to them and which ones are
not. It has already become apparent that as
telephone and typewriter operators women, as a
class, are better fitted than men. They have, in
general, greater patience for details and quickness of perception in these fields. Similarly, in
architecture some have already achieved conspicuous success. One who has observed the insufficient closet space in modern apartments and

kitchenettes witn the icebox in front of the stove, is inclined to wish that male architects would consult their mothers or wives more freely. In law and medicine results are not yet clear. We shall presently possess more extensive data in all fields for surer conclusions.

A second result may be, that many women, instead of leaving the home, will be forced back into it. This movement will be accelerated if the granting of equal pay for equal work and a universal application of the minimum wage take place. There are a great number of positions, especially those where personality is not a vital factor, where employers will prefer women when they can pay them less; but if they must give equal pay, they will choose men. Hence the tendency of the movements mentioned is to throw certain classes of women back into the home. The home of the future, however, will have lost much of the drudgery and monotony once associated with it. The ingenious labor-saving devices, like the bread-mixer, the fireless cooker, the vacuum cleaner, and the electric iron, the propagation of scientific knowledge in the rearing of children, and wider outlets for outside interests, will tend to make domestic life an exact science, a profession as important and attractive as any other.

The home is not necessarily every woman's sphere and neither is motherhood. Neither is it every woman's congenital duty to make herself attractive to men. The "woman's pages" of newspapers, filled with gratuitous advice on these subjects, never tell men that their duty is fatherhood or that they should make themselves attractive or that their sphere is also the home. Until these one-sided points of view are adjusted to a more reasonable basis, we shall not reach an understanding. They are as unjust as the farmer who ploughs with a steam plow and lets his wife cart water from a distant well instead of providing convenient plumbing.

Women who are fitted for motherhood and have a talent for it can enter it with advantage. There is a talent for motherhood exactly as there is for other things. Other women have genius which can be of greatest service to the community in other ways. They should have opportunity to find their sphere. If this is "Feminism," it is also simple justice. One reason that we are at sea in some of the problems of the women's-rights movement, is that the history of women has been mainly written by men. The question of motherhood, the sexual life of women, and the position of women as it has been or is likely to be affected by their sexual characteristics, must be more exactly ascertained before definite conclusions can be reached. At present there is too much that we don't know. We need more scientific investigations of the type of Mr. Havelock Ellis's admirable *Studies in the Psychology of Sex*[1] and less of pseudo-scientific lucubrations like Otto

[1] Philadelphia, 1906. The F. A. Davis Company.

Weininger's *Sex and Character*. When human
society has rid itself of the bogies and nightmares,
superstitions and prejudices, which have borne
upon it with crushing force, it will be in a better
position to construct an ideal system of government. Meanwhile experiments are and must be
made. Woman suffrage is not necessarily a reform; it is a necessary step in evolution.

One venerable bogey I wish to dispose of before
I close. It is that the Roman Empire was ruined
and collapsed because the increasing liberty given
to women and the equality granted the sexes under
the Empire produced immorality that destroyed
the State. The trouble with Rome was that it
failed to grasp the fundamentals of economic law.
Slavery, the concentration of land in a few hands,
and the theory that all taxation has for its end the
enriching of a select few, were the fallacies which,
in the last analysis, caused the collapse of the
Roman Empire. The luxury, immorality, and
race-suicide which are popularly conceived to have
been the immediate causes of Rome's decline and
fall, were in reality the logical results, the inevi-
table attendant phenomena of a political system
based on a false hypothesis. For when wealth
was concentrated in a few hands, when there
was no all-embracing popular education, all in-
centives to thrift, to private initiative, and hence
to the development of the sturdy moral qualities
which thrift and initiative cause and are the product of, were stifled. A nation can reach its

maximum power only when, through the harmonious cooperation of all its parts, the initiative and talents of every individual have free scope, untrammeled by special privilege, to reach that sphere for which nature has designed him or her.

———

NOTE: The official organ of the National American Woman Suffrage Association is *The Woman's Journal*, published weekly. The headquarters are at 505 Fifth Avenue, New York City.

England has two organisations which differ in methods. The National Union of Women's Suffrage Societies has adopted the constitutional or peaceful policy; it publishes *The Common Cause*, a weekly, at 2 Robert Street, Adelphi, W. C., London. The "militant" branch of suffragettes forms the National Women's Social and Political Union, and its weekly paper is *Votes for Women*, Lincoln's Inn House, Kingsway, W. C.

The International Woman Suffrage Alliance issues the *Jus Suffragii* monthly at 62 Kruiskade, Rotterdam.

A good source from which to obtain the present status of women in Europe is the *Englishwoman's Year Book and Directory for 1914*, published by Adam and Charles Black.

INDEX

A

Adultery, under Roman Law, 19–22; laws modified by Justinian, 68–69; among Germanic peoples, 80, 86, 87; see also under various States.

Age of Consent, under English Law, 138–139; in the United States, 155–156, 167–168, 275; see also under various States.

Alabama, 175–176

Apostles, teachings about women, 55–57

Arizona, 176–177

Arkansas, 177–178

Attainder, bills of, in Roman Empire, 35–37; laws of Arcadius, Honorius, and Constantine, 75–76; of Pope Innocent III, 116

B

Breach of Promise, under Roman Law, 12; modification by Constantine, 72; by Justinian, 73

Business, women in, under Roman Empire, 29; in England, 143; in the United States, 173–174; see also under each State.

C

California, 178–180

Chastisement, right of husband to chastise wife under English Law, 125–127

Christ, teachings about women, 52–53

Colorado, 180–181

Connecticut, 181–182

Consent of women to marriage, under Roman Law, 10; opinions of Church Fathers, 60; enactments of Christian Emperors, 74

Crimes against women, under Roman Law, 41–42, 76; among Germanic peoples, 94–97; under English Law, 138–139

Curtesy, defined, 174; under English Law, 127–129; see also under various States.

Custom, power of, 266–269

D

Delaware, 182–183

Discrepancy in wages paid to women, 280–283

District of Columbia, 183–184

Index to Supplementary Chapter